JOHN IRWIN is Assistant Professor of Sociology at Sonoma State College, Rohnert Park, California. He is coauthor, with Donald Cressey, of "Thieves, Convicts, and the Inmate Culture," and has been closely involved in studies of convicts and other deviants for the past fifteen years.

THE FELON

John Irwin

Prentice-Hall, Inc. 

Englewood Cliffs, N.J.

C–13-314237-X; P–13-314229-9. *Library of Congress Catalog Card Number 76-96973.* Printed in the United States of America.

Current printing (last number):
10 9

PRENTICE-HALL INTERNATIONAL, INC. (*London*)
PRENTICE-HALL OF AUSTRALIA PTY. LTD. (*Sydney*)
PRENTICE-HALL OF CANADA, LTD. (*Toronto*)
PRENTICE-HALL OF INDIA PRIVATE LIMITED (*New Delhi*)
PRENTICE-HALL OF JAPAN, INC. (*Tokyo*)

This book is dedicated
to the more than 200,000 convicts
presently "doing time"
in the United States

ACKNOWLEDGMENTS

Grateful acknowledgment is made to the following for permission to use quotations appearing in this book:

Ace Publishing Corporation, for *Junkie* by William Burroughs; Barrie & Rockliff, Alfred A. Knopf, Inc., and Piri Thomas, for *Down These Mean Streets* by Piri Thomas; The Bobbs-Merrill Company, Inc., for *The Effectiveness of a Prison and Parole System* by Daniel Glaser; Malcolm Braly, Hutchinson & Co., Little, Brown and Company, and A. P. Watt & Son, for *On the Yard* by Malcolm Braly, copyright © 1967 by Malcolm Braly; Lenore L. Cahn, for *The Sense of Injustice* by Edmond Cahn; Jonathan Cape Limited and McGraw-Hill Book Company, for *Soul on Ice* by Eldridge Cleaver, copyright © 1968 by Eldridge Cleaver; Jonathan Cape Limited and The Macmillan Company, for *Manchild in the Promised Land* by Claude Brown, copyright © 1965 by Claude Brown; William Chambliss, University of Washington, for a taped interview with a retired safe burglar; College and University Press Services, Inc., for *Whiz Mob* by David Maurer; Coward-McCann, Inc., and Ann Elmo Agency, Inc., for *The Riot* by Frank Elli, copyright © 1966 by Frank Elli; Doubleday & Company, Inc., for *Hustler* by Henry Williamson and *Scotsboro Boy* by Haywood Patterson and Earl Conrad; The Free Press, for *Urban Villagers* by Herbert Gans; Grove Press, Inc., Alex Haley, and Hutchinson & Co., for *The Autobiography of Malcolm X*, with the assistance of Alex Haley, copyright © 1964 by Alex Haley and Malcolm X, copyright © 1965 by Alex Haley and Betty Shabazz; Dr. Henry L. Hartman, for "Interviewing Techniques in Probation and Parole"; Life Magazine, for "The Reentry Crisis" by Richard Stolley, © 1965 Time Inc.; McGraw-Hill Book Company, for *Soldier to Civilian* by G. C. Pether; Dr. Walter B. Miller and The Society for the Psychological Study of Social Issues, for "Lower-Class Culture as a Generating Milieu of Gang Delinquency," *The Journal of Social Issues* 14: 5–19; Harold Ober Associates Incorporated, for *My Life in Crime* by John Bartlow Martin, copyright 1952 by John Bartlow Martin; Prentice-Hall, Inc., for *Stigma* by Erving Goffman, © 1963; The Society for the Study of Social Problems, for "Thieves, Convicts, and the Inmate Culture" by John Irwin and Donald R. Cressey, *Social Problems* 10: 142–55; Paul Takagi, for "Evaluations and Adaptations in a Formal Organization"; The University of Chicago Press, for *The Jack-Roller* by Clifford Shaw and *The Professional Thief* by Edwin H. Sutherland; The University of Illinois Press, for "The Stranger: An Essay in Social Psychology" by Alfred Schutz, *The American Journal of Psychology,* May 1944; and The University of Minnesota Press, for *The Probation Officer Investigates* by Paul Keve, © copyright 1960.

PREFACE

An acknowledgment of my indebtedness for this book must go back to the origin of my interest in the felon. This began with my association with Donald Cressey who inspired my original interest in sociology, supplied the foundation for my theoretical perspective, and facilitated my career in sociology in many concrete ways. In a similar and no less a manner, I am indebted to Lewis Yablonsky. In acquiring the final version of a theoretical perspective which underpins the study, I am deeply indebted to Herbert Blumer, Erving Goffman, and David Matza.

A group of "experts" worked with me for two years, and without their help I doubt if the study would have been possible. I am naming only a few of these persons. They are Lawrence Harsha, Ed Roberts, Philip Brylke, Gene Davenport, Verdi Woodward, Ed Deriso, Herb Zeigler, and Paul Proget. There were many others whom I haven't named.

Many persons have read and commented on various parts of the manuscript. For their important help I acknowledge my indebtedness to David Matza, Sheldon Messinger, Elliot Studt, Robert Sommers, Michael Sanford, Jacqueline Wiseman, Don Gibbons, Marvin Scott, and Ted Davidson.

I was supported during the greater part of this study by a Woodrow Wilson Dissertation Fellowship. I received additional financial, secretarial, and other forms of assistance from the Parole Action Study, supported by O.L.E.A. Grant no. 24953 and administered by Elliot Studt at the Center for the Study of Law and Society, University of California. The Center, directed by Philip Selznick and Sheldon Messinger, also allowed me full use of its facilities throughout the study.

CONTENTS

INTRODUCTION

This book began as a study of parole. Almost immediately, however, the boundaries were expanded to encompass the extended "career" of the felon. The reason for this expansion was not simply the meandering interest of the investigator. Rather, it became apparent when research on parolee behavior began that to understand this phase of the felon's life it would be necessary to examine earlier phases, because the felon's parole experiences are shaped for him to some extent by orientations he acquires in prison.[1] Furthermore, his position in the prison world is related to his preprison life.[2]

The career of the felon, therefore, became the major theme of the study. Typically, the felon's career begins with some degree of contact with other criminals or deviants who are involved in one of the existing behavior systems of crime or deviance. These systems will be described in the first chapter. Through this contact he acquires a criminal identity and perspective (or identities and perspectives). That is, he acquires a set of beliefs, values, understandings, meanings and self-definitions relative to one or more criminal life styles.

Equipped with this perspective and identity, he passes through arrest, sentencing, imprisonment, and release. Any new phase in his career is structured for him to some degree by meanings, definitions, and understandings he brings to this phase from perspectives gathered earlier. In summary, there is a strand of continuity through the prison and even into future postprison years which is explained by the criminal perspective and identity acquired early in the career and which is overlaid with other deviant identities that obtain in prison.

This does not mean that it is an inevitable, single-track career, with the person coming into contact with, and gaining commitment to, some

1. Jerome Skolnick has pointed out that an individual's orientation to the prison social system has an impact upon his parole experience. "Toward a Developmental Theory of Parole," *American Sociological Review* (August, 1960), p. 543.

2. John Irwin and Donald Cressey contend that prison behavior systems, prison roles or identities, stem not exclusively from prison conditions, but to some degree are determined by the culture the inmate brings to prison. "Thieves, Convicts and the Inmate Culture," *Social Problems* (Fall, 1962), pp. 142–55.

criminal behavior system and then having this commitment steadily strengthened as he comes into more intense contacts with other criminals and official agents of social control. On the contrary, it will be shown how the original commitment is often weak and confused, how at various stages, especially in some unsettling and ambiguous situations he encounters—such as the arrest and sentencing experience described in chapter 2—the identities and perspectives become very muddled. At these stages many felons grapple for alternate life styles and some find them. Usually, however, they do not, or they do not succeed in them. Often this represents a failure on the part of the official agents whose policies and acts usher the felons along the criminal or deviant path rather than opening up acceptable alternatives for them. Usually, this is due to the officials' failure to understand the felon's viewpoint, their misinterpretation of the felon's acts and responses, and the continuation of their own misguided policies.

The second important discovery of the study, and the secondary theme of the book, is the obstacle-course nature of the felon's life once he is arrested. In looking at his passage through the various phases in this way, i.e., as the negotiation of an obstacle course, more is meant than that the prisoner has problems or that his life is difficult, since we would expect the prisoner's life to be difficult. I mean that he is faced with a series of difficulties which have been purposely placed in his path. They weren't placed there simply to make his life hard. Almost always they were raised for the purpose of furthering some correctional goal, very often one of control. We presently can't say too much about this, except where the measures are obviously excessive. Sometimes the goal is punishment, though this motive is usually disguised as something which is less objectionable. We must uncover the real goal in these cases. What is more important, however, is that often the goal is that of helping or rehabilitating the felon. For instance, the parole system discussed in chapter 7 has the official dual purpose of surveillance and help for the ex-prisoner. Its success in surveillance is problematic, and I am convinced that it is almost a complete failure as an aid to the ex-prisoner. In fact, it exists for the most part as a serious obstacle which he must surmount even when he is trying to return to a noncriminal life.

A second unique feature of the felon's difficulties, a feature which makes them like the obstacle course, is that many of them are hidden, screened by ignorance or subterfuge. Many of the recurring pitfalls are either completely unknown, misunderstood or falsely described. The reentry problems discussed in chapters 5 and 6 are of this nature.

A common dimension in the nature of these obstacles and the ignorance which surrounds them is the disparity of perspectives of the officials and the felons. The programs and policies obstructing the felon's progress instead of facilitating it are planned and implemented from an official or conventional viewpoint. The official image of the felon, the explanations of his acts, the definition of the programs themselves are quite different than the felon's view of these same things. By the same token, the felon acts according to a set of categories and understandings foreign to the officials. He interprets and responds to their programs in a fashion unanticipated and not understood by them. They in turn dig down into their perspectives and find additional mistaken reasons for his unexpected acts. The lack of understanding continues and new ineffective programs are introduced. The basic problem is a lack of understanding of the felon's own views. A major goal of this study will be to present this viewpoint.

CONCEPTUAL FOUNDATIONS

In playing out the two major themes of the study—the career and the obstacle course—three concepts are germane: perspective, identity, and behavior system. *Perspective* refers to the set of subcultural beliefs, values, meanings, and world view carried by some group of actors.[3] *Identity* is one's self-conception relative to a particular subcultural perspective.[4] For example, there is a group or collectivity of persons who sometimes think of themselves as "thieves," "dope fiends," "hustlers," or "heads," and who during these times share, interact upon, and negotiate a set of understandings, meanings, values, beliefs, and symbols relative to an explicit thief's, dope fiend's, hustler's or head's life style. The membership of such groups fluctuates, and any one member can move in and out of the life and act upon other perspectives and identities, criminal or noncriminal. Thieves, for instance, intermittently or permanently drop out of crime and become "family men," "working men," "businessmen," or some other identity.

The subcultural perspective and identity emerge among a group of actors who are brought together for some length of time and interact together around some common interest or enterprise. Their behavior through time becomes routinized and patterned, and a unique subcultural system is generated. This group and the shared dimensions which emerge in the interaction are sometimes referred to as a behavior system.[5]

3. The concept of perspective used here has been taken from a discussion on perspectives by Tamotsu Shibutani, "Reference Groups and Perspectives," *American Journal of Sociology* (1955), pp. 562–69.

4. In many uses of identity it relates to culture. For instance see Erik Erikson, "The Concept of Identity in Race Relations: Notes and Queries," *Daedalus* (Winter, 1966), p. 149. Here we are relating it to subculture.

5. This version of behavior system was presented first by Edwin Sutherland. See *Principles of Criminology* (New York: J. B. Lippincott Co., 1939). It was further developed by A. B. Hollingshead, "Behavior Systems as a Field for Research," *American Sociological Review* (1939), pp. 816–22. Most of the recent uses bear little relationship to these earlier versions. Behavior system has become a system of patterns recognized

In our case the focus of the group is usually a criminal one. This is not always the case, however. There are two identities prevalent in prison which are not "criminal"—the "lower-class man" and the "square john." The differences in their origin and patterns will be dealt with throughout the book. For the most part, however, we are concerned with criminal behavior systems, perspectives, and identities.

One last characteristic of behavior systems must be emphasized here. Though membership fluctuates, though commitment on the part of the members is highly variable, and though individuals alternately or simultaneously participate in other systems, a particular system continues to exist because the members themselves, and some broader group of other persons, are explicitly aware of the system, or at least of many aspects of it, and they tend to act towards it as an entity and towards its components—the definitions, meanings, and understandings of which it is constituted. What is being emphasized is that these are natural systems which exist to some extent because people are aware of them and act towards them.

DESIGN OF THE STUDY

Actual research on felons began in June, 1966, after the California Department of Corrections approved the study and I was granted permission to enter the California prisons and interview inmates, attend preparole functions, study the inmate files, interview parole agents and parole administrators, and attend all other parole functions.[6] At this time, while the topic of the study was still limited to parole, I decided to select a sample of approximately one hundred persons sequentially released from California prisons on parole to the San Francisco and Oakland parole districts, to interview some of these before release and in the first few months after release, and to interview the total sample at the end of a year. Even though the scope of the study broadened while prerelease interviews were being conducted, this original sampling and interviewing plan was followed.

The sample chosen contained every parolee from all California prisons released on parole to San Francisco and Oakland parole districts during the period of July 1 to August 15, 1966—a total of 116 convicts. The

by social scientists rather than a system which emerged among a group in interaction. See for instance Ruth Shoule Cavan, *Criminology*, 3rd ed. (New York: Thomas Y. Crowell Company, 1962); and Marshall B. Clinard and Richard Quinney, *Criminal Behavior Systems* (New York: Holt, Rinehart and Winston, Inc., 1967).

6. I must emphasize that the California Department of Corrections extended me great cooperation at all times during this study. At no time was I denied access to any records or functions under the control of the Department. Furthermore, the general attitude of all Department members whom I met was always extremely gracious and cooperative.

records of all 116 men were examined, and 41 were interviewed prior to release from prison. Between August 15, 1966, and the summer of 1967, 34 of those who had been interviewed prior to release were seen again, some quite frequently, especially during the first several months following their release.

During the fall of 1966, after the scope of the study had broadened from parole to the career of the felon, a group of convicts at San Quentin was organized by myself and a Correctional Counselor at San Quentin for the purpose of pursuing our individual research interests. This group, which varied in size through the months from ten to fifteen inmates, was a source of new ideas and concepts, and a check on the validity of emerging descriptions and explanations.

Further, in order to investigate the later phases of the felon's career, a series of interviews of fifteen ex-convicts, also not in the original sample and who had remained out of prison for many years, was undertaken in the spring of 1967.

The final stage of the study was an attempted follow-up interview of the original 116 persons who were released in 1966. Seventy of the 116 were actually contacted during the summer of 1967 and administered a 180-item interview.

SOFT DATA

The more "rigorous" techniques, procedures, and instruments employed in the study produced a rather flimsy and brittle skeleton of "hard" data upon which "softer," but I think "heavier," data were draped. I believe the latter have more strength and life. Furthermore, the techniques which produced the bulk of the "soft" data—unstructured interviews of participants, exemplary types, and experts; use of fictional and nonfictional accounts; group discussions of issues and concepts; and finally, my own impressions and opinions based upon a wide variety of contacts with criminals and ex-criminals, convicts and ex-convicts, keepers and cops—are more consistent with the general perspective of the study. As will be seen in the following pages, this study is concerned primarily with the socially constructed perspectives, realities, and moral systems of groups. These phenomena emerge and exist because persons in interaction, in order to make sense out of their surroundings and to achieve their personal goals, must be able, and to some extent are able, to know what is on each other's minds. The shared perspectives, realities, and moral systems which emerge because of these two factors are best sought, therefore, by participating in the type of interaction and relying on the human capability—*verstehen*—which produces and sustains them.[7]

7. This theoretical perspective is founded on some of the seminal concepts in sociology presented by Max Weber—especially *verstehen*—and Emile Durkheim—es-

CLOSING REMARK

In closing this introductory statement, allow me to answer the major criticism which I anticipate will be inspired by the general approach or particular aspects of this study: namely, that an analysis which focuses on the perspective of the actor, subcultural patterns, and shared meaning worlds remains at the level of the ideal-typical, far above concrete behavior, and therefore misses most of the real behavior. To a great extent this criticism is true, but no more true of this approach than of most others. For instance, Parson's remarks of social system analysis, "We simply are not in a position to 'catch' the uniformities of dynamic process in the social system except here and there," [8] are true of any systematic attempt to catch uniformities in human behavior. I contend that approaching the phenomenon principally through the actors' shared abstractions comes closer to the concrete reality than most other approaches.

---

pecially *collective representations*. It also borrows heavily from the work of George Simmel, especially the paper, "How Is Society Possible?" in *A Collection of Essays, with Translations and a Bibliography*, ed. Kurt H. Wolff (Columbus, Ohio: Ohio State University Press, 1939). It is more directly related to the ideas of George Herbert Mead, *Mind, Self and Society* (Chicago: University of Chicago Press, 1934); Herbert Blumer, "Society as Symbolic Interaction," in Arnold Rose, ed., *Human Behavior and Social Processes* (Boston: Houghton Mifflin Company, 1962); Samuel Strong, "Social Types in a Minority Group—Formulation of a Method," *American Journal of Sociology* (March, 1943); and Alfred Schutz, *Collected Papers*, Vol. I., ed. Maurice Natanson (The Hague: Martinus Mijnoff, 1962).

8. See Talcott Parsons, *The Social System* (London: The Free Press of Glencoe, 1951), p. 21.

I

CRIMINAL IDENTITIES

The first stage of the criminal career is the person's involvement with a criminal behavior system and the acquisition of a criminal perspective and identity. Most imprisoned felons have had some contact and some involvement with criminal systems prior to arrest. Some, however, have not, and this distinction must be emphasized. Not all felons are "criminals"; that is, not all felons have a criminal identity. Some persons are convicted of a felony, sent to prison, and released without ever identifying with criminal behavior systems. This chapter will describe the major behavior systems with which entering felons into California prisons have had contact. Changes in commitment to these systems, the effects of commitment, and the future career courses will be treated in ensuing chapters.

It must be kept in mind that the *systems* are being described. Many persons have contact with more than one system and the systems themselves, because of cultural diffusion, interchange of members, and common background characteristics, are overlapping. Therefore, though relatively pure types do exist, classifying many felons neatly according to their involvement with one system is difficult. The clearest and perhaps most important distinction is that between the various criminal systems and the two noncriminal ones—the square john and the lower-class "man." Within criminal systems, the distinctiveness and exclusiveness of membership varies. This variation will be discussed in the descriptions of the systems which follow.

In spite of this overlap in the life routines of actual felons, the task of describing the systems in their ideal-typical form is being undertaken because they do exist as relatively distinct entities in the minds of some of the participants, and they operate, therefore, distinctly and differentially on an overall and long-term basis.

To lend weight to my own conceptions of the internal characteristics and the interrelationships of these systems, maximum use is made of the accounts, analyses, and descriptions of other writers.

THE THIEF

Probably the oldest existing criminal system is that of the "thief." This system, which presently seems to be fading, has been highly influential in the general criminal world and the prison. As we shall see in chapter 3, it established certain dominant themes in the prison milieu which are still operative.

MAJOR THEMES OF THE THIEF'S WORLD

The dominant theme of the thief system is the "big score," a large sum of money stolen usually in a safe burglary or armed robbery. The big score, as Cloward and Ohlin describe it,

> quickly transforms the penniless into a man of means—is an ever-present vision of the possible and desirable. Although one may also achieve material success through the routine practice of theft or fraud, the "big score" remains the symbolic image of quick success.[1]

Armed robbery has remained one of the principal methods of obtaining the big haul. Formerly safe burglary was another principal method, but advanced safe and police technologies have reduced its importance. Other methods, however, have emerged to replace it. For instance, with the widespread use of payroll checks and existence of check cashing facilities after World War II, the big check score became common. In this "caper" several thousand dollars of payroll checks are cashed by a small team working usually on Friday, Saturday, and Sunday. But with the increased difficulty in cashing payroll checks, this score has become less prevalent. Car-theft operations are another type of big score. Likewise, a large check or bank account withdrawal which involves the thief's posing as a businessman and interacting with bank officials is a popular type of big score. It can be expected that as types of big scores are prevented by new precautionary measures and technology, others will emerge and the thief will continue to pursue the large sums of money which can be taken in one big caper.

The second major theme is that of "rightness," or "solidness," which involves the personality attributes of honesty, responsibility, and loyalty. A thief, to be considered "all right" by his peers (something which is extremely important to him), must meet his obligations, pay his debts, keep his appointments, and, most importantly, *never* divulge information to anyone which may lead to the arrest of another person. His character, his "rightness," is one of the most important dimensions of his life. For

1. Richard Cloward and Lloyd Ohlin, *Delinquency and Opportunity* (New York: The Fress Press, 1960), p. 22.

instance, a convict who had considerable contact with the system of the thief, and who identified himself as a thief, in describing his release plans emphasized the fact that he had good character.

I won't have no trouble getting started out there. I gotta lotta friends in the bay area. I mean friends I've had for years. Good people. Squares. Even though they know I'm a thief, they know that I'll never let them down. I never steal from a friend. And they can count on me. These are people that I've done a lotta favors for and they've helped me, too. (Interview, Soledad Prison, June 1966)

This 53-year-old man, who has served six months for safe burglary, eight years for a large armed robbery and another six years for safe burglary involving explosives, wrote me a letter in which he described his experience on his first day out of prison. His description of an incident on a train and his impressions of the general morality of contemporary society are relevant to the thief's conceptions of good character.

Aside from above mentioned, I noticed a little boy, having difficulty to reach a paper drinking cup. *No one* moved to help him. I was in the middle of the car, and got up to help him. Other passengers looked at me when I sat down, after doing this something that I didn't even give a second thought.

John, what has happened to people? Now I can understand what I have been reading in regards to those that will stand by and not caring about no one but their immediate families. (Letter from parolee, dated June 22, 1966)

Other thieves and persons studying this system have commented on the importance of good character, "solidness," or "rightness," in the system of the thief.[2]

Another important facet of thievery is "coolness." Coolness has two dimensions. First is the ability to keep one's composure in the face of difficulties encountered on capers. The following account of an armed robbery reveals this facet:

I had all these people lined up against the wall on one side of the place but the bartender was behind me and I had to keep one eye on him. Well, this motherfucker decided that he had a chance to get a pistol he had behind the bar, so he went for it. Now I had to swing around and take my attention off these people and bring him back under control. Things could've got out of hand right there. But I was cool, man. I stuck that fucking shotgun in his face and told that motherfucker to freeze! Then I whipped around to those other people and kept them under control. Finally I got everybody calmed down and under control and I went on and got them in the ice box and then made the manager open the safe. (Interview, San Quentin, March 1968)

2. For instance, see Cloward and Ohlin, *Delinquency and Opportunity,* p. 23. Also see the autobiography of a thief, Jack Black, *You Can't Win* (New York: The Macmillan Company, 1927), pp. 112–13.

Second, coolness is involved in the day-to-day living of the thief. The good thief lives in an unobtrusive manner, careful not to draw unwanted attention and "heat."

Man, a good thief don't want to draw no heat. He can't be flashing his roll, showing up in a new suit every day, hanging around the same places, spending money, so everyone will know he ain't working and will start asking questions. This is just asking for trouble. A good thief don't let nobody but his partners know how much money he's got. He keeps a good cover so squares will think he's working and won't ask questions. (Field notes, San Quentin, September 1967)

Finally, a dimension which was once more important, but is disappearing as the thief system itself fades, is that of skill. To get a sense of its former importance, and also of the age of this system, we turn to the autobiography of a "yegg" (thief) in the last century. Jack Black describes "Foot-and-a-Half George," a pioneer safe cracker:

This grizzled old yegg was a by-product of our Civil War. Apprentice to a village blacksmith, he was drafted into the army, where he learned the disruptive force of powder, and many other things useful to him in his profession of safe breaking. His rough war service, his knowledge of mechanics and explosives combined to equip him for what he became—one of the pioneers of safe breaking. From black powder he turned to dynamite and afterward was one of the first to "thrash out the soup"—a process used by the bums and yeggs for extracting the explosive oil, nitroglycerine, from sticks of "dan," or dynamite. He boasted that he had never done a day's work outside of prison since he was mustered out of the army, except one year in a safe factory in the East where he went deliberately and worked for starvation wages to learn something of the construction of a very much used make of safe and its lock.[3]

A wide variety of other skills have been involved in thievery. Presently, because of the increased use of forged documents and electronic devices in the big scores, photographic and electronic skills are valued. Also "fronting" skills (the ability to dissemble with composure and adeptness) have been and are still highly valued, since these skills are often employed in big scores. For instance, Jack Black and a partner discuss a potential score:

"Kid," he said, "I read in the papers some time ago that a man named Charlie Rice, in New York City, put on a cheap, black alpaca coat, put his cap in his pocket, and with a pencil on his ear walked into a bank and behind the counter where there were twenty clerks at work. Unnoticed, he picked up twenty-five thousand dollars in bank notes and walked out.

"That suggested to me that I can walk into this jewelry store some evening before Christmas when they will have an extra force of clerks employed, and go behind the counter if I am dressed like a clerk. If I can get behind the

3. Jack Black, *You Can't Win,* pp. 108–9.

counter you can surely get in front of it. I will put a tray of stones out for your inspection, and you will walk out with it." [4]

The World View of the Thief

The thief believes that he lives in a generally corrupt and unjust society, and that he and other thieves are actually among the few honest and trustworthy people. For instance, a thief comments on his life style:

The way I see it a guy has several ways to go in this world. If he's not rich in front, he can stay honest and be a donkey. Only this way he works for someone else and gets fucked the rest of his life. They cheat him and break his back. But this guy is honest.

Now another way is he can start cheating and lying to people and maybe he can make himself a lot of money in business, legally I mean. But this guy isn't honest. If he's honest and tries to make it this way he won't get nowhere.

Another way he can make it and live a halfway decent life and still be honest is to steal. Now I don't mean sneaking around and taking money or personal property from assholes who don't have nothing. I mean going after big companies. To me this is perfectly honest, because these companies are cheating people anyway. When you go and just take it from them, you are actually more honest than they are. Most of the time, anyway, they are insured and make more money from the caper than you do.

Really, I think it is too bad it is this way. I mean it. I wish a guy could make a decent living working, which he can't do because those people who have it made got that way fucking the worker. And they are going to keep it that way. And all that crap about having to have laws protecting property. These are just laws set up by those people who got all the property and are going to make sure they keep it. (Interview, San Quentin, October 1967)

A thief interviewed by a sociology class comments on honesty and corruption:

I never did envy anybody that was a member of society, frankly. I haven't got a hell of a lot of use for society. Not when I've been takin' care of those members of your society—district attorneys and judges. I just don't dig this society. I just got the wrong definition or something along the line pertaining toward it. I believe a man should be honest, don't misunderstand me.[5]

From Sutherland's study of the professional thief, we borrow a thief's comments on honesty in American society:

I would like nothing better than to live in England the rest of my life if I could get a legitimate job there. I like the climate in spite of all the howls you hear about it. I like the beauty of their lawns and houses and castles. I like the simple way in which they live. And most of all I like to keep honest in England, because everyone else is honest. But it would not be so easy to stay

4. Ibid., p. 173.
5. Taped interview of 56-year-old retired safe burglar, University of Washington.

honest here in the United States, because so few other people would keep me company in honesty.[6]

THE HUSTLER

Hustling is a system of theft quite distinct from that of the *thief*. It is presently carried on mainly by Negroes in large urban centers, who, because of segregation and prejudice, have had minimal contact with lower-class Irish, Italians, Jews, and Poles who have carried the traditions of the thief in the large cities.

Negroes have acquired their own system of theft. It has its own values, beliefs and its own styles of stealing, styles which were picked up in the South from a variety of grifters, short-con men, flimflam men, pool hustlers, pimps, and gamblers, who regularly toured rural areas and, while "beating" rural Negroes, were also imparting these forms of theft.[7] Moreover, in the cities Negroes were the victims of various semilegitimate and illegitimate hustlers—loan sharks, salesmen and gamblers. So styles of "hustling" have been familiar to the Negro for decades while the styles of heavy theft have remained remote.

Major Themes of Hustling

The major theme of hustling is "sharpness." Sharpness has two dimensions: (1) sharpness in language and intellectual skills and (2) sharpness in appearance. The language-intellectual-skills component is the ability to dupe, to outwit through conversation. Sharpness in appearance is maintaining a good "front"—sharp clothes, car, and physical appearance. For instance, a convict in my sample who considered himself a hustler commented on his own sharpness, "smoothness," or "slickness."

> I always went in for "smooth" crime. I didn't like no violence. Only suckers go that violent route. I rip a cat off with my conversation. Ya really got to be slick to do that.
>
> Outside, I stay sharp. I mean, I dress sharp, always make a good impression.

6. Edwin H. Sutherland, *The Professional Thief* (Chicago: University of Chicago Press, 1937), p. 181.

7. Grifting is a behavior system of theft which has often been confused with that of "heavy" theft. It differs in that it involves various types of con games, rather than direct forms of theft. Furthermore, grifters and other con men do not value the thief's conception of good "character" and trust. For descriptions of grifting or confidence men see Sutherland, *The Professional Thief*; David W. Maurer, *The Big Con* (New York: Bobbs-Merrill Co., Inc., 1940); David W. Maurer, *Whiz Mob* (New Haven: College & University Press, 1964). Don Gibbons has distinguished between the professional thief and the professional "heavy," a distinction which corresponds to that being made here between the grifter and the thief. See Donald Gibbons, *Society, Crime, and Criminal Careers* (Englewood Cliffs, N. J.: Prentice-Hall, Inc., 1968), pp. 246–57.

I always liked good clothes. Stacy Adams shoes, silk suits, a nice lid. I always spend a lot of money for clothes. Soon as I get out, I'm gonna get me some good clothes. A cat has to look good to feel good, and when he feels good he can make himself some money. He can beat those fools better. (Interview, San Quentin, July 1966)

The second major theme in hustling is hustling itself. In this sense hustling connotes being "on the hustle"—being alert, always ready for a chance to make money, and ready to beat a mark. Hustling is a 24-hour-a-day enterprise. Hustlers must steal or "take care of business" constantly. Malcolm X has described this aspect of hustling:

Full-time hustlers never can relax to appraise what they are doing and where they are bound. As is the case in any jungle, the hustler's every waking hour is lived with both the practical and the subconscious knowledge that if he ever relaxes, if he ever slows down, the other hungry, restless foxes, ferrets, wolves, and vultures out there with him won't hesitate to make him their prey.[8]

A related theme in hustling is the absence of trust. This dimension separates it most clearly from the system of the thief. The hustler believes that everyone is worthy of being taken, that everyone is ready to steal from everyone else if the opportunity presents itself and one must guard against being taken. It is a dog-eat-dog world, where there is little trust even among the hustlers themselves. Malcolm X comments on trust among hustlers:

What I was learning was the hustling society's first rule; that you never trusted anyone outside of your own close-mouthed circle, and that you selected with time and care before you made any intimates even among these.[9]

Henry Williamson, a hustler, describes the lack of trust among his peers.

Now they say that there ain't no honor among thieves, and this proves it because Jesse was holdin' out, and I was holdin' out! When it all got divided up, Delmos got three packages, and as far as he knew we only got three. We divided twenty dollars of the sixty or seventy that I got, me holdin' out forty or fifty! [10]

Styles of Hustling

There are two main styles of making money in hustling. The first of these is the short con. Remember that the hustler is different from the grifter or the con man. Although hustlers borrow some of the traits of the confidence man, they do not have the technical skill or the organizational capacities to execute the big con, the main forte of the con-

8. *The Autobiography of Malcolm X* (New York: The Macmillan Company, 1965), p. 109.
9. Ibid., p. 87.
10. Henry Williamson, *Hustler* (New York: Avon Books, 1964), p. 130.

fidence man. They do not have direct contact with these more skilled operators to learn the intricate techniques of the larger, more elaborate con games. Furthermore, the cutthroat, trustless relationships between hustlers prevent them from executing long term, elaborate schemes, so they have learned short-con games from grifters. These are con games which take only one or two people and can be executed with swiftness, usually in no more than a few hours.

There are a variety of short con games, but they all have one central theme: leading the mark to believe that he will obtain a sum of easy money, often by cheating one of the operators. Playing on the mark's greed, the operators maneuver him into a position where his own money is taken. For instance, a very old con game is the "pigeon drop." This game involves the discovery—by one of the players or the player and the mark simultaneously—of a wallet or envelope full of money. The mark is enticed to produce a comparable sum of his own in order to show good faith. The discovered sum and the mark's own money are placed together and a wallet or envelope stuffed with paper is secretly substituted. This is given to the mark for safekeeping while the player or players complete some required transaction. Then the mark is "blown off"; that is, left with the false money.

Other short con games are even less elaborate than this; for example, "greasy pig" or "three-card monte," which involve guessing which shell the pea is under or which card is a certain card. The hustler with deft hand motions, verbal deception, and sometimes the aid of a partner, allows his marks to win until the bets are high and then prevents them from guessing correctly.

The second main style of hustling is pimping or "macking." In macking, the mack has a "stable" or "string" of whores. His job is keeping the girls clothed, out of jail, healthy, and working. He is able to keep his stable because without him they would be harassed and robbed by police, prosecuted by the courts, robbed by "tricks," and generally unable to keep any order in their chaotic lives. Furthermore, they earn respect and prestige by being part of the stable of a high prestige "mack."

The mack drives a long car—a Cadillac (presently a "hawk"—a Cadillac El Dorado), dresses "sharp" (Italian silk suits are the present fad), and keeps his hair processed. He has a large roll of bills which he "flashes" constantly. When he is not "taking care of business"—that is, bailing his girls out of jail, seeing his lawyer, taking his girls to work, or spending leisure time with his girls—he usually is passing time in the company of other macks in one of their "hawks," a barber shop where he has his hair processed or at some coffee house, cafe, or bar where macks "hang out."

Though these are the ideal forms of hustling, not all hustlers are short-con men or pimps. Some hustlers engage in strong-armed robbery, armed robbery, burglary, picking pockets, and boosting. For instance, Malcolm X describes some of the hustlers in Harlem:

Jumpsteady was called that because, it was said, when he worked in white residential areas downtown, he jumped from roof to roof and was so steady that he maneuvered along window ledges, leaning, balancing, edging with his toes. If he fell, he'd have been dead. He got into apartments through windows. It was said that he was so cool that he had stolen even with people in the next room. I later found out that Jumpsteady always keyed himself up high on dope when he worked.

Fewclothes had been one of the best pickpockets in Harlem back when the white people swarmed up every night in the 1920's, but then during the Depression, he had contracted a bad case of arthritis in his hands. His finger joints were knotted and gnarled so that it made people uncomfortable to look at them.[11]

These latter forms of theft are not characterized by the major theme of hustling—that is, theft through conversation—but they are classified as hustling because they exhibit other aspects of hustling. They are day-to-day, survival types of theft, and there is still no trust among the hustlers—each will steal from the other if he has the chance.

The World View of the Hustler

To the hustler, the world is made up of those who take and those who are taken. They did not make it this way, but this is the way it is, so the sensible course for a man is to be one of those who take and try to keep others from taking from you:

There's a mark born every minute and a con man every hour. The con man is born to take care of the marks. Of course, I am a con man. There really are only two classes of people—marks and con men. I decided early in life that the angle boy gets the worm. I didn't make the rules. I just try to live by them. I'd rather be a con man than a mark.

You know how it goes in this dog-eat-dog world. You got to take the other guy before he takes you. You know, the real sharpies outwit the marks. Of course, it all depends on how you get ahead. My way was no different from, say, a lawyer or businessman. You know, a lawyer has a license to steal.[12]

THE DOPE FIEND [13]

The "dope fiend," "hype," or "junkie" is a person who for an extended period has used an opiate—morphine or heroin, but mostly

11. *The Autobiography of Malcolm X,* pp. 89, 90.

12. As quoted in Julian Roebuck, "The 'Short Con' Man," *Crime and Delinquency* (July 1964), pp. 241, 243.

13. The label "dope fiend" is that used most frequently by heroin addicts themselves. Although it possesses derogatory connotations for others, it doesn't for addicts. For this reason, and because it is the "natural" label, it will be used frequently throughout this book.

heroin. This use of drugs is the dominating aspect of his life. Securing money for drugs, finding drugs, and shooting drugs have crowded out all other facets. An ex-addict describes this dominance:

> When you're hooked, man, nothin' else matters. It's like putting all your worries in a spoon, cooking them up and sucking them up into a dropper and then sticking them in your arm. As long as you got stuff and you're loaded, you just don't care about nothin'! When you don't have any and you're sick, well, nothin' but getting some more gaw is on your mind. In a way it really makes life simple for ya. (Field notes, March 1967)

Irrespective of former history, former subcultural identities, once "hooked," the physiological effects and other exigencies of drug use take over and certain patterns emerge. During his addiction, the dramatic impact of drugs and the differential contact with other dope fiends cause the drug user to acquire the dope-fiend identity as his major identity. Even when he is not addicted, he is still primarily a dope fiend. The drug-addict adage "once a dope fiend, always a dope fiend" reflects this dominance of the dope-fiend identity, more than the physiological addictive aspects of the opiates.

Major Themes of the Dope-Fiend World

All the themes of this system are derived from the one dominant dimension—drug use. For instance, one major theme is "hooked." Being hooked is more than the physiological condition or the association of withdrawal symptoms with drugs stressed by Lindensmith.[14] It is the realization that one is now into or back into the full life of the dope fiend, and that he must now plan to secure drugs regularly, hustle daily, avoid arrest, and struggle to maintain some level of health while addicted.

"Scoring" is the second dominant theme. Scoring sometimes is an easy, inconsequential act, but it can be an excruciating, nerve-wracking, time-consuming operation. Often, days on end are taken up in finding "the bag man"—somebody who has drugs to sell. William Burroughs, a former drug addict, describes scoring:

> Of course, it often took me a long time to score.
>
> When I first hit New Orleans, the main pusher—or "the Man," as they say there—was a character called Yellow. Yellow was so named because his complexion was yellow and liverish-looking. He was a thin, little man with a dragging limp. He operated out of a bar near the NMD hall and occasionally chocked down a beer to justify sitting in the bar several hours a day. He was out on bail at the time, and when his case came to trial he drew two years.
>
> A period of confusion followed, during which it was difficult to find a score. Sometimes I spent six or eight hours riding around in the car with Pat, waiting

14. Alfred R. Lindensmith, *Opiate Addiction* (Bloomington, Indiana: Indiana University Press, 1947), p. 72.

and looking for different people who might be holding. Finally, Pat ran into a wholesale connection, a dollar-fifty per cap, no less than twenty.[15]

Scoring can be and often is one of the most undesirable and painful aspects of drug life. For instance, one dope fiend ruminating on his drug life stated:

Man, when I think of all the motherfucking hours I wasted of my life waiting for the connection. I can remember times that I stood at one corner for eight hours waiting for some asshole to come back with my stuff. I couldn't leave 'cause he had my last bread or I couldn't leave because I was afraid that I would miss him. So I just stood there, maybe in the fucking cold, waiting, steady watching every car. Man, don't you know that that is a miserable existence. (Field notes, San Francisco, August 1966)

Another theme is "fixing." It is the fix that cures the sickness, and it is the fix that is the central part of the whole dope life. A dope fiend, when asked about fixing, answered:

Ya, fixing is pretty damn important to the dope fiend. I can remember a lotta times, the hassles involved in fixing. A bunch of guys nervously arguing over who goes first. Or guys watching each other, making sure they don't get burnt. Ya know, until you see that bubble of blood come up in the dropper and watch the stuff disappear down the needle, you're nervous as hell. No, fixing sticks in your mind. I guess there's a lot of ritual in it too. (Interview, San Quentin, March 1967)

Related to fixing is the theme of sickness. It is avoiding sickness which propels the junkie. Burroughs comments on junk sickness:

It is possible to detach yourself from most pain—injury to teeth, eyes, and genitals present special difficulties—so that the pain is experienced as neutral excitation. From junk-sickness there seems to be no escape. Junk-sickness is the reverse side of junk-kick. The kick of junk *is* that you have to have it. Junkies run on junk-time and junk-metabolism. They are subject to junk-climate. They are warmed and chilled by junk. The kick of junk is living under junk-conditions. You cannot escape from junk-sickness any more than you can escape from junk-kick after a shot.[16]

The fourth dominant theme in the junkie's life is hustling. The price of drugs, the fact of rapidly increasing tolerance of drugs, and the physically debilitating aspects of drug use make it virtually impossible to support a habit while working. One must hustle. Dope fiends steal in all the ways that thieves and hustlers steal; but what distinguishes their theft from that of other thieves is that the dope fiend, because of his addiction, because of his need of a consistent supply of money and drugs and because of his inability to sustain extended periods with no money, tends to be pettier, less ambitious, less polished, more desperate, and

15. William Burroughs, *Junkie* (New York: Ace Books, 1953), p. 76.
16. Ibid., p. 92.

more impulsive. William Burroughs describes some of the addict-hustlers, some successful, some not:

> Louis was a shoplifter who had lost what nerve he ever had. He wore long, shabby, black overcoats that gave him all the look of a furtive buzzard. Thief and junkie stuck out all over him. Louis had a hard time making it. I heard that at one time he had been a stool pigeon, but at the time I knew him he was generally considered right.
>
> George was a three-time loser. The next time meant life as an habitual criminal. His life narrowed down to the necessity of avoiding any serious involvements. No pushing, no stealing; he worked from time to time on the docks. He was hemmed in on every side and there was no way for him to go but down.
>
> "The Fag" was a brilliantly successful "lush-worker." His scores were fabulous. He was the man who gets to a lush, never the man who arrives on the scene when the lush is lying there with his pockets turned inside out. A sleeping lush—known as "flop" in the trade—attracts a hierarchy of scavengers. First come the top lush-workers like "the Fag," guided by a special radar. They only want cash, good rings, and watches. Then come the punks who will steal anything. They take the hat, shoes, and belt. Finally, brazen, clumsy thieves will try to pull the lush's overcoat or jacket off him.
>
> Lonny was pure pimp. He was skinny and nervous. He couldn't sit still and he couldn't shut up. As he talked, he moved his thin hands which were covered on the backs with long, greasy black hairs. He was a sharp dresser and he drove a Buick convertible. But he wouldn't hesitate to hang us up for credit on a two-dollar cap.[17]

Of course many addicts support their habits by selling drugs. In fact, at some time in their addict life, all dope fiends at least dabble in "pushing." For some, though, this is their only hustle.

A final major theme is the obverse side of the effects of drugs. Opiates reduce one's needs, other than the need for drugs, to near nothingness. Appetites shrink and die. Burroughs comments on the loss of appetites and drives:

> Junk short-circuits sex. The drive to non-sexual sociability comes from the same place sex comes from, so when I have an H or M shooting habit I am non-sociable. If someone wants to talk, O.K. But there is no drive to get acquainted. When I come off the junk, I often run through a period of uncontrolled sociability and talk to anyone who will listen.[18]

Besides reducing the appetites, opiates induce a feeling, an attitude which perhaps is more important than the short-lived euphoria or the relief from withdrawal symptoms. This feeling, which may be related to the loss of appetites, is a feeling of "not caring." Mainly, the dope fiend doesn't care what others think of him. Consequently, devoid of appetites and of the essential social ingredient of caring what others think of oneself, the dope fiend's world is unsocial, individualistic, and isolationist.

17. Ibid., pp. 42–43.
18. Ibid., p. 106.

Such social contacts and ties as there are tend to exist only for the sake of securing drugs. This is true even of the ubiquitous sexual union. Because of habit, of the need for *some* companionship, and of the need to have someone hustle for them—to turn tricks or boost—dope fiends often have "ol' ladies." These relationships are usually short-lived and devoid of sex and compassion.

World View of the Dope Fiend

The dope fiend believes that life is for the most part dull, mundane, routine, or just aggravating. Drugs and the drug life offer the only escape from this dull and routine life. A San Francisco dope fiend describes the life:

> It is adventuresome to be an addict. Cowboys and Indians at the Saturday matinee didn't have a life that was any more exciting than this. The cops are the bad guys, you are the glorious bandit.
>
> The chase is on all day long. You awaken in the morning to shoot the dope you saved to be well enough to go out and get some more. First you have to get some money. To steal you have to outwit those you steal from, plus the police. It is very exciting.
>
> Now you have the cagey process of converting the stolen goods into dope and when you succeed in all of this you go home and regard yourself for a good day's caginess with a nice big fix.
>
> There are very few vocations offered to me in this society that can be as exciting as the vocation of drug addiction.[19]

A major world concern of the dope fiend is the legalization of drugs. The dope fiend feels that he has been unjustifiably denied a legal supply of drugs and, therefore, has been forced to take risks with the law (which he often loses) and to live a life of desperation, ill-health, and deprivation. This belief ignores the fact that it is this life, constituted of scoring, fixing, and hustling, that fills out his life and gives it meaning.

THE HEAD

A radically different system of drug use which exists parallel to the dope-fiend system is that of the head. The head uses a variety of drugs which have recently been labeled "psychedelic"—marijuana, peyote, mescaline, LSD, and methamphetamine. A major underlying difference in the two systems stems from the different drugs used. Mainly, excluding methamphetamine for the moment, the psychedelic drugs are not addictive and are relatively inexpensive. It is possible, therefore, to be a head and yet live a "normal" economic life. This is due simply to the matter of drug supply, because both the head and the dope fiend can function

19. *San Francisco Sunday Examiner and Chronicle,* April 16, 1967, Sec. 1, p. 2.

in a work setting. Both experience some impairment—the head experiences some reality distortion and the dope fiend some psychological and physiological apathy—but given a constant supply of drugs both are perfectly capable of functioning in most employment situations.

In the years prior to 1960, before the discovery and availability of the new drugs—peyote, LSD and methamphetamine—the head system was more cohesive and homogeneous and mainly confined to the lower class. But now some different population segments have come into the behavior system, which has resulted in considerable splintering of the system, and at present the head system is not a cohesive and homogeneous one. In fact, it may be fragmenting into several systems. For the present, however, we will consider it as one system with some internal differences which are related to the different drugs used. This will be done because to some extent there are important commonalities and similar emphases in all the drugs and the patterns surrounding them. Moreover, there is considerable overlap in usage of the various drugs. Many heads use all the psychedelic drugs regularly. Others use one primarily, but use the others with some frequency. And many others settle on one of them after going through periods of use of the others. Finally, there is considerable contact between groups specializing in different psychedelic drugs.

Major Themes of the Head's World

The major theme uniting all the various psychedelic drug-using groups together into one system is the emphasis in their drug use and their life style of seeking new and exotic experiences. Instead of seeing their drugs as something which "fixes" them—which cures their sickness or brings them to a state where they have no cares—they see drugs as mind expanders or pathways to new experiences. A reporter for the *San Francisco Chronicle,* after a short study of "heads," describes this emphasis:

> For the true "heads," drugs are paints on the palette of introspective possibilities to be mixed according to mood, need and fancy.[20]

Weed heads. The major theme of marijuana users, or weed heads, the oldest strand in the head system, is that of "coolness." Coolness to heads has three related facets. It connotes maintaining composure, control, and being in good taste. Moreover, it connotes maintaining politeness and smoothness, and avoiding violence and harshness in interpersonal relations. For instance, William Burroughs notices that tea heads (another term for weed heads) were "brought down" by straightforward, and therefore, crude business transactions:

> Tea heads are not like junkies. A junkie hands you the money, takes his junk and cuts. But tea heads don't do things that way. They expect the peddler

20. Nicholas Van Hoffman, *San Francisco Chronicle,* August 24, 1966, p. 14.

to light them up and sit around talking for half an hour to sell two dollars' worth of weed. If you come right to the point, they say you are a "bring down." In fact, a peddler should not come right out and say he is a peddler. No, he just scores for a few good "cats" and "chicks" because he is viperish. Everyone knows that he himself is the connection, but it is bad form to say so. God knows why. To me, tea heads are unfathomable.[21]

In a comparison of different drug users, Allan G. Sutter confirms this aspect of coolness:

It is "uncool" to engage in senseless violence or gang fighting. Two types of "cool people" describe their reactions to violence differently. The first is a "mellow dude" who uses "weed" for social purposes:

> See the people I know, after they got hip to weed and climbed out of that rowdy trip, they just squared off completely you know. They wanted to jump sharp, enjoy themselves and be mellow instead of getting all brutalized.[22]

Finally, "coolness" suggests meticulousness and fastidiousness in dress and appearance. Weed heads value their "threads" [clothes] and their "short" [car] highly and give considerable attention to both.

Acid heads. The two unique central themes of acid heads are tolerance and spontaneity. Simmons and Winograd in describing the emergence of the "hang-loose ethic" among the youth "scene" (of which LSD use is an integral part) emphasize spontaneity and tolerance:

As part and parcel of the importance placed on directly experiencing oneself and the world, we find that *spontaneity,* the ability to groove with whatever is currently happening, is a highly valued personal trait. Spontaneity enables the person to give himself up to the existential here and now without dragging along poses and hangups and without playing investment games in hopes of possible future returns. The purest example of spontaneity is the jazz musician as he stands up and blows a cascade of swinging sounds.

Another facet of the hang-loose ethic is an untutored and unpretentious *tolerance.* Do whatever you want to as long as you don't step on other people while doing it. A girl is free to wet her pants or play with herself openly while she's up on an acid trip and no one will think less of her for it. A man can stand and stare at roadside grass blowing in the wind and no one will accuse him of being the village idiot. If you like something that I don't like, that's fine, that's your bag: just don't bring me down.[23]

Both spontaneity and tolerance appear to be related to LSD experiences. This drug seems to break down, temporarily at least, one's categorization

21. Burroughs, *Junkie,* p. 31.

22. "The World of the Righteous Dope Fiend," *Issues in Criminology* (Fall 1966), p. 188.

23. J. L. Simmons and Barry Winograd, *It's Happening* (Santa Barbara, Calif.: Marc-Laird Publications, 1966), pp. 15–16.

of the world, and therefore its continued use makes him less rigid and more spontaneous.

Meth heads. The "meth head," or "speed freak," is the hardest to relate to the general head system. In many ways, "speed" is antithetical to the other drugs in that it produces hyperactivity and to some extent its use results in dependency. Though one does not experience the actual withdrawal symptoms associated with opiates, one becomes extremely depressed after withdrawal. Furthermore, extended use seems to produce extreme paranoia, so that it isn't possible to continue a "normal" life while using methamphetamine regularly.

However, in many other ways it is a part of the head system. There is some overlap in the collectivities who use speed and the other head drugs, as well as an overlap in the major subcultural dimensions. For instance, the main theme of the speed freak is heightened and intensified experience, although this often becomes merely the desire to escape boredom or depression. These intense and heightened experiences, however, have a bizarreness to them. After prolonged use of the drug—crystals, speed or meth—the meth head will develop temporary psychosis characterized by extreme paranoia and erratic behavior. Several heads, dope fiends, and other criminals have commented on the behavior of meth heads:

That speed is some bad shit man, I'm not goin for that anymore. It took me months to get my head straightened out. I'm still not sure I'm all right.

I don't like being around one of those meth heads. The cat's always talking and jerking. They're fucked up, man. They walk up to a policeman and leap in his arms, telling him, "you got me!" The bull hadn't even noticed them before.

A little bit of speed is all right. But when you keep taking it, it fries your brain. The first thing you know you're running across roof tops, thinking everybody's after you. (Field notes, San Quentin, June 1967)

The World View of the Head

Heads feel that there is nothing immoral in the use of drugs—that is, the drugs that they use. (They sometimes feel that the hard drugs or opiates are, if not immoral, harmful.) Besides feeling that it is not immoral, they feel that it is beneficial. In fact, they believe and publicly contend that the use of drugs like marijuana and LSD would improve the relations between people and world conditions in general, since the use of these drugs would enhance people's insight into themselves and social situations. For example, several heads comment on the social benefits of drugs:

If these greed heads would just turn on once in awhile they wouldn't fuck over everyone like they do.

Squares'd come off that terrible hate trip they're on most the time if they got high more.

I think everyone should have at least one trip [on acid]. They'd understand themselves better. And maybe they'd get rid of a lot of their hangups. They'd relate to other people better. (Field notes, San Francisco, Summer 1966)

The acid heads, besides believing that drugs are beneficial and that "turning on" would cause many people to remove their "hangups," are quite critical and disapproving of conventional society on moral grounds. Simmons and Winograd present a collage of statements gathered in their experiences with the new acid heads:

To the widespread charges that they are being immoral, irresponsible, and irreverent, they turn about and reply: "Look at you, blowing up whole countries for the sake of some crazy ideologies that you don't live up to anyway. Look at you, mindfucking a whole generation of kids into getting a revolving charge account and buying your junk. (Who's a Junkie?) Look at you, needing a couple of stiff drinks before you have the balls to talk with another human being. Look at you, making it with your neighbor's wife on the sly just to try and prove that you're really alive. Look at you hooked on *your* cafeteria of pills, and making up dirty names for anybody who isn't in your bag, and screwing up the land and the water and the air for profit, and calling this nowhere scene, the Great Society! *And you're gonna tell us how to live?* C'mon, man, you've got to be kidding.[24]

THE DISORGANIZED CRIMINAL

More potential criminals emerge from delinquent groups in lower- and working-class urban segments than are, in fact, absorbed into the specialized criminal systems previously described. Many, in fact the majority of delinquents, though they are available for specialized criminal careers, never become part of any relatively cohesive system.[25] We must remember that the systems we are talking about, though they are natural systems (that is, they exist in the everyday world), are nebulous. Their dimensions are not spelled out clearly in a manual or brochure for interested parties. Their dimensions for the most part exist in the minds of the system members, in conversations between fellow members, and in conversations between fellow members and outsiders discussing the system. But here they are never complete, static, or coherent. They are continually being negotiated and changed. Consequently, it takes some skill merely to be able to learn the dimensions of the system when in contact

24. Simmons and Winograd, *It's Happening,* pp. 27–28.

25. Cloward and Ohlin have suggested that lack of opportunity is an important factor in delinquents not moving into thief systems (*Delinquency and Opportunity,* Chapter 6). David Matza has characterized the delinquent world as one of confusion and lack of coherence (*Delinquency and Drift* [New York: John Wiley & Sons, Inc., 1964]).

with it. Many are not able to identify the system or keep up with its frequent changes. Many delinquents pass into adulthood still in the state of confusion, not only moral confusion, vacillating between commitment to conventional value and criminal values, but cognitive confusion, unable to piece together a cohesive social world.

Disorganized criminals, who make up the bulk of convicted felons, pursue a chaotic, purposeless life, filled with unskilled, careless, and variegated criminal activity.

I was working at anything I could get. I wasn't looking for a special field, 'cause I hadn't found anything that captivated my interest. Mostly I was working around automobiles.

I spent a lot of time with the fellows, hanging around on the corner, riding around in cars, going to clubs and parties and dances.

I only planned to steal something a couple of times. Most of the time I'd be riding around with the fellows and somebody would say let's break in this place. (Interview, Soledad Prison, June 1966)

Others have recognized this common criminal pattern. For instance, Don Gibbons describes the semiprofessional property offender who engages in various simple and uncomplicated property crimes such as strong-armed robberies, holdups, burglaries, and larcenies.[26] Julian Roebuck and Ronald Johnson, when typing 400 convicted Negro felons, discovered a "jack-of-all-trades" offender which was their largest category.[27] This type of offender had a record of crimes lacking sophistication, planning, or pattern. These writers hypothesize that certain personality attributes, frequent incarceration, and lack of contact with seasoned criminals explain this lack of specialization and skill.

Major Themes of the Disorganized Criminal's World

Although these offenders are unskilled and unspecialized, they do participate in a criminal behavior system. It is a much less cohesive and coherent system, but it does have common dimensions and a tenuous identity and perspective. For instance, its major dimension is "doing wrong" or "fucking up." Early in his life, the disorganized criminal is committed to "doing wrong"—breaking rules, and getting into trouble. Henry Williamson, when he was young and participating in a variety of criminal activities, related that doing wrong was his favorite pastime:

I really didn't pay girls too much attention for a good little while. I saw them and I didn't see them. See, I always loved what I was doin' otherwise more. I like to go out and . . . I don't know, just be with guys. I guess I really just like to be goin' out and doin' wrong. That's all it were. I would be getting

26. Gibbons, *Society, Crime, and Criminal Careers,* p. 258.
27. "The Jack-of-all-Trades Offender," *Crime and Delinquency* (April 1962).

more enjoyment out of that than sittin' up in the show. Now I wouldn't get no enjoyment out of doin' wrong until after I had did it. I liked to just sit back and think about what I had did.[28]

One facet of "doing wrong" or "fucking up" is a devil-may-care attitude. The disorganized criminal often presents a great deal of bravado in the face of arrest or danger. Roebuck recorded the following statement from a disorganized criminal:

Once I got started, I had to go on with it . . . break on in and take the chance. You start thinking about the bread and you got to go. When I'm there set to go, the rollers [police] just got to get me, if they get me. The bust [arrest] just have to come.[29]

Another facet of this theme is self-defeatism. The disorganized criminal often believes that he is "born to lose," that he can't avoid "trouble," and that no matter how hard he tries, something will happen and things will go bad for him.[30]

Man, it don't matter how good things are goin' for me. You know, I may have a nice little job and everything running along smooth and I'll fuck it up. I'll fuck it up somehow. I always do. Like some cat can come along with a nice little caper and take me along. We'll get busted. It seems like I've been fucking up so long that it's always going to be like that. (Interview, San Quentin, March 1967)

This dimension—doing wrong—is very similar to "trouble," a focal concern of the lower class described by Walter Miller.[31] He stressed that keeping out of trouble is a dominant concern of the lower class; however, he also mentions that getting into trouble can be valued.

The second important theme of the disorganized criminal is his readiness or availability for criminal pursuits. The disorganized criminal is easily moved by his own impulse or others' encouragement to commit law infractions. Roebuck characterizes them as "docile, easygoing fellows," who "were easily talked into taking appreciable risks for small 'scores.' "[32]

Being available is a major characteristic of their day-to-day life. For instance, William Burroughs describes a group of disorganized criminals who frequented a certain New York bar:

This bar was a meeting place for 42nd Street hustlers, a peculiar breed of four-flushing, would-be criminals. They are always looking for a "set-up man," some-

28. Williamson, *Hustler,* p. 35.

29. Roebuck and Johnson, "The Jack-of-all-Trades Offender," p. 178.

30. The phrase "born to lose" is often tattooed in crude amateur style on the hand or arm of the disorganized criminal.

31. Walter Miller, "Focal Concerns of Lower-Class Culture," in Louis A. Ferman, Joyce L. Kornbluh, and Alan Haber, eds., *Poverty in America* (Ann Arbor: The University of Michigan Press, 1965), p. 263.

32. Roebuck and Johnson, "The Jack-of-all-Trades Offender."

one to plan jobs and tell them exactly what to do. Since no "set-up man" would have anything to do with people so obviously inept, unlucky, and unsuccessful, they go on cooling off as dishwashers, soda jerks, waiters, occasionally rolling a drunk or a timid queer, looking, always looking, for the "set-up man" with a big job who will say, "I've been watching you. You're the man I need for this set up. Now listen. . . ." [33]

Sheldon Messinger and Egon Bittner, in a study of professional crime in "West City," developed the concept of criminal labor force when they discovered large numbers of unsophisticated criminals who "hang around" various locations in the city waiting for work in crime.[34]

World View of the Disorganized Criminal

The disorganized criminal doesn't have a unique world perspective. For the most part he shares many of the components of the thieves' and hustlers' world view. But more than likely, in the same way that he was unable to learn the dimensions of these more sophisticated systems, he is also unable to develop a cohesive world view.

Besides having mixed up components of these other systems—such as the belief in the general corruptness of society or the dog-eat-dog society—he is likely to still possess much of his lower-class perspective, especially the dimensions of "toughness," "trouble," "fate," and "excitement" described by Walter Miller.[35]

STATE-RAISED YOUTH

One "criminal" system which is represented in the prison world is a system which develops and for the most part exists only in prison. This is the system of the state-raised youth. Many persons come to an adult prison after one or more commitments to the California youth prisons—Whittier, Preston, and Tracy. In these institutions they have come into contact with the intense and pervasive youth-prison behavior system, and it is very probable that they have taken on some of the dimensions of the state-raised identity.

Major Themes of the State-Raised System

The major theme of this system is related to "toughness"—the focal concern of the lower class described by Walter Miller. In the youth prison, which has a high concentration of delinquents committed to this concern,

33. Burroughs, *Junkie*, p. 20.
34. Sheldon L. Messinger, "Some Reflections of 'Professional Crime' in West City" (unpublished manuscript), p. 15.
35. Miller, "Focal Concerns of Lower-Class Culture," pp. 261–69.

toughness is raised to extreme heights. Violence is accepted as the proper mode of settling any argument, and one must be ready to resort to and face violence. One state-raised youth described to me his transaction with another inmate in youth prison.

State-Raised Youth. I was talking to my friend and this dude came over to us and wanted to know when I was gonna give him two cartons I owed him. I told him I was busy talking to my friend here and I would straighten him out later. He kept on and started getting a little salty. This got me hot, not 'cause he wanted the cigarettes, 'cause I righteously owed him the stuff. But the motherfucker was gettin' on my nerves. So finally I told him, "You know what, Man, I don't owe you no cigarettes." He told me, "Listen Man, you be here with the stuff in an hour." I told him, "I'll be here."

Interviewer. So what happened?

State-Raised Youth. Well, I went and got my stuff [weapons] and met the motherfucker.

Interviewer. What happened?

State-Raised Youth. I piped him. Laid his head open. He didn't fuck with me after that. (Interview, Soledad Prison, June 1966)

The second theme of the state-raised system is a clique-forming propensity. In the hostile, violence-prone prison world, youths usually band together in small cliques. To some extent this is for protection, to some extent it is an extension of the gang-forming behavior of the delinquent youth. For the most part these are loose-knit, constantly shifting cliques. But occasionally in the youth prison or later in adult prison a group of these youths will form a tight-knit clique and will share possessions, steal together, participate in prison rackets, and exert some force over other inmates and other inmate cliques. For instance, Claude Brown tells of his clique in a New York youth prison:

Within six months after I had moved into Aggrey House, most of the guys who had been in Carver House with me had been transferred to Aggrey. I had my old gang from Carver and some bigger cats who were already in Aggrey when I got there. I was raising twice the hell that I had raised in Carver House, and Simms wasn't smiling now.[36]

In a prison in Hawaii during a period of disorganization, McCleery reports that a group of "reform-school graduates" took over the prison for a short time:

Although other groups were emerging, the common background and attitudes of the reform-school group gave it a cohesiveness all out of proportion to its size. This group turned for its leadership (and established as its heroes) to two types of men whose status had been restricted by the traditional structure of the prison community: the most powerful and aggressive of older inmates, and new

36. Claude Brown, *Manchild in the Promised Land* (New York: The Macmillan Company, 1965), p. 201.

inmates who reached the prison with newspaper reputations for violent criminality.[37]

This syndicate was able to organize in this way largely because of the clique-propensity acquired by these youths in the youth prisons. Furthermore, in a given state (such as California or New York) which has a rather extensive system of youth prisons, by the time a state-raised youth comes to adult prison he has acquired a wide range of contacts with other state-raised youths with whom he may organize cliques.

A third theme of the state-raised youth is prison homosexuality. This homosexuality is somewhat unique to youth and adult prisons. There is a set of homosexual roles in prisons which become important categories in the state-raised youth perspective. The first of these is the "punk" or "kid" who is indigenous to the prison milieu. It is believed in prison that the punk or kid would not necessarily be a homosexual if he had not come to prison, but because of his passive, submissive, and feminine youthfulness, he is "turned out" by older aggressive homosexuals, or "jockers." Besides punks and jockers, there are queens in prison who are "real" homosexuals.

These homosexual roles are especially important to the state-raised youths because it is likely that they have spent the greater portion of their postpubertal years in a captive society away from females. They frequently enter into various sexual unions with other males. Some make use of a punk or queen occasionally as a sexual release considered slightly superior to masturbation. Others enter into a permanent relationship—a jocker-kid relationship—with a homosexual.

Moreover, a great deal of the time of the inmates in youth prisons is taken up in play related to homosexuality. In the verbal "dozens," where homosexuality is imputed to each other, or in "grab ass," where in aggressive play-acting each makes homosexual advances towards the other, the manhood of each is being challenged constantly.

The state-raised youth with years of this type of experience is unduly sensitive to homosexuality. He is quick to impute homosexuality to others and to prove his own masculinity. Furthermore, he has acquired a set of sexual meanings and definitions which are hard to reconcile with the sexual meanings of nonprison worlds.

The last important theme in the state-raised youth's world is the "streets," a concept which has a much different meaning for him than for other criminals. "The streets" is some place where you temporarily sojourn and engage in wild, abandoned pleasures. A state-raised youth described some of his escapades to me:

While I was in Whittier I ran off a couple of times. You know, we would hear

37. Richard McCleery, "The Governmental Process and Informal Social Control," in Donald Cressey, ed., *The Prison* (New York: Holt, Rinehart and Winston, Inc., 1961), p. 177.

that there was gonna be some wild party over in Bellflower—somebody's brother who visited him would tell him about it. And then we'd hit the fence that night. We were laying to get to that party and lap up that good booze and fuck them young bitches and maybe smoke some dope. But they'd catch us before we'd get anywhere and all we'd get is some more time. (Interview, Soledad Prison, June 1966)

For these youths, "the streets" is a category within the prison world. Releases from prison are seen as short vacations from prison. At times, a small clique of state-raised youths who have been released in the same time period will form on the streets and then live out the escapades they had planned in prison. These groups tend not to stay out of prison very long because their activities are blatant and bizarre.

The World View of the State-Raised Youth

The world view of these youths is distorted, stunted, or incoherent. To a great extent, the youth prison is their only world, and they think almost entirely in the categories of this world. They tend not to be able to see beyond the walls. They do conceive of the streets, but only from the perspective of the prison. Furthermore, in prison it is a dog-eat-dog world where force or threat of force prevails. If one is willing to fight, to resort to assault with weapons (or if he has many friends who will do so), he succeeds in this world.

Other than this, the world is made up of people with power—people who run the prison systems and enforce the rules or the people behind them who are being protected by the police, but little is known about how this works except that there is probably little chance of "beating 'em."

THE "MAN" IN THE LOWER CLASS

Now we turn to a noncriminal behavior system which produces a few felons. This is the lower class. Several writers have characterized the lower class as a unique behavior system or as possessing a unique cultural tradition. For instance, Walter Miller has described the separate tradition of the lower class in the United States, and Oscar Lewis has observed that there tends to be a common culture—the culture of poverty—among all people "who are at the very bottom of the socio-economic scale." [38] Herbert Gans has described the lower-class stratum as a behavior system and characterizes the man in the lower class thusly:

38. Walter Miller, "Lower-Class Culture as a Generating Milieu of Gang Delinquency," *Journal of Social Issues* (1958); Oscar Lewis, *The Children of Sanchez* (New York: Vintage Books, 1961).

For the lower-class man, life is almost totally unpredictable. If they have sought stability at all, it has slipped from their grasp so quickly, so often, and consistently that they no longer pursue it. From childhood on, their only real gratifications come from action-seeking, but even these are few and short-lived. Relationships with women are of brief duration, and some men remain single all their lives. Work, like all other relationships with the outside world, is transitory. Indeed, there can be no identification with work at all. Usually, the lower-class individual gravitates from one job to another, with little hope or interest of keeping a job for any length of time. His hostility to the outside world therefore is quite intense, and its attempts to interfere with the episodic quality of his life are fought. Education is rejected by the male, for all of its aims are diametrically opposed to action-seeking.[39]

The lower class is the cradle for many of the criminal behavior systems described previously. But apart from supplying members for these systems, it sends some of its "normal" members to adult prisons, even though they have had no extensive involvement with criminal behavior systems and, in fact, consider themselves as honest and noncriminal persons. This is because lower-class values are such that felony commission is likely even in normal lives of the lower class member. For instance, Walter Miller, after identifying focal concerns of this segment states:

Following cultural practices which comprise essential elements of the total life pattern of lower-class culture automatically violates certain legal norms.[40]

Other writers have recognized that the lower class, or segments of it, constitutes a subculture of violence where assaultive acts and murders are relatively frequent.[41]

Major Themes of the Lower Class

The central theme of this identity, and that which is related to occasional felonious behavior, is "manhood," or *"machismo."* In the lower class, manhood is proven by the demonstration of physical prowess and courage, and the willingness to resort to physical violence when threatened. Oscar Lewis in describing *machismo* in the culture of poverty emphasizes lack of fear.[42] Claude Brown describes manhood in the Harlem ghetto:

I had a bloody nose; they'd kicked my ass good, but I didn't mind, because they hadn't taken my quarter. It wasn't the value of the money. It couldn't have been. It was just that these things symbolized a man's manhood or principles.

39. Herbert Gans, *Urban Villagers* (New York: The Free Press, 1962), p. 246.

40. Miller, "Focal Concerns of Lower-Class Culture," p. 269.

41. See, for example, Henry A. Bullock, "Urban Homicide in Theory and Fact," *Journal of Criminal Law, Criminology, and Police Science,* XLV (January–February 1955); Marvin E. Wolfgang, *Patterns of Criminal Homicide* (Philadelphia: University of Pennsylvania Press, 1958); and Gibbons, *Society, Crime, and Criminal Careers,* p. 354.

42. Lewis, *The Children of Sanchez,* p. xxvii.

That's what Johnny Wilkes used to like to call it, a man's principles. You don't mess with a man's money; you don't mess with a man's woman; you don't mess with a man's family or his manhood—these were a man's principles, according to Johnny Wilkes.[43]

The second theme of the "man" in the lower class is that of action seeking or "hell-raising." Walter Miller identifies excitement as a focal concern of the lower class:

For many lower-class individuals the rhythm of life fluctuates bewteen periods of relatively routine or repetitive activity and sought situations of great emotional stimulation. Many of the most characteristic features of lower-class life are related to the search for excitement or "thrill." Involved here are the highly prevalent use of alcohol by both sexes and the widespread use of gambling of all kinds—playing the numbers, betting on horse races, dice, cards. The quest for excitement finds what is perhaps its most vivid expression in the highly patterned practice of recurrent "nights on the town." This practice, designated by various terms in different areas ("honky-tonkin'," "goin' out on the town," "bar-hoppin' ") involves a patterned set of activities in which alcohol, music, and sexual adventuring are major components.[44]

The combination of these two—manhood and action-seeking—often result in the commission of a misdemeanor or felony. "Trouble," as suggested by Walter Miller, is often the culmination of the action-seeking episode. A lower-class man describes his crime:

I weren't doin' no good. Been drinkin' and talkin' all that violence. I thought this here woman took my money so I cut her. She hit me with her shoe first though.

I never stole though. If I were to steal I could of got in the union like I wanted to. (Interview, Soledad Prison, June 1966)

World View of the Lower Class

There are two important dimensions in the general world view of the "man" in the lower class. The first of these is the belief in fate. To a great extent he believes things are determined for him and that he doesn't have much control over the direction of his life. Walter Miller has described this dimension:

Many lower-class individuals feel that their lives are subject to a set of forces over which they have relatively little control. These are not directly equated with the supernatural forces of formally organized religion, but related more to a concept of "destiny," or man as a pawn of magical powers. Not infrequently this often implicit world view is associated with a conception of the ultimate futility of directed effort towards a goal: if the cards are right, or the dice good

43. Brown, *Manchild in the Promised Land,* p. 256.
44. Miller, "Focal Concerns of Lower-Class Culture," p. 269.

to you, or if your lucky number comes up, things will go your way: if luck is against you, it's not worth trying.[45]

The second dimension is the dichotomy between themselves and "them," the people with power, the people with money who run things. "They" can't be trusted since they do not care about the lower-class person; in fact, all they seem to want to do is exploit him and control him. This distrust of "them" results in a distrust of the many institutions of the conventional society which the lower-class people see working in the advantage of "them." Oscar Lewis describes this distrust in the culture of poverty:

A critical attitude toward some of the values and institutions of the dominant classes, hatred of the police, mistrust of government and those in high position, and a cynicism which extends even to the church gives the culture of poverty a counter quality and a potential for being used in political movements aimed against the existing social order.[46]

THE SQUARE JOHN

Many "conventional" persons are sent to prison. In other words, many persons who have had no contact with criminal behavior systems, and in fact have always considered themselves upstanding citizens, are convicted of felonies. The "man" in the lower class, though he doesn't consider himself a criminal, does not consider himself a conventional person. Too much of his normal, accepted behavior violates the law and he is generally too antagonistic towards people in high positions and the government for him to identify with conventional society. There are, however, many persons convicted of felonies who are members of working-class or middle-class strata who conceive of themselves as noncriminal, ordinary citizens, who, perhaps, have made a "mistake" or have a serious "problem."

Many studies have described the law-breaking behavior of conventional people and have stressed their lack of criminal commitment and their lack of contact with other criminals. For instance, in a study of check forgery, Lemert discovered one class of forgers which contained almost 30 per cent of a sample of convicted forgers who "have acquired normal attitudes and habits of law observance" and who "come from a class of persons we would ordinarily not expect to yield recruits to the criminal population." [47] Donald Cressey describes a class of offenders—embezzlers —who, although they conceive of themselves as conventional people,

45. Ibid., p. 267.
46. Lewis, *The Children of Sanchez*, p. xxvii.
47. Edwin Lemert, "An Isolation and Closure Theory of Naïve Check Forgers," in *Human Deviance, Social Problems, and Social Control* (Englewood Cliffs, N. J.: Prentice-Hall, Inc., 1967), p. 102.

steal when they have an unshareable problem, an opportunity to steal, and are able to adjust their conceptions of self as trusted persons though they are taking funds entrusted to them.[48] Don Gibbons, in describing criminal role careers, has included several types of offenders—professional "fringe" violators, one-time losers, statutory rapists, aggressive rapists, violent sex offenders, nonviolent sex offenders, murderers, and homosexuals—who conceive of themselves as conventional, noncriminal people.[49]

Emergence of the Square John Identity

When these "conventional" offenders come into contact with "criminals" in city jails and prison, they discover that they are quite different. They discover, possibly for the first time, that there are persons who not only systematically engage in crime, but who also have a system of beliefs and values, as well as an ideology, which justifies crime. They find it difficult to understand these criminals, who often offend their conventional sensibilities. They discover that, though they themselves have been convicted of a felony and will be imprisoned, they are not criminals. They accept the label criminals use for them—square johns. In doing so, they are recognizing, sometimes for the first time explicitly, their participation and identification with the conventional world. Often they had taken their membership in conventional society and their attendant conventional perspective for granted. They had "identified" themselves in other ways—by their occupational, class, or family position. But now in the midst of "foreigners," their conventional identity is thrown into relief. When this happens, the conventional perspective they had taken for granted often becomes more explicit, more crystallized, and in fact, purer—that is, more consistently conventional and more puritanical.

Major Dimensions of the Square John Identity

This identity and perspective differs from the criminal identities in some very important dimensions, most of which are related to conventional moral norms. For instance, the square john shares the conventional society's belief in property rights, and he is more apt to uphold the value of working for a living and obeying the legal code.

The square john differs from the criminal in that he has no familiarity with certain criminal values which are important in prisons, such as "do not inform on others." He is not apt to find "snitching" or "snitches" repugnant. Furthermore, he has difficulty learning the concept of "do your own time," which is somewhat natural to most criminals.

48. Donald Cressey, *Other People's Money* (New York: The Free Press, 1963), p. 30.
49. Gibbons, *Society, Crime, and Criminal Careers,* chapters 14 and 15.

Most importantly, the square john does not consider himself a criminal. He is able to consider himself an "honest" person (even though he has been convicted of a felony which sometimes involves theft) because (1) he was not in fact guilty (many square johns persist in denying guilt of any crime, a denial which can have two forms, denial of the crime, as in the case of homosexuals who deny that homosexual behavior is in fact a crime, or denial of the commission of the crime); (2) he committed the felony under the extreme pressures of a circumstantial "problem"; or (3) he committed the crime under the pressure of a psychological "problem."

The World View of the Square John

The square john shares conventional society's perspectives, displaying the same variations that exist in this broad segment. He is, however, apt to be relatively conservative, and racially prejudiced. There seems to be a relationship between theft and assault in the case of conventional people and conservative attitudes.

CLASSIFICATION OF FELONS ACCORDING TO CRIMINAL BEHAVIOR SYSTEMS

A sample of 116 persons released on parole in 1966 when classified according to the behavior systems had the following distribution:[50]

System	*Per Cent*
Thief	8
Hustler	7
Dope fiend	13
Head	8
Disorganized criminal	27
State-raised youth	15
Lower-class "man"	6
Square john	16
Total	99

The illustration below may be useful in visualizing some of the relationships between the various systems. Roughly, the relative age of involvement of the individual with the system is indicated by its position from left to right. The relationship in recruitment between the systems is indicated spatially. Furthermore, the relative size and cohesiveness of each system is indicated by size and shading.

50. See the Appendix for the instrument used to classify felons according to these behavior systems.

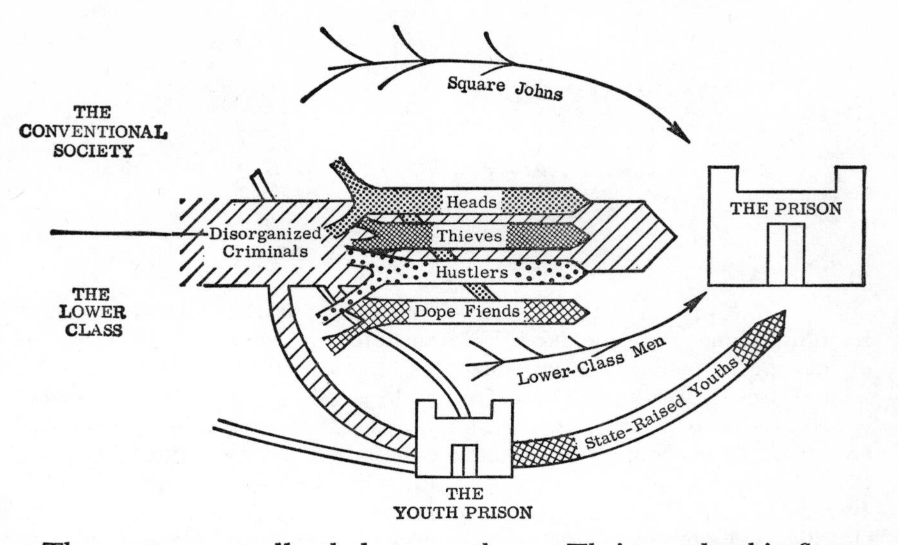

These systems are all nebulous to a degree. Their membership fluctuates and many individuals are ambivalent in their identity relative to the system. In spite of this, these systems exist and tend to maintain some degree of cohesiveness and consistency. This is possible because some collectivity at a given time is active in the system and is to some degree following the patterns of the system and articulating its dimensions. Furthermore, they exist because some persons who are in contact with them, either by direct participation or by interacting with participants, tend to conceive of each system as an entity and are able to delimit the boundaries of that system and to propagate it.

Patterns of identification with these systems vary considerably. Some people alternately become involved in them and then participate in other systems. However, many maintain their identification relative to one of them, and many others strengthen their commitment to one of them when arrested and imprisoned. Their identity, therefore, relative to the system with which they have had more contact, is likely to influence greatly their life in prison as well as their future after release.

2

THE PRISON EXPERIENCE:
Classification and Sentencing

The primary official task of the prison is the detention of the felon for a length of time. Next in importance, presently, is his correction, or, in current penological language, his "treatment." In California, as in many states with progressive correctional systems, there are two processes which are essential to the correctional task. These are classification and sentencing. This chapter will examine these two processes and attempt to demonstrate that in both cases the outcome is far from a total success. In fact, instead of furthering the "treatment" of the felon, in many cases classification and sentencing actually promote self-disorganization, a sense of injustice, and increased commitment to criminal values and beliefs. A major reason for this, it will be argued, is that the official agents approach these tasks from a position of ignorance, insensitivity, or intolerance of the experiences and perspectives of the felons they are attempting to correct. In attempting to understand the actual effects of these processes, we will avoid this mistake by examining classification and sentencing from the standpoint of the felon.

CLASSIFICATION

Only a minority of felons are strongly and exclusively committed to a deviant behavior system when arrested, convicted, and imprisoned. The majority, even a majority of "criminals," have participated to some degree in both criminal and conventional systems and are to some extent ambivalent in commitment.[1] The process of being diagnosed and classified by official agents, however, tends to polarize those who stand in the middle, ambivalent between a deviant commitment and a conventional commitment. Probably most of the relatively uncommitted shift towards

1. Gresham Sykes and David Matza first emphasized the tentativeness of commitment of delinquents to criminal values in "Techniques of Neutralization," *American Sociological Review* (December 1957); in the field of corrections, see Stanton Wheeler, "Socialization in Correctional Communities," *American Sociological Review* (October 1961), Peter G. Garabedian, "Social Roles and the Process of Socialization in the Prison Community," *Social Problems* (Fall 1963), and Daniel Glaser, *The Effectiveness of a Prison and Parole System* (Indianapolis: Bobbs-Merrill Co., 1964), pp. 54, 95. All have examined the tentative commitment to criminal values.

a deviant identity. Some, however, do shift towards a conventional one, or remain ambivalent.

Treatment Philosophy

This polarization of identities is to some extent related to the infusion of treatment philosophy into the sentencing and classification of prisoners. Treatment philosophy has brought about a shift in focus in the handling of criminals. Currently in sentencing and classifying a felon, the felon himself instead of the felony is the focus. The criminal act is seen more as a symptom or an indicator of the criminal's character or personality. For instance, a probation officer writes:

> A profound and exciting thing is happening in our lifetime. After persisting for centuries in an eye-for-eye, tooth-for-tooth concept of criminal justice, our society's philosophy of crime and its control is now making a massive turn in the direction of an individualized handling of offenders that the time regularly considers the offender himself, and not just his offense.[2]

So, instead of merely punishing a man for his crime, society seeks to determine what kind of person he is and to understand why he committed the act or acts. This interest in the "causes" of his behavior precipitates or enhances a corresponding interest on the part of the offender himself. While the court and the prison officials probe into his past and his psyche, he must conduct his own inquiry and discover answers which are acceptable to himself. Shaping his inquiry, however, is one important concern which is absent from that of the officials—he must to some extent strive to maintain some dignity, some self-respect as he reaches new conclusions about himself.

The official diagnostic agents employ, and intentionally or inadvertently make available to the felon, several personality models and attendant explanations for his criminality. From the felon's standpoint, however, the models they use are undignified and at times unfeasible. Therefore, he more often turns to a deviant perspective which does offer him a feasible and dignified explanation for his criminal behavior and his criminal position in the world.

Presentencing Experiences

The formal examination of the person's character and past occurs after the individual has been through certain poignant and disorienting experiences, experiences which have rendered him more receptive to reinterpretations of his past behavior. These experiences begin with arrest, when the suspect is taken to a city jail and left, sometimes for hours, in

2. Paul Keve, *The Probation Officer Investigates* (Minneapolis: University of Minnesota, 1960), p. 3.

a holding cell or in a booking office while the slow process of formal booking and fingerprinting is completed. If this process takes place in a large city, the suspect finds himself in the company of a fairly large group of silent and disgruntled newly arrested persons. The booking-room officers who are working in close proximity process scores of incoming prisoners daily and, therefore, tend to maintain an insulation of formality or ferocity in order to withstand the frequent supplications from the mass of incoming prisoners. The suspect's most importunate entreaties go unnoticed, unanswered, or harshly repulsed. To gain permission to make a single telephone call, as is his legal right, often takes considerable persistence on the part of the prisoner:

> They took us upstairs. There was six of us all together. Five men and a woman. They put all the men in a cage, a 6 x 6 cage. Two walls were concrete, two were chicken wire. We were there six hours. There was no place to sit down, no place to lay down. All you could do was stand or squat. Everybody was involved in their own little thing, trying to figure out how bad it was for them, trying to figure out what they were going to do.
>
> They treated us just like an animal in a cage, a pet. We were ignored. You were ignored most of the time. When they wanted to give us some attention they did it at their discretion. There we were for six hours—while they did paper work and fingerprinted us. There was one that always wanted to show that no matter how he loosened up he was always in charge. Like, he went over to the wall and he would read us our rights: "You have the right to remain silent as long as you can stand the pain," or he would walk by the cage and take out his gun and flip open the cylinders and spin it and then stick it back in the holster, you know, and then look over and grin.
>
> You start thinking what does this all mean, why was I arrested. You know, why couldn't I've read the signs, you know. I felt that there were signs and if I'd read them properly I could've avoided the whole thing. It was like my whole world collapsed. You know how they say a dying man feels, that his whole life passes in front of him. Well, I got a feeling something like that.[3]

From the booking room he is transferred to a small felony tank or to a "bull pen" which houses all offenders, from drunks to felony prisoners. Two, three, or four chaotic days follow. The prisoner is taken from his cell for frequent trips to the offices of the investigating officers, for visits with friends or relatives, for arraignment, a preliminary hearing, and consultation with a lawyer. During this time, through the occasional phone calls he is granted, through visits with friends and family, and through messages carried by departing prisoners or his lawyer, the prisoner often grapples furiously to effect certain action, to complete plans, to fulfill unfulfilled responsibilities, to tie together some of the loose ends of his torn life on the outside.

Then the pace slows down, his efforts succeed or fail, the People's case against him is established, and the slow court proceedings take over. He

3. Taped interview of person recently arrested for the first time, April 1968.

is transferred to a county jail where he is housed in larger "tanks" with other prisoners who are also waiting for trial or are serving county jail sentences. Here 30, 40, 60, or possibly 120 days pass by slowly, punctuated only by periodic counts, infrequent visits, and two or three notoriously bad daily meals.[4] The hours are spent crowded with other prisoners in narrow aisles in front of the cells or in small day rooms. He plays cards, dominoes, reads, and sleeps; or with a small group of other prisoners, he "trips" or "shoots the bull." Alternately, each member of the group attempts to break the monotony with some story from his reading, his fantasies, or from his or his friends' biographies. In this way over a period of time, each prisoner's repertoire of knowledge, experiences, stories, ideas, and opinions is exhausted. In this period, the bad food, the poor air, lack of sunlight and exercise, and the low morale have an overwhelming impact upon the man's general health, which in turn impinges upon his mood and consciousness.

Some persons who are sent to prison avoid this period of incarceration by posting bail, but they are a minority.[5] Even posting bail, however, doesn't prevent all the disorganizing effects of arrest and conviction. One often loses his job through arrest, and because of time taken up in court appearances and because of the fact of his arrest itself finds it difficult to find new employment. Furthermore, the arrest usually disrupts his normal social life. All of his personal contacts will be different to some degree. He still must face formal and informal inquiries into his past and into his personality on the part of those who are searching for reasons for his downfall.

These experiences—arrest, trial, and conviction—threaten the structure of his personal life in two separate ways. First, the disjointed experience of being suddenly extracted from a relatively orderly and familiar routine and cast into a completely unfamiliar and seemingly chaotic one where the ordering of events is completely out of his control has a shattering impact upon his personality structure. One's identity, one's personality system, one's coherent thinking about himself depend upon a relatively familiar, continuous, and predictable stream of events. In the Kafkaesque world of the booking room, the jail cell, the interrogation room, and the visiting room, the boundaries of the self collapse.

While this collapse is occurring, the prisoner's network of social relations is being torn apart. The insulation between social worlds, an insulation necessary for the orderly maintenance of his social life, is punctured. Many persons learn about facets of his life that were previously unknown to them. Their "business is in the streets." Furthermore, a multitude of

4. Of the 70 felons interviewed in a follow-up interview, 47 per cent had spent at least three months in city and county jails before being sent to prison on their last conviction.

5. In the sample of 70, only 12 per cent were released on bail during their last court proceedings.

minor exigencies that must be met to maintain social relationships go unattended. Bills are not paid; friends are not befriended; families are not fed, consoled, advised, disciplined; businesses go unattended; obligations and duties cannot be fulfilled—in other words, *roles* cannot be performed. Unattended, the structure of the prisoner's social relations collapse.

During this collapse a typical thought pattern often occurs. The arrested person usually reviews his immediate past and has second thoughts about the crime or crimes, or about the complex of behavior related to the crime. Facing the collapse of his personal world, the eventuality of conviction of a felony and a long prison term, he is very prone to express extreme regret. "Why did I do it?" "If only I hadn't done that." "Why did I get into this mess?" "If only I had another chance." All these typify his thinking. Regret and remorse probably reach the greatest intensity in the first few days when the impact of the disjointed experience is the greatest, but this type of reflection on his past continues throughout the presentencing phase.[6]

In this situation, the person, feeling extreme regret, disoriented in his thinking about himself in relation to a meaningful world, witnessing the collapse of his social relationships, in a position of disrespect in regard to the formal structure of society, begins to struggle to fit the pieces of himself back together, to restore himself to dignity in his own eyes and possibly in the eyes of some group of others. This struggle does not take place in isolation. If he is in jail awaiting trial and sentencing (which is true of the great majority), he is in constant and close interaction with a group or a variety of groups of prisoners; if he is out on bail, he is interacting with his family, his former friends, and acquaintances. After conviction he is generally in contact with the official investigator of the court—the probation investigator. This is most likely to be true of the middle range of convicted persons, those who have not made a positive commitment before entering jail and whom we are most interested in here. The committed often bypass the investigation or are legally ineligible for probation. It is the middle-range felon who has an ambiguous criminal past that is the most likely to be investigated by the probation department.

After sentencing he is transferred to a state prison. In California, he is transferred first to one of the reception-guidance centers. There he

6. Investigating police officers usually are questioning a suspect in this period and take advantage of his regret, his desire to win approval or forgiveness, and his searching for means to undo his acts and to restore things to their former state. By implied or expressed promises to help "straighten things out," to extend efforts in his behalf, they very often succeed in getting a surprising degree of cooperation from the suspect. Often, this cooperation works against him and aids in his conviction. It sometimes results in his alienation from his friends, whom he possibly betrayed in his cooperation. This becomes very important to him when he is abandoned by the police officers and is left alone to make his way in jail or prison.

remains for approximately six weeks while he goes through diagnosis, classification, and orientation.

Passing from the county jail to prison is another disorganizing event. Again the daily routine is shattered, and he is thrust into totally new surroundings. A new process of being moved like a pawn begins. The first day he is stripped, bathed, reclothed, fingerprinted, and photographed. In the ensuing days he is examined, interviewed, and tested. All this takes place while he is facing the foreign, possibly hostile, prison world. Furthermore, he is embarking on a prison term of indeterminable length.

In the first weeks at the reception-guidance center he is being observed almost constantly by people who will make an evaluation of him, an evaluation which will be influential in determining the course of his prison life. The custodial officer in his cell block, the correctional counselor who leads the daily or weekly group sessions, the psychologist and vocational counselor who interview him at least once will all make an evaluation and a recommendation for his prison "program." These evaluations are the most complete that will be made during his prison sentence, and they are referred to periodically throughout his sentence by classification committees who decide which institution he will be transferred to and his "custody" in that institution, and by the Adult Authority, who will make the eventual determination of his sentence; consequently, he is motivated to be sensitive to and careful towards these evaluators.

The investigations conducted in these two settings, the jail and the prison, may have an important impact upon his struggle to reconstruct his identity. He may be strongly motivated to learn the court's and the prison's interpretation of him only for pragmatic reasons, so that he may maximize his ability to manipulate his own destiny. More often, however —and this is especially true of the less committed criminals—he is pulled into a dialogue about himself. He will try to learn their interpretation of him, experiment with it, and finally accept or reject it. We must look closely, therefore, at the probation investigation and the prison diagnosis and classification processes, for they are influential in the felon's reconstruction of himself.

California Probation Investigation

In California, all convicted persons who are legally eligible for probation (unless the defendant himself explicitly waives a probation hearing and seeks immediate sentencing) are referred to the probation department and assigned to an investigating probation officer.

> . . . and in every felony case in which the defendant is elegible for probation, before any judgement is pronounced, and whether or not an application for probation has been made, the court must immediately refer the matter to the

probation officer to investigate and to report to the court, at a specific time, upon the circumstances surrounding the crime and concerning the defendant and his prior record, which may be taken into consideration either in aggravation or mitigation of punishment.[7]

As it is narrowly defined in the California Penal Code, the probation investigation serves to supply the court with information "upon the circumstances surrounding the crime and concerning the defendant and his prior record which may be taken into consideration either in aggravation or mitigation of punishment." In reality, however, it is much more broadly conceived. The main task of the investigation is to produce a report containing a recommendation for granting probation or denial of probation, a summary of the social history of the defendant, a description of the crime, and an evaluation which tends to support the recommendation. Though the criteria upon which this recommendation is made are not formally stated in the California Penal Code, they have been formulated in other documents. For instance, in the *Standards and Guides for Adult Probation,* the following list of factors important to the probation officer's recommendation are suggested:

(1) The offense: its nature and circumstances (possibly a clue to the personality of the offender). Was it part of an established behavior pattern or a result of unusual circumstances? Was it against property? If it was against a person, was it attended by violence or injury?
(2) Established patterns of behavior: emotional and psychic drives; offender's attitude toward himself and his situation; his awareness of the need for change and his will to change; his ability to use help to modify his conduct and adjustment.
(3) Age at which delinquent behavior first began and the character and persistence of such behavior (which are more important than age at time of offense).
(4) Offender's stability, motivation, achievement, and capacity, as reflected in his history of education, employment, military service, and leisure activity.
(5) Offender's attitude toward people, authority, and orderly social restraints and prospects for modifying those that are incompatible with a law-abiding life.[8]

Interviews with probation officers in Alameda County revealed that a major concern in their recommendation was the supervisability of the defendant on probation. These investigators develop this concern and considerable knowledge related to supervisability in the two years they must serve as supervising probation officers before they may be promoted to investigations.

7. Section 1203, *California Penal Code.*
8. National Council on Crime and Delinquency, *Standards and Guides for Adult Probation,* A Report of the Committee on Standards for Adult Probation Professional Council (New York, 1962), pp. 43–44.

All but a few of the above criteria for granting or denying probation are underpinned by two interrelated conceptions: (1) the person's character or personality and (2) the reason he committed the crime. Some conception of these two is necessary to answer the recommendations made in the *Standards and Guides for Adult Probation*. At least an "intuitive" conception of them is required to assay the supervisability of a defendant. So a central function of the probation investigation is the formation of these two conceptions.

Case Evalutions and Classification in California Prisons

The two dominant concerns of the case evaluation and classification at the reception-guidance centers are essentially the same as those of the probation investigation; that is, producing some conception of the person's character or personality and the causes of his criminal acts. For instance, the statute authorizing the establishment of the diagnostic centers and supplies guidelines for the diagnosis clearly reflects these central concerns:

The work of the clinic shall include a scientific study of each prisoner, his career and life history, the cause of his criminal acts and recommendations for his case, training and employment with a view to his reformation and to the protection of society.[9]

The Department of Correction's Manuals used by personnel involved in classification and case evaluation emphasize personality assessment and evaluation of his past behavior, especially his criminal behavior.

Definition of Classification:

The classification process is a systematic study of the individual inmate which must include:

(a) A complete evaluation of the individual's past development, present needs and behavior, and his potential for the future.
(b) Use of this information in the better understanding of the inmate; in developing the individual's resources for rehabilitation; in providing a realistic, integrated program of custody, treatment, training, institutional assignments, and housing.[10]

The psychologist is responsible for evaluating the intellectual and personality make-up of individuals received for diagnostic study in the Reception-Guidance Center. In the examination of the individual, he ordinarily utilizes interview techniques, psychological test data, and the available file material. He assumes the major responsibility for the selection and administration of test instruments, and the recording and reporting of test results.

The personality evaluation should be based on a dynamic formulation which

9. Section 5079, *California Penal Code*.
10. State of California, *Inmate Classification Manual of the Department of Corrections* (1963), paragraph CL-II-00.

will be useful in explaining the individual's pattern of behavior in interpersonnel situations as it applies to his relations to persons in authority, family members, and peers.

The basic goal of the social evaluation is to present a brief but complete picture of the social and personal dynamics underlying the individual behavior, including his criminal behavior.[11]

The Impact of the Investigation

I am suggesting that these investigations have an important impact on the felon's own attempts to reorient himself. Of course, in order for this to be true, the conclusions reached in the investigations must be known to him. In the case of the probation investigation there is some likelihood that the interpretations of the probation will become known to the defendant. This is so in part because the investigation—which entails, in Alameda County for instance, two interviews of the defendant and a written application for probation in which the defendant tells his story of the offense, why he thinks he should be granted probation, and his biography—forces the defendant into interaction with the investigator. Even if the investigator remains "passive" and "neutral," he must probe certain selected areas which seem important to him and frame certain questions in a particular way in order to elicit the particular information he is seeking. In doing this he unavoidably gives clues about his thinking in regard to the man's life and crime, but the interaction very often becomes much more than a mere investigation. It is conceived by many involved in probation investigation as the beginning of the treatment process and, therefore, a freer exchange of opinions occurs.

Treatment should begin with the first interview with the defendant, not await the court's disposition.[12]

It is because I stoutly believe the investigation to be the beginning of the treatment process that the interview techniques will be discussed here.[13]

In practice the initial interview may extend over two or three sessions with the probationer.* It has two main goals: (1) developing a relationship and

* In many instances the initial interview is that in which the probation officer begins his social (or presentence) investigation. The same principles enunciated in this article apply to the prospective probationer as well as to the probationer.[14]

11. State of California, *Manual of Procedures for the Cumulative Case Summary of the Department of Corrections* (1963), paragraphs CS-IV-00, CS-IV-01, CS-VIII-03.

12. *Standards and Guides*, p. 32.

13. Keve, *The Probation Officer Investigates*, p. 21.

14. Henry L. Martman, "Interviewing Techniques in Probation and Parole," *Federal Probation*, September 1963.

(2) obtaining a picture of the probationer and his developmental background from which the probation officer can draw some inferences as to the dynamics of the probationer's antisocial behavior.

In addition to the feedback that occurs in the actual interviews, the convicted felon has other forms of access to the opinions of the probation investigator. In California, he may legally see the probation report, since it is a public document, although instances of a defendant requesting to see it are extremely rare. The lawyer, however, has the report at the sentencing hearing and he may have read it before this time. He, therefore, may relate its contents to the felon. Furthermore, the probation officer often talks to the wife, other relatives, or other interested parties. They may become cognizant of his interpretations and relate them to the defendant. Some felons receive a prison sentence after having been granted probation, supervised for a period, and then having had probation revoked for various reasons. They very likely become cognizant of the investigating probation officer's view and the elaborated view of the supervising probation officer during the supervision period and subsequent investigations. Finally, the report follows the felon to prison and is used by prison counselors in guiding their interviews with the new inmate. So the felon has several means of access to the interpretations of his behavior formed by the probation officer.

In the case of the evaluation and classification which takes place at the reception-guidance centers, it is more certain that he will become aware of the evaluations made of him. Here he is in more intense and extended interaction with the evaluators. Furthermore, the psychologist and the vocational counselor who make an important evaluation are often intense and overt in their penetration of the person's personality and character. The felon is now an imprisoned individual and he is to be subjected to a treatment routine, of which these initial interviews are the opening phase. Therefore, the interviewers tend to pull the convict into interaction with them and into a dialogue about the convict's self.

Apart from contacts with the official agents, the convicted felon also interacts with other prisoners who, through their own contacts with these same agents, are somewhat knowledgeable of the explanatory models used by them. This is the case in the jail setting where many prisoners have been subjected to these evaluations in former settings—other jails, mental hospitals, and prisons—and it is more true in the reception-guidance centers. There, these modes are actually frequent topics of discussion in the daily group sessions.

The investigation, therefore, may supply the convicted felon with one model for the reconstruction of his identity, a model based upon conceptions of him formed by court and prison officials. The felon may or may not find this model acceptable or tenable, and may or may not be motivated to accept it. He must, however, if he becomes cognizant of it, reckon with it in the reconstruction of his identity, since it represents to him the view "they" have of him—"they" being those who have almost unlimited power over his life. Furthermore, it becomes the view held by some of his family, his friends, or other interested parties who rally around the court and the prison officials, and are active in the construction of this view.

The Models

Before trying to explore some of the factors involved in the rejection or acceptance of the officially constructed view, let me first describe the four personality models most often used to understand the criminal and his acts. These descriptions of the personality or character and the attendant explanation of the criminal behavior were gleaned from the records of forty-three convicts interviewed before release on parole. After the four models were selected, a random sample of fifty case files of parolees in Region II—the San Francisco Bay Area—were read to test the applicability of the models and to obtain a frequency distribution of their use.

Emotional disturbance. The first model, which is by far the most frequently used, is that of emotional disturbance. In this view the person is seen to have serious emotional problems, conflicts, and/or pathological relationships with family members—father or mother—which lead to his engaging in aggressive, self-destructive, and/or socially harmful behavior. The following are some examples of the use of this model taken from the probation reports and reception-guidance center evaluations of convicted felons in California:

> This defendant of average intelligence has a history of dependency upon alcohol, probably resulting from feelings of inadequacy and insecurity from childhood. (County Probation Report)

> In summary, S. is an immature individual who apparently has little insight into his personality problems and a fairly low threshold as far as frustration tolerance is concerned and easily resorts to the use of narcotics. (Cumulative Summary, Inmate Records, California Department of Corrections)

This emotional disturbance model was employed 33 per cent of the time by probation officers, 67 per cent of the time by correctional counselors, and 74 per cent of the time by prison psychologists.

Moral unworthiness. The second most frequently used model is that of moral unworthiness. Here the person is seen as an individual of low moral character who, though he is cognizant of right and wrong, follows his own self interests at the expense of others. In scientific language he is a psychopath or sociopath.

> This 31-year-old defendant was subject to juvenile authorities, disciplinary action while in the Army, and in 1959 was committed to State Prison because

of burglary, second degree, involving the taking of property from homes. He was subject to parole supervision until September 1964. He gives the impression of being intelligent and reflective. He cannot give a satisfactory explanation of his involvement in the present offenses, and his claim to innocence is not believable. There were no extenuating or mitigating circumstances surrounding the offense. Undoubtedly, the defendant knew the consequences of criminal behavior if caught and was willing to take risks in driving from San Francisco to Walnut Creek with the co-defendants as passengers in order to steal. This deputy suspects that the offense was motivated by greed, a desire for more in the way of tangible possessions than his earnings would permit. (County Probation Report)

In summary, this inmate is seen as a hedonistic, self-centered, impulsive young man with a delinquent and sociopathic orientation. Because of his defensiveness and inability to form close interpersonal relationships he will undoubtedly go through the present period of incarceration unchanged. (Cumulative Summary)

Moral unworthiness was employed 33 per cent of the time by probation officers, 6 per cent of the time by correctional counselors, and 5 per cent of the time by prison psychologists.

Subculture carrier. The third model is that of a subculture carrier. Here the person is seen to have been basically normal, but to have become involved in a delinquent or criminal group and to have gotten into trouble because he followed the patterns of this group.

The defendant does not appear to be aggressively antisocial. There is little question that he drinks to excess, and apparently drifts with a group in the Fillmore District that is low in motivation. This defendant appears to be a good natured individual who has no great desire to change his pattern of living. His history of delinquency is such that it can be anticipated that he will continue to be at least a petty offender for some time to come. (County Probation Report)

After moving to California to join his family, B., at the age of 16, evidently came into contact with a different sub-culture which had an important influence on his social adjustment. This is shown by his Rap Sheet which starts about that time and B. has piled up an impressive record of arrests in a relatively short time. Some of the charges imply violence and it appears feasible to suppose that this has been one way for B. to try to achieve the status which has been thoroughly impressed upon him from home.

There was no evidence of any psychosis, or any evidence of any marked neurotic tendencies. He admits getting into many difficulties through the years, but he looks on this as a means of social recognition within the subculture in which he was living in the East Bay Area. He views, and probably correctly, that much of his difficulty was a need for acceptance, which meant going along with the group with which he was associating and to be a rather "big-shot" among that group. (Cumulative Summary)

This explanation was applied much less frequently than the preceding two. Probation officers used it 22 per cent of the time, correctional counselors 12 per cent, and prison psychologists 9 per cent.

Phenomenological model. The final view, one which is employed rather rarely, is a phenomenological explanation. Here the person's acts are explained in terms of the motives of the person himself. Ofter the person is seen to be a basically normal person who was faced with extreme circumstances, circumstances which perhaps do not excuse his acts, but make them understandable to the evaluator. For instance, he stole money because he needed it for a certain reason.

Appearing before the court is a 25-year-old, married caucasian American male who has pleaded guilty to three counts of felony checks. He readily admits his complicity in the offense, attributing his behavior to employment failure and subsequent financial pressures. As opposed to the usual case of this nature, the defendant makes no attempt to hide his illegal behavior. He has been extremely cooperative with the police and with the Probation Department. He is definitely beginning to establish a dangerous pattern of check writing, upon review of his prior criminal record, but it is noted that a majority of the checks were utilized for the purchase of food, and the defendant did make some attempt to rationalize his behavior at the time by entering a total in his checkbook, as opposed to writing checks for a considerable amount of cash, and he apparently made attempts to obtain funds for restitution by contacting his parents. (County Probation Report)

In summary, S. is a first offender who appears to have been aggravated to the breaking point by a long series of events which included marriage to a carefree, unsympathetic, and perhaps unappreciative wife. He apparently was very much in love with the woman and, in an extraordinary fashion, was able to overlook or tolerate behavior which would have caused immediate aggressive action by most men. Later when S. found himself not only rejected in an indirect way, but in a position where he could not express love for his wife through his children, he lost all sense of self-control. (Cumulative Summary)

This model, which does not necessarily infer pathology or moral unworthiness, and therefore is the most palatable, is seldom offered. It was used in only 11 per cent of the cases by probation officers, 6 per cent by correctional counselors, and 3 per cent by prison psychologists.

Acceptance or Rejection of the Models

The influence of these models on the felon's self-reorganizational efforts is related to (1) their being offered and/or known to him, (2) their being tenable given his particular history, (3) the degree of contact he may have had with subcultural systems which offer explanations for his criminal behavior, and (4) the compatibility of the particular model with any strong beliefs or values the felon may possess. For instance, a person who has had some degree of contact with a deviant belief system (and this is true of most felons), the emotionally disturbed model which is offered most often and is usually feasible is to a degree incompatible with and far less dignified than the rationale offered for criminal activities by most deviant belief systems. The model of emotional disturbance locates some of the mainsprings of his acts outside his conscious self—in the unconscious or the emotional realm. This suggests that the individual is to a degree incapable of controlling his own action, and this seems acceptable only to persons who do not have beliefs which justify and supply alternate explanations for their actions.

Conventional people, middle-class people who have had little or no involvement with criminal behavior systems, who tend to find criminal explanations more repugnant than that of emotional disturbance, will tend to accept this view of themselves more readily. The middle-class person is generally more receptive of psychological and psychiatric explanations.

The morally unworthy or sociopathic model is acceptable to few persons. Only truly sociopathic or psychopathic people—people with no regard for the opinions or feelings of others except insofar as they affect their progress towards immediate goals—can accept this view of themselves. This model is more apt to be employed in the case of the more criminally involved, since the motives of this type of person are less likely to be understood by the evaluators, and evil motives or sociopathy are more likely to be inferred.

The phenomenological model is feasible and acceptable to most felons. It is seldom offered, however. The reason for this is that in order for the evaluator to explain criminal acts in terms of the offender's own motives, the evaluator would have to understand these motives and then feel that they were justified to some extent. For those felons who in the context of their criminal activity were operating according to criminal dimensions, it is doubtful that the evaluator will have this understanding or see the justifications. In the case of the less criminally involved, the middle-class or conventional felon, it is more likely that the motive will be understood. In the case of the extreme-circumstances version of the phenomenological model, it is true that the evaluator has seen some justification.

This leaves the subculture model, which is also given very infrequently. It is only given in the case of the more heavily involved criminals, where the evaluator has strong evidence of extended involvement with deviant peers. The application of this model by the evaluators does not offer the felon an explanation. It merely refers him to the source of his distorted, antisocial beliefs and values. The use of this model seldom results from the evaluators' perception of the world view of the subculture carrier and a resultant explanation of the acts and the criminality from this viewpoint. (This would actually imply the use of the phenomenological model.) They merely recognize that the person has come under the influence of people who have different patterns.

Polarization

The effect of the various investigations and evaluations is, therefore, to polarize the population of felons. Most of those with some previous involvement with criminal systems who are familiar and have at least flirted with criminal identities and criminal perspectives finally move towards a stronger commitment to a deviant perspective and identity, although in the initial stages of the prison career (arrest, conviction, probation investigation, and classification-evaluation) they remain ambivalent—in fact, more ambivalent than they were prior to arrest. This is not simply the effect of coming into differential contact with deviant systems in the jail and prison setting. It is partly because, in that stage when they are most disorganized, most doubtful about their past commitments, and therefore most receptive to alternate interpretations of their behavior and alternate views of themselves, they are usually offered only undignified, denigrating, or completely repugnant alternatives. Consequently, they are apt to reembrace deviant explanations with renewed commitment.

In the case of those who have had little or no contact with criminal systems—and this is particularly true of "middle-class" felons—the models offered by the evaluators are usually more acceptable than criminal ones, especially when they are trying to identify with the evaluators in the situation. These persons generally move to a stronger conventional commitment and are able to do this by accepting a tainted view of themselves.

Though the majority move in one of these two directions, there are still some who move in neither direction. For various reasons, such as insufficient contact with any cohesive deviant world and an inability to learn or general reluctance to accept the other models, having a commitment to both a deviant and a conventional world which leaves them suspended between the two, these persons continue to vacillate or to remain confused.

SENTENCING AND THE SENSE OF INJUSTICE

The current system of determining the actual sentence of the felon in California, like that of classification, has not greatly furthered the correctional goal. One reason for this is that it is a major source of anger, resentment, and a profound sense of injustice against the conventional society. This sense of injustice, we believe, is related to increased loss of commitment to the conventional society.[15]

15. A relationship between the sense of injustice and commitment to criminal values has been discussed by many writers. In the 1920s, observers of the emerging juvenile

The Sense of Injustice in California Prisons

Adult criminals have felt some sense of injustice for various reasons for many years. This feeling stemmed, first, from their perception of the inequality in the social circumstances in which they were born, grew up, and competed as adults.[16] Second, they perceived inequality and unfairness because of corruption and class bias in the way they were handled by law enforcement agencies and the courts. However, the sense of injustice based on these two reasons may not have been as extreme as, and certainly was different in kind than, that which is appearing today. Formerly, criminals tended to accept the inequality of their social circumstances because it was consistent with their world view. As they saw it, society always had some at the top and some at the bottom, and it was just their misfortune to be at the bottom. Furthermore, they could not strongly resent the inequality of treatment resulting from corruption and bias because they knew that if they were in a position to receive or offer bribes of special favor they too would do so. Presently, convicts, like many other deviant and nondeviant segments, are acquiring a basically more critical perspective on society and some of its institutions and organizations. This shift in perspective has produced a new, profound sense of injustice.

Treatment: The Promise and the Disillusionment

To fully comprehend the new perspective and the attendant sense of injustice we must look at the recent development of the treatment ideal in the California correctional system. During the 1950s and on into the 1960s, treatment philosophy has guided the remarkable expansion of the California penal system. While the state increased its prisons for adult males from three to its present ten, a major concern has been education,

---

court system warned of the possible effects of perceived unfairness on the juvenile's criminal career. See Roscoe Pound, *Cleveland Crime Survey* (Cleveland: Cleveland Foundation, 1922); Zechariah Chaffee, Jr., Walter Pollak, and Carl Stern, "Unfairness in Prosecutions," *National Commission on Law Observance and Enforcement: Report of the Prosecution* (Washington, D. C.: Government Printing Office, 1931). David Matza has emphasized the sense of injustice in explaining the neutralization of conventional morality and the corresponding growth of commitment to criminal values among juveniles handled by the juvenile court. See *Delinquency and Drift* (New York: John Wiley & Sons, Inc., 1964), chapters 4 and 5. More recently, Edwin Lemert, examining the relationship between injustice and commitment, focused on stigmatization and the denial of deviants as a major source of the sense of injustice. See *Human Deviance, Social Problems, and Social Control* (Englewood Cliffs, N. J.: Prentice-Hall, Inc., 1967), pp. 43–44.

16. Cloward and Ohlin explore the relationship between commitment to criminal values and the sense of "unjust deprivation" in *Delinquency and Opportunity*, pp. 117–24.

vocational training, and various forms of therapy. It must be agreed that California has led this nation, perhaps the world, in experimentation with the treatment philosophy.

During this twenty-year history, the general convict and administrative attitude towards treatment has shifted drastically. In the early years, in the period just after 1950, with the possible exception of some solidly entrenched custody-oriented staff and administrators and some strongly committed criminals, the treatment era was welcomed with general enthusiasm. The convicts especially responded to the promise of treatment. During their term in a California prison, they were led to believe that they would be able to raise their educational level to at least the fifth grade and much higher if they desired, to learn a trade, to have physical defects, disfigurations, and tattoos removed or corrected, and to receive help in various individual or group therapy programs in solving their psychological problems. In effect they were led to believe that if they participated in the prison programs with sincerity and resolve they would leave prison in better condition than they entered and would generally be much better equipped to cope with the outside world.

From the outset, however, some people recognized inherent difficulties in implementing treatment in prison. David Powelson and Reinhard Bendix, writing in 1951, identified a basic therapeutic flaw in the prison situation, where custody concerns were necessarily primary and the moral depravity of the prisoner must be assumed in order to legitimate custody.[17] They further warned of the danger that existed in disguising custody concerns as treatment. Donald Cressey and Lloyd Ohlin recognized potential difficulties in implementing treatment in prison because of organizational obstacles stemming from the multiple and possibly conflicting goals of the prison.[18]

Presently, the flaws in the treatment in prison have become glaringly apparent; in fact, a general disillusionment has set in and has now become widespread among convicts. In a recent interview of seventy California felons who had been released on parole in the summer of 1966, 57 per cent stated that the treatment programs were not effective. When asked what was the main purpose of the treatment programs, 55 per cent agreed that the main purpose was to get more money from the State for more prisons, and 28 per cent felt that the main purpose was to control inmates.

This disillusionment appears to be the result of the following factors. First, the convicts believe that the treatment programs have failed. Their criterion for failure is the same used by the department and criminologists

17. Harvey Powelson and Reinhard Bendix, "Psychiatry in Prison," *Psychiatry*, Vol. XIV (1951).

18. Donald Cressey, "Limitations on Organization of Treatment in the Modern Prison," and Lloyd Ohlin, "Conflicting Interests in Correctional Objectives," in Social Science Research Council, *Theoretical Studies in Social Organization of the Prison* (pamphlet, March 1960).

—rates of recidivism. The convicts believe that recidivist rates have not been lowered, in fact, that they have risen in the last fifteen years. Sixty-two per cent of those interviewed believed that presently less than 35 per cent of all releasees stay out of prison.

Second, the convicts doubt the motives of the implementors of treatment. As Powelson and Bendix had warned, convicts now tend to view the whole treatment program as a grand hypocrisy in which custodial concerns, administrative exigencies, and punishment are all disguised as treatment.

Third, they have reacted to the sickness image of themselves which underpins the treatment ideal. This view that they are emotionally disturbed has proven to be less dignified and more humiliating than that of moral unworthiness.[19] At least the morally depraved are responsible for their own actions, whereas the emotionally disturbed are considered incapable of willful acts.

The final source of disillusionment has been the convicts' recognition that the staff and the administrators are also disillusioned. This has become increasingly apparent in the last two or three years. The final convincer was the abandonment of many programs in progress or in the planning stages after Governor Reagan took office in 1967. This has generally been interpreted by the convicts as confirmation from above that the system has failed.

Disillusionment and the Sense of Injustice

Replacing hope and accompanying disillusionment is a sense of injustice of new proportions. In many ways this sense of injustice is a result of treatment. In pursuing treatment, the convicts have acquired a new perspective and in implementing treatment the state has transferred extraordinary unchecked powers to the Adult Authority, powers which, now that the treatment ideal has been brought into question, seem unfair and, in fact, unconstitutional.

This new perspective which has emerged among a significant and growing portion of convicts seems to be primarily the result of their participation in education and therapy programs.[20] In pursuing education and

19. Erving Goffman describes a similar reaction on the part of the mental patient who, under constant psychiatric evaluation in which his views of self are brought into question, often clings to a self which is outside of the one the hospital can give or take—an amoral self. See *Asylums* (Garden City, N. Y.: Anchor Books, 1961), p. 169.

20. The more relativistic and generally critical perspective which is emerging among convicts is not developing in isolation, but is being influenced and is related to a general trend among broader segments of the American population; e.g., those segments active in civil rights and peace demonstrations and the new bohemian segments. Recently, actual interaction between these segments and the convicts was initiated when issues of the *Outlaw,* an underground newspaper published in San Quentin, fell into the hands of the *Berkeley Barb,* an organ for these new discontented segments. The

in seeking insights into their own psychology and their relationship to society, the convicts have absorbed a great deal of the cultural relativism of the social sciences and humanities. With a relativistic perspective they no longer assume that the basic structure of society is necessary and good and that it is merely corruption on the part of particular officials or the natural disadvantage of some classes which lead to injustice. Now, when it is convenient, they penetrate one layer deeper and question the structure or aspects of the structure itself.[21] In California in particular, their critical attention is focused on the indeterminate sentence law and the parole board, known as the Adult Authority.[22]

This parole board had acquired great judicial powers while the convicts passed through the stages of hope and disillusionment and developed in their passing a new perspective on society. The Adult Authority acquired the power to make the final determination of sentence, to retract this determination and refix the sentence at any future date, to release on parole, and to return to prison from parole. None of these powers are checked by review or appeal. It was generally agreed at the time when the Adult Authority gained these powers that they were necessary to implement rehabilitation. It was believed that in a system of individualized treatment whereby an inmate would be subjected to a rehabilitative routine and then released when it was determined that he had been rehabilitated or when it appeared that his chances of not returning to crime were at a maximum, a panel of experts should have great discretionary powers to make the final determination of sentence.[23]

Berkeley Barb followed with a series of editions beginning January 26, 1968, featuring convict grievances expressed in the *Outlaw* and seeking support for a strike which was called for in issues of the *Outlaw*.

21. It must be noted that the convicts for the most part are still politically conservative and racially prejudiced. Their critical "outsider" perspective has not yet freed them of their narrower world views because it is segmental. They tend to invoke more liberal, humanistic, culturally relativistic precepts in context where they feel that existing structures are directly hurting *them*.

22. Preceding the February 1968 demonstration, the *Outlaw* listed ten "demands," five of which focused directly on practices of the Adult Authority (see *Berkeley Barb*, February 1968, p. 1). Contrast this with the eleven demands of the 1952 Michigan State Prison rioters, of which only one referred to parole board practices and nine referred to conditions in prison (John Bartlow Martin, *Break Down the Walls* [New York: Ballantine Books, 1954], pp. 93–94).

23. It has become increasingly apparent to all involved that this goal, at least with the present state of knowledge, is impossible to achieve. As evidence for this view, I refer to the following statements of Richard McGee, Chief Administrator of the California Department of Corrections, in *Organization of State Correctional Services in the Control and Treatment of Crime Delinquency*, Publication of the State of California Youth and Corrections Agency, May 10, 1967, p. 159:

> *Sentencing Decisions of Parole Boards*
> The four state parole boards have a most complicated as well as agonizing decision to make on every offender:
> (1) While there is an enormous amount of information in the offender's case file, these are difficult to read and interpret, and do not present clear-cut conclusions.

In effect, however, the parole board in California has never completely achieved this ideal. Except for the original Adult Authority panel, it has never been a panel of experts as it was originally conceived and defined by the Legislature.[24] Indications of rehabilitation, a lofty ideal, have never been the chief concern in determining a convict's sentence. Amount of time served for particular crimes has always been the primary factor, and the degree of variability of sentences because of indications of rehabilitation has always been very limited.

During the 1950s, however, when the spirit of treatment was at its height, these powers seemed appropriate. Now that the disillusionment has set in, these powers seem to some, particularly the convicts, excessive and unjust. Currently, the convicts do not view the determination of sentence as a therapeutic decision, but a judicial one, and judicial decisions, they believe, should be made according to traditional concepts of fairness and constitutional concepts of justice. The convicts, though they still tend to accept the fact that the society, in the name of law and justice, has the right to imprison them, are becoming increasingly adamant that this same society should itself obey its own notions of fairness and justice in setting the length of sentence.

In focusing their attention on the sentencing process, the convicts are becoming more knowledgeable in actual points of law, especially constitutional law, and they have identified many regular procedures of the Adult Authority which in their opinion are in violation of constitutional precepts of justice. These are mainly (1) the right to due process, (2) guarantees against *ex post facto* enforcement of the law, and (3) guarantees against cruel and unusual punishment.

---

(2) The staff who know the inmate best are required to present descriptive and evaluative reports on the subject but, in the case of adult prison inmates, are not allowed to recommend a disposition.

(3) It is extremely difficult to assess change in an individual in a 10- to 30-minute interview.

(4) There is doubtful correlation between behavior in an institution and behavior in the community. In fact, conformity in the institution setting may be related to excessive dependency and may portend parole failure.

24. In 1944, when the present Adult Authority was formed, the Legislature wrote, "One member shall be an attorney-at-law, one have had practical experience in handling adult prisoners, one a sociologist in training and experience" (Paragraph 5075, *California Penal Code*). In 1951, when two members were added, it was stated that these two new members should have "had all or any one of these qualifications: Paragraph 5075 (1951)." During the period 1945–51, the board had three members who had extensive police experience. One of these persons had a degree in law, but there was no sociologist. After 1953, the paragraph quoted was deleted, and exact composition of the board was not spelled out. The fact that the board had never conformed to the original guidelines (and that it would be difficult for it to do so) was probably the major consideration in changing this paragraph.

Denial of Due Process

The convicts believe that in many cases the Adult Authority actually convicts men for crimes without due process. This occurs in cases where a man is held accountable and made to serve extra time for crimes which were not charged against him and/or crimes for which he was not guilty. It is possible for the Adult Authority to give a person an additional sentence for these crimes because of the leeway which exists in most indeterminate sentences. For instance, many crimes, such as first-degree robbery, first-degree burglary, and second-degree murder, have maximum sentences of life. Most sentences have at least a maximum of ten years. Since the average sentence served by all first termers is two and a half to three years, it is clear that the Adult Authority has enough margin to pile additional sentences on top of the normal sentence for a particular crime.[25]

In most cases where the convict feels that crimes of which he was not convicted are having an influence on the amount of time served, he received this impression from statements made by the board members who referred directly to other crimes mentioned in probation, police, or parole-violation reports.

In the following case description a convict at San Quentin felt that he had been denied due process. This is the convict's own version of his case and the Adult Authority proceeding and is not presented here as a factual account. Since we are exploring the sense of injustice being experienced by the convicts, their own accounts are our concern:

S. was convicted for second-degree burglary and served two years. While on parole, he states that his relations with his parole agent were not good even though he was working steadily and conforming to parole regulations. After completing eighteen months on parole he was arrested two blocks from his home at 11:00 P.M. He was on his way home from a nearby bar where he had just spent two or three hours. The police were looking for someone who had committed a burglary several blocks away about an hour earlier. When they discovered that S. had a record for burglary he was taken to jail and charged with this crime. When his alibi was established and there was no evidence to connect him with the crime except for his being in the neighborhood, the judge dismissed the charge and admonished the arresting officers.

S.'s parole was cancelled, however, and he was returned to prison. When he appeared before the A.A. for a parole-violation hearing he was asked if he knew why he had been returned. He replied that he did not. The A.A. member became irritated with him and told him that just because he "beat the charge" in court did not mean that he was not guilty, and that the best thing he could do was to admit that he was guilty. He refused to do this and tried to explain to the member that the judge clearly believed him to be innocent and that he could prove this from the transcript of the preliminary hearing.

25. The Department of Corrections' statistics reveal that the average time served by all men who were released for their first time in 1965 was 33.9 months.

S. was denied parole consideration and postponed for another year. The next year he brought the transcript of this case to the hearing and the member said that he did not want to read it and that it made no difference to him anyway. He was guilty as far as they were concerned. Once again he was denied parole and scheduled for another hearing in a year. (Interview, San Quentin, December 1967)

Ex Post Facto Enforcement

The United States Constitution states that "no bill of attainder or *ex post facto* law shall be passed." [26] Lon L. Fuller in his book *The Morality of Law* states that:

A retroactive law is truly a monstrosity. Law has to do with the governance of human conduct by rules. To speak of governing or directing conduct today by rules that will be enacted tomorrow is to talk in blank prose.[27]

In California prisons many inmates feel that they have confronted this monstrosity. They believe that the Adult Authority, again applying the wide discretionary powers and manipulating the vast time margins at its disposal, enforces laws retroactively.

L. served two years for burglary. Shortly after release from prison in 1959, he returned to the use of narcotics. He had used both marijuana and heroin in moderation since his mid-teens, but never had a narcotics arrest nor was there any indication in this record of heavy involvement in narcotics traffic. In 1959 after becoming addicted he became involved in drug traffic in order to support his habit. Four months later he was arrested with nine ounces of heroin. He pled guilty to a charge of possession and was given the maximum term allowed —1 to 10 years. This, however, was imposed consecutively to the sentence—1 to 15 years—that he was serving, so in effect, he returned to prison with a sentence of 1 to 25, of which he had served a little more than 2 years. After serving three years he felt that there was some chance of having his term fixed and being granted a parole date. (The average time served for opiate convictions of men released in 1965 with one prior jail or prison sentence was 44.1 months.) At this board appearance the subject of sales was brought up by the A.A. members and it was implied that he was going to serve the time usually given a seller of narcotics.

L. returned to the board with four years and felt that he should be granted a parole at this hearing. The subject of sales was brought up again and at this time L. tried to explain that he was addicted and that his trafficking in drugs was merely a way of maintaining his habit. At this time an A.A. member told him that the "public has spoken" and now wants narcotics addicts to serve more time. The more stringent laws which were passed in 1961 were a mandate from the public to hold narcotics offenders in prison. L. returned that these new laws did not apply to him, because he was sentenced in 1959 under the

26. Article I, Section IX, Paragraph 3.
27. *The Morality of Law* (New Haven: Yale University Press, 1964), p. 53.

old laws. L. felt that this was retroactive enforcement of the law. L. still has not been released on parole after serving more than eight years. At each board appearance the subject of sales and the more stringent narcotics laws are brought up. (Interview, San Quentin, December 1967)

Cruel and Unusual Punishment

The Constitution also prohibits cruel and unusual punishment. However, it does not supply guidelines for defining it. The concept seems necessarily culture-bound. In prisons, cruel and unusual punishment is decided by comparing a particular sentence with "normal" sentences in a general class of crimes. When one serves much more than the norm for his particular crime—allowing for the peculiarities of his crime—or when one serves more time for what is generally considered a less serious crime than is normal for a more serious crime, then he usually experiences the sense of injustice from cruel and unusual punishment.

P., a Mexican-American heroin-user, has a long history of arrests related to drug use: misdemeanor "marks," paraphernalia arrests and a felony conviction for possession of a small quantity of heroin. In 1960 he was stopped and searched as he was leaving the toilet facility of a skid-row hotel. He was found to be in possession of a hypodermic needle and an eyedropper. An examination of his arms revealed a number of puncture wounds, some fresh. He was booked under a charge of "Suspicion of Narcotic Act, Felony." Under interrogation P. admitted his addiction, the extent of same, and the fact that he had just prior to arrest "shot-up" a half a gram of heroin. The paraphernalia found in his pocket was forwarded to the forensic chemist who, after testing, stated that the residue scraped from the eyedropper was a substance containing heroin.

Felony charges of possession of heroin were brought against P. He pled not guilty. There was no narcotic substance in evidence at the trial as the amount found in the eyedropper had been scarcely detectable and all of it was used in the chemist's test. The trial resulted in a guilty verdict. In view of his prior convictions he was given the maximum sentence of 2 to 20 years.

When last contacted P. had made five appearances before the Adult Authority, having served more than six years. He would have served seven years when he made his next appearance. In his last appearance the A.A. told him that his request for parole was premature since he was a recidivist for narcotic offenses. P., who professes that he had never been anything but a "boot-and-shoe hype"—a drug addict who is involved in petty theft to support his habit—feels that he is being made to serve an extremely long sentence. (Interview, San Quentin, December 1967)

Convicts in California prisons are particularly sensitive to this injustice because they feel extremely vulnerable. The criteria for the determination of sentence are unknown to them and there are examples in the prison population of men serving unduly long sentences for reasons which are not apparent. Furthermore, the convicts do not know how much time they will serve until the end of their sentence, since it is not fixed until that time. They spend the majority of their sentence with some fear that they too might be serving a cruel and unusual sentence, and thus they share the sense of injustice of others who are actually receiving unduly long sentences.

DESERT

Besides these precepts of justice which are spelled out in the Constitution, there are other conceptions of justice which are part of our Western cultural tradition and about which the convicts are becoming increasingly sensitive now that they are attitudinally in a position to question the morality of the penal system. For instance, Edmond Cahn, in exploring the various dimensions of the sense of injustice, includes the concept of desert:

> The law is regarded as an implement for giving men what they deserve, balancing awards and punishments in the scale of merit. As *general* merit is so difficult of admeasurement, legal action is usually expected to relate to particular merit: that is, to the right, duty or guilt acquired in a specific circumstance.[28]

A violation of just desert occurs when an individual receives the punishment for the crimes of others or receives extraordinary punishment for his crime because of other contingencies not directly related to his particular crime. In former years (prior to the establishment of the indeterminate law in California), when sentencing was done by the judge of the local superior court, it was believed that men were often given more than their just desert for particular crimes because of the pressure on the judge from an outraged local public. This seems to have been one of the major motives for the passage of the indeterminate sentence law. Presently, however, many California convicts feel that they still are receiving more than their just desert because of the acts of other persons. They believe that when crimes in the same general class as theirs are committed on the outside and receive undue public attention, they have less chance of receiving a parole. Many have reported that these outside crimes are discussed in the board appearances.

> D., an armed robbery offender, appeared before the Adult Authority after serving 4½ years. He felt that because of his crime, the time served, his past record and his institutional record, he should be paroled at this time. However, approximately two months prior to this board appearance an armed robbery had occurred which because of having excessive violence received considerable news media coverage. Furthermore, many statements by law enforcement officers and political leaders had followed which requested harsher treatment of armed robbers. At D.'s board appearance, very little was said about his progress in prison; instead the conversation turned to the recent violent robbery and the attendant publicity given to this crime. D. was not granted a parole at

28. *The Sense of Injustice* (New York: New York University Press, 1949), p. 16.

this time and was scheduled to return for another board appearance when he had served 5½ years. Needless to say, D. felt that he was being punished for the acts of other persons. (Interview, San Quentin, December 1967)

The Sense of Injustice and Commitment

Most men in California receive a sentence very close to the norm for their particular crime and probably no factors other than their particular crime and institutional record enter into the determination of their sentences. However, they are aware of instances of the injustices described above, since they are a dominant and frequent topic of conversation among convicts. All convicts feel extremely vulnerable to the types of injustices they hear about, and the sense of injustice is contagious and its effects are profound. Edmond Cahn has described this contagion as one of the important basic human responses.

> Finally, the sense of injustice is no mere generic label for the concepts already reviewed. It denotes that sympathetic reaction of outrage, horror, shock, resentment, and anger, those affections of the viscera and abnormal secretions of the adrenals that prepare the human animal to resist attack. Nature has thus equipped all men to regard injustice to another as personal aggression. Through a mysterious and magical empathy or imaginative interchange, each projects himself into the shoes of the other, not in pity or compassion merely, but in the vigor of self-defense.[29]

The response on the part of the convicts towards the perpetrators of the injustice, the Adult Authority, the Department of Corrections, and the conventional society is presently—as Cahn describes above—a growing resentment and anger. This resentment and anger certainly weaken the felon's already damaged ties to conventional society and in many cases return him to criminal behavior systems. It is very likely that such feelings are currently directing many felons in prison towards an increasingly important deviant system—political radicalism. The importance of this unconventional life style in the prisons will be discussed in chapters 3 and 4.

29. Ibid., p. 24.

3

THE PRISON EXPERIENCE:
The Convict World

EXISTING STUDIES

The thirty years of prison research following Clemmer's pioneer work has produced considerable knowledge of the convict's social world. The great bulk of this knowledge, however, is not directly suited for my purpose, which is to produce an understanding of the extended career of the felon. The prison phenomena must be looked at with an eye toward postprison behavior. The characteristics of the prison social organization described in former studies, if they are in fact accurately described, may or may not be relevant for this purpose. Besides having a shifted focus, the present study was undertaken in the California prison complex which has unique features and has recently gone through important changes. For these reasons and because of some general inaccuracies of former studies, it is necessary to present a revised and updated description of convict social organization. In presenting this description an attempt will be made to synthesize some of the major findings of thirty years of prison research. Let me briefly review some of the important findings of former studies.

The Convict Social Organization as a Social System

After the 1940s and the work of Parsons and others on the social-system model, a view of convict behavior as a system of normatively interlocked "roles" emerged. Actually the description of prison roles began in the 1930s with Hans Riemer's identification of the "politicians" and "right guys" as leaders of the prison community.[1] Schrag elaborated the description of roles, and then Gresham M. Sykes dealt explicitly with the convict social organization as a social system composed principally of argot roles.[2] Sykes describes a social system made up of "rats," "center men," "gorillas," "merchants," "wolves," "punks," "fags," "ball-busters,"

1. Hans Riemer, "Socialization in the Prison Community," *Proceedings of the American Prison Association* (1937), pp. 151–55.
2. Clarence Schrag, "Social Types in a Prison Community" (unpublished master's thesis, University of Washington, 1944); *Society of Captives* (Princeton: Princeton University Press, 1958).

"real men," "toughs," and "hipsters." This system of normatively interlocked roles is a functional system which emerged to cope with the exigencies of living in prison, a living situation which is characterized by Sykes, and Sykes and Messinger as the "pains of imprisonment":[3]

To account for the contours of this system, Sykes and Messinger identified the situation to which it must adapt and the goals which it must attain—the minimal things that it must do for the convicts. First, it must help to mitigate the loss of dignity, prestige, and feeling of moral worth that the individual suffers upon incarceration. Secondly, the important problem of material deprivation must be coped with. Lastly, the system must cope with the problem of heterosexual deprivation and the concomitant problem of living side-by-side with other deviants who are possibly repugnant and dangerous to each other.[4]

A social system which emerges to cope with these exigencies must do so in a setting in which an overseeing formal structure demands a minimum degree of order. This formal organization, the prison administration, cannot allow excessive violence, escapes, and riots.[5] Even though this is a totalitarian organization, it is not true that the administration has the raw force available to ensure control without resorting to informal means of social control.[6]

The system is able to exist partly because it actually accommodates the official system. Certain special privileges are granted by the administration to inmate leaders in exchange for order. The "politician" is often involved in a direct conspiracy where lip service is paid to the convict code while the convicts are secretly betrayed for the "politician's" personal gain. The "right guy" is afforded special consideration even though he appears to be completely hostile to the administration because, by his enforcement of the convict code, he in effect helps to control other convicts.[7] The activities of the homosexual and "merchant," if they are sufficiently discreet, are tolerated by the official organization because this is one method of regulating activities in two very explosive areas—sex and the supply of scarce material goods.

The key activities of the role incumbents of this system depend upon the total convict population's adherence to two maxims of the prison code—do your own time and don't inform on another convict. Ostensibly these norms are in opposition to those of the administration, but close scrutiny reveals that adherence to them serves the administration's

3. Gresham Sykes and Sheldon Messinger, "Inmate Social System," Social Science Research Council pamphlet (March 1960), p. 19.

4. Sykes and Messinger, "Inmate Social System," pp. 14–16.

5. See Richard Cloward, "Social Control in the Prison," Social Science Research Council pamphlet, pp. 22–28.

6. See Clarence Schrag, "Some Foundations for a Theory of Correction," in Donald Cressey, ed., *The Prison* (New York: Holt, Rinehart and Winston, Inc., 1961), pp. 338–40.

7. Sykes and Messinger, "Inmate Social System," p. 34.

purposes. In fact, the administration is involved explicitly in inculcating and enforcing these norms.[8]

This system not only serves the administration's purposes and the purposes of a few convict leaders, but it is also rewarding to the average convict. Besides maintaining order and, therefore, protecting him from the dangers of chaos—the war of all against all—adherence to the norms of this system helps to bolster his dignity, his wounded self-respect. The system has the appearance of solidarity, cohesion, and opposition to the official system and, in turn, the conventional society. It is a rejection of the rejectors.[9]

Carrying the functional-structural approach further, the proponents of this description of the convict social world argued that the system was of indigenous origin. If it emerged to meet the exigencies of imprisonment and to adapt to the situational characteristics, especially the one laid down by the official structure—that of maintaining a minimum of control—then a structural-functional argument is best served by asserting that the characteristics of the system take shape within the situation itself, free of influence from external factors.

A potential contradiction to the indigenous origin concept is avoided by suggesting that former internalized values and norms, former identities, and former statuses are erased upon entering prison. This is accomplished through various ceremonies to which the new prisoner, the "fish," is subjected.

The indigenous-origin theory of the convict social system was questioned by Irwin and Cressey.[10] They observed that (1) many convicts, especially the "thief," bring with them a commitment to a subculture which is not stripped from them, and, in fact, prepares them for life in the prison; and (2) many convicts, again especially the "thief," have an identity within and orient their behavior while in prison toward the larger criminal world of which the prison world is an important part. The convict system of norms, they suggest, are to a great extent a version of age-old criminal norms and values. The "right guy" role is not indigenous to the prison, but, rather, has its origins in the criminal world.

They further suggest that many of the purely "convict" patterns emerge

8. Cloward, "Social Control in the Prison," pp. 24–25.

9. McCorkle and Korn, "Resocialization Within Walls," *The Annals* (May 1954), p. 88.

10. John Irwin and Donald Cressey, "Thieves, Convicts, and the Inmate Culture," *Social Problems* (Fall 1962). Two studies of women's prisons—David Ward and Gene Kasselbaum, *Women's Prison* (Chicago: Aldine Publishing Co., 1965), and Rose Giallombard, *Society of Women* (New York: John Wiley & Sons, Inc., 1966)—have revealed social systems with radically different role types and patterns. This further tends to refute the purely indigenous-origin theory of the convict social system. If the patterns of the system emerged to cope with the pains of imprisonment, and if former orientations have no influence on convict patterns, we would expect similar social systems in all prisons which had similar deprivations.

in youth institutions and are carried into the adult prison as the reform-school youths graduate to adult prisons. The system of roles, values, and norms that exist in the adult prison are the result of two converging subcultures—the thief subculture and the "convict" subculture, both of which emerge in other social settings.

Several points of disagreement with structural-functional interpretations of convict behavior are suggested by the Irwin and Cressey study. First, the patterns that emerge are not entirely indigenous in origin. Second, a convict entering prison does not have his former identities relative to other subcultures blotted out. Third, in addition to a single convict social system to which convict behavior is oriented, there are less encompassing social phenomena which are the focal points of convict behavior—in the Irwin and Cressey study, the thief subculture and the "convict" subculture. Finally, convict behavior as adaptive behavior cannot be understood merely as an adaptation to the prison situation. The thief, for instance, adapts to a large world of which the prison was merely a part.

Another possible weakness of the "social system" interpretations is that the proponents of this perspective overlooked Clemmer's principal finding—that 53.5 per cent of the convicts associate in primary or semi-primary groups. Clemmer actually identified fourteen primary or semi-primary groups in a random sample of 190 inmates.[11] In his description, these groups to some extent stand in opposition to the rest of the population. Furthermore, the group members' involvement with each other, especially in the case of the primary groups, was very pervasive. How does this social phenomenon blend with the interpretation of convict behavior as a social system? The structural-functional studies failed to take up this point.

CONVICT SOCIAL ORGANIZATION IN CALIFORNIA PRISONS

Background Variables

Before presenting a description of the convict social world which emphasizes those aspects that have the greatest relevance for the career of the felon and which attempts to reconcile the various findings of former studies, the unique features of the California prison system must be mentioned. Some of these have an important bearing on the convict social organization. First, California has six prisons in its complex of ten institutions which have cell blocks and gun towers, and which can hold convicts who require maximum custody. In addition, each of these six have

11. Donald Clemmer, *The Prison Community* (New York: Holt, Rinehart and Winston, Inc., 1940), p. 135.

"adjustment centers," blocks of cells in which convicts are segregated from the rest of the population twenty-four hours a day and remain alone in their cells most of these hours. Troublesome convicts, therefore, can either be transferred to another prison and/or placed indefinitely in adjustment centers. The administration can thus effectively employ expulsion from the convict social system as a means of control.[12]

Second, some of the California prisons have very large populations. San Quentin varies from 3,000 to 5,000; Folsom is in the range of 2,500; Soledad—in three satellite institutions—has a population of 3,500; Vacaville and Tracy each have populations of about 1,500. Besides this, as mentioned above, there are many transfers from prison to prison. One effect of these large populations and numerous transfers is that few convicts are well known by a significant number of other convicts, and consequently few have "roles" in regard to the prison as a whole.

Finally, the California prisons for the last fifteen years have been introducing programs and changes of policy according to a "treatment" penal ideology. The first change was the establishment of the indeterminate sentencing system which leaves the final determination of an individual's sentence, within limits prescribed by law, in the hands of the Adult Authority. The Adult Authority, in making their decisions, have available a variety of data gathered throughout an individual's prison and preprison career. This method of determining the actual time to be served has an important impact upon the convict in respect to his prison behavior. Generally, the convict desires to present a favorable view of his progress in prison and/or remain largely inconspicuous to the prison administration. This, among other things, has driven a wedge into convict solidarity.

The next "treatment" program which affected convict social organization was the establishment of group counseling. After 1955 this program grew until a majority of convicts at some time in their prison career now participate. Group counseling takes many different forms; some groups are led by trained personnel (sociologists, psychologists, and psychiatrists) some by untrained personnel (guards and various prison-free personnel). The groups vary greatly in the regularity of their meetings; some meet once a week, some as often as every day. An overall effect of these meetings is that convicts learn more about administrative concerns, problems, and policies, and the staff has learned more about convicts' affairs. Some of the reluctance to talk to the prison authorities—"the bulls"—has disappeared. Communication in general between the convicts and the administration has increased.

The treatment emphasis has resulted in the institution of various forms of physical, psychological, and vocational therapy. Prison trade

12. See the discussion of the limitations of expulsion as a means of social control in most prison settings in Cloward, "Social Control in the Prison," pp. 22–23.

schools and high schools have expanded. One prison primarily for the purpose of training and educating younger convicts and another, a hospital prison, with an expanded psychiatric staff and a psychiatrist superintendent, were opened. This emphasis on treatment and the growing availability of educational and vocational training facilities have further eroded convict solidarity. Furthermore, these programs have encouraged a new mode of adaptation to incarceration, which will be the focus of the discussion later.

Existing Patterns

A social system, such as that described by Sykes, Sykes and Messinger, Cloward, and McCleary, though it exists, is not the most important social phenomenon in the prison life of most convicts in California prisons. The prison populations at the various prisons are too large. Thus, only a very small group of convicts in any one prison are known well by enough convicts to constitute their having a role in regard to the prison as a whole. Furthermore, the California prison administrators have succeeded, it seems, in preventing the existence of convict cohesion. This is the result of (1) the practice of transferring or segregating men who seem to have too much power and are seen as a threat to the prison policies and current programs; (2) the indeterminate sentence system which serves as a very powerful control mechanism and thus makes it unnecessary to rely on informal means of control; and (3) the treatment programs which have made incursions into convict solidarity. The convict population in California tends to be splintered. A few convicts orient themselves to the prison social system and assume roles in regard to the prison, and a few others withdraw completely, but the majority confine their association to one or two groups of convicts and attempt to disassociate themselves from the bulk of the population. These groups vary from small, close-knit, primary groups to large, casual groups. They also vary greatly in the basis of formation or focus. Many are formed on the basis of neighborhood and/or racial ties, others on the basis of shared criminal identities, especially in the case of thieves, dope fiends, heads, and hustlers, but the great majority of the groups are formed on a rather random basis. Many convicts who cell together or close to each other, who work or attend school together, maintain friendship ties which vary greatly in strength and duration.

The type of group affiliations the convict forms, the impact of this group participation, and the general impact of the prison experience upon his extended career are related to a wide range of factors, some systematic, some relatively random. Presently four of these factors seem to stand out. These are (1) his preprison identity, (2) his prison adaptive mode, (3) his race-ethnicity, and finally (4) his relationship to perspective and identity of the "convict." The following paragraphs will focus primarily on the prison-adaptive modes, but the relationship between these modes and criminal identities will be considered. Race-ethnicity and the convict perspective will be treated later in the chapter.

Prison-Adaptive Modes

Many studies of prison behavior have approached the task of explaining the convict social organization by posing the hypothetical question—how do convicts adapt to prison? It was felt that this was a relevant question because the prison is a situation of deprivation and degradation, and, therefore, presents extraordinary adaptive problems. Two adaptive styles were recognized: (1) an individual style—withdrawal and/or isolation, and (2) a collective style—participation in a convict social system which, through its solidarity, regulation of activities, distribution of goods and prestige, and apparent opposition to the world of the administration, helps the individual withstand the "pains of imprisonment."

I would like to suggest that these studies have overlooked important alternate styles. First let us return to the question that theoretically every convict must ask himself: How shall I do my time? or, What shall I do in prison? First, we assume by this question that the convict is able to cope with the situation. This is not always true; some fail to cope with prison and commit suicide or sink into psychosis. Those who do cope can be divided into those who identify with and therefore adapt to a broader world than that of the prison, and those who orient themselves primarily to the prison world. This difference in orientation is often quite subtle but always important. In some instances it is the basis for forming very important choices, choices which may have important consequences for the felon's long term career. For example, Piri Thomas, a convict, was forced to make up his mind whether to participate in a riot or refrain:

> I stood there watching and weighing, trying to decide whether or not I was a con first and an outsider second. I had been doing time inside yet living every mental minute I could outside; now I had to choose one or the other. I stood there in the middle of the yard. Cons passed me by, some going west to join the boppers, others going east to neutral ground. The call of rep tore within me, while the feeling of being a punk washed over me like a yellow banner. I had to make a decision. *I am a con. These damn cons are my people . . . What do you mean, your people? Your people are outside the cells, home, in the streets. No! That ain't so . . . Look at them go toward the west wall. Why in hell am I taking so long in making up my mind? Man, there goes Papo and Zu-Zu, and Mick the Boxer; even Ruben is there.*[13]

This identification also influences the criteria for assigning and earning prestige—criteria relative to things in the outside world or things which

13. Piri Thomas, *Down These Mean Streets* (New York: Alfred A. Knopf, Inc., 1967), p. 281.

tend to exist only in the prison world, such as status in a prison social system or success with prison homosexuals. Furthermore, it will influence the long term strategies he forms and attempts to follow during his prison sentence.

It is useful to further divide those who maintain their basic orientation to the outside into (1) those who for the most part wish to maintain their life patterns and their identities—even if they intend to refrain from most law breaking activities—and (2) those who desire to make significant changes in life patterns and identities and see prison as a chance to do this.

The mode of adaptation of those convicts who tend to make a world out of prison will be called "jailing." To "jail" is to cut yourself off from the outside world and to attempt to construct a life within prison. The adaptation of those who still keep their commitment to the outside life and see prison as a suspension of that life but who do not want to make any significant changes in their life patterns will be called "doing time." One "does time" by trying to maximize his comfort and luxuries and minimize his discomfort and conflict and to get out as soon as possible. The adaptation made by those who, looking to their future life on the outside, try to effect changes in their life patterns and identities will be called "gleaning."[14] In "gleaning," one sets out to "better himself" or "improve himself" and takes advantage of the resources that exist in prison to do this.

Not all convicts can be classified neatly by these three adaptive styles. Some vacillate from one to another, and others appear to be following two or three of them simultaneously. Still others, for instance the non-copers mentioned above, cannot be characterized by any of the three. However, many prison careers fit very closely into one of these patterns, and the great majority can be classified roughly by one of the styles.

Doing time.

When you go in, now your trial is over, you got your time and everything and now you head for the joint. They furnish your clothing, your toothbrush, your toothpaste, they give you a package of tobacco, they put you up in the morning to get breakfast. In other words, everything is furnished. Now you stay in there two years, five years, ten years, whatever you stay in there, what difference does it make? After a year or so you've been . . . after six months, you've become accustomed to the general routine. Everything is furnished. If you get a

14. "Gleaning" is one term which is not natural to the prison social world, and the category itself is not explicitly defined. Convicts have recognized and labeled subparts of it, such as "intellectuals," "programmers," and "dudes on a self-improvement kick," but not the broader category which I have labeled gleaners. However, whenever I have described this category to convicts, they immediately recognized it and the term becomes meaningful to them. I chose the term gleaning because it emphasizes one very important dimension of this style of adaptation, the tendency to pick through the prison world (which is mostly chaff) in search of the means of self-improvement.

stomachache, you go to the doctor; if you can't see out of your cheaters, you go to the optician. It don't cost you nothing.[15]

As the above statement by a thief indicates, many convicts conceive of the prison experience as a temporary break in their outside career, one which they take in their stride. They come to prison and "do their time." They attempt to pass through this experience with the least amount of suffering and the greatest amount of comfort. They (1) avoid trouble, (2) find activities which occupy their time, (3) secure a few luxuries, (4) with the exception of a few complete isolates, form friendships with small groups of other convicts, and (5) do what they think is necessary to get out as soon as possible.[16]

To avoid trouble the convict adheres to the convict code—especially the maxims of "do your own time" and "don't snitch," and stays away from "lowriders"—those convicts engaged in hijacking and violent disputes. In some prisons which have a high incidence of violence—knifings, assaults, and murders—this can appear to be very difficult even to the convicts themselves. One convict reported his first impression of Soledad:

The first day I got to Soledad I was walking from the fish tank to the mess hall and this guy comes running down the hall past me, yelling, with a knife sticking out of his back. Man, I was petrified. I thought, what the fuck kind of place is this? (Interview, Soledad Prison, June 1966)

Piri Thomas decided to avoid trouble for a while, but commented on the difficulty in doing this:

The decision to cool myself made the next two years the hardest I had done because it meant being a smoothie and staying out of trouble, which in prison is difficult, for any of a thousand cons might start trouble with you for any real or fancied reason, and if you didn't face up to the trouble, you ran the risk of being branded as having no heart. And heart was all I had left.[17]

However, except for rare, "abnormal" incidents, convicts tend not to bother others who are "doing their own number." One convict made the following comments on avoiding trouble in prison:

If a new guy comes here and just settles down and minds his business, nobody'll fuck with him, unless he runs into some nut. Everyone sees a guy is trying to do his own time and they leave him alone. Those guys that get messed over are usually asking for it. If you stay away from the lowriders and the punks and don't get into debt or snitch on somebody you won't have no trouble here. (Interview, San Quentin, July 1966)

To occupy their time, "time-doers" work, read, work on hobbies, play cards, chess, and dominoes, engage in sports, go to movies, watch TV,

15. Maurer, *Whiz Mob*, p. 196.

16. Erving Goffman has described this mode of adaptation, which he calls "playing it cool" (*Asylums*, pp. 64–65).

17. Thomas, *Down These Mean Streets*, p. 280.

participate in some group activities, such as drama groups, gavel clubs, and slot car clubs, and while away hours "tripping" with friends. They seek extra luxuries through their job. Certain jobs in prison, such as jobs in the kitchen, in the officers' and guards' dining room, in the boiler room, the officers' and guards' barber shop, and the fire house, offer various extra luxuries—extra things to eat, a radio, privacy, additional shows, and more freedom. Or time-doers purchase luxuries legally or illegally available in the prison market. If they have money on the books, if they have a job which pays a small salary, or if they earn money at a hobby, they can draw up to twenty dollars a month which may be spent for foodstuffs, coffee, cocoa, stationery, toiletries, tobacco, and cigarettes. Or using cigarettes as currency they may purchase food from the kitchen, drugs, books, cell furnishings, clothes, hot plates, stingers, and other contraband items. If they do not have legal access to funds, they may "scuffle"; that is, sell some commodity which they produce—such as belt buckles or other handicraft items—or some commodity which is accessible to them through their job—such as food items from the kitchen. "Scuffling," however, necessitates becoming enmeshed in the convict social system and increases the chances of "trouble," such as conflicts over unpaid debts, hijacking by others, and "beefs"—disciplinary actions for rule infractions. Getting into trouble is contrary to the basic tenets of "doing time," so time-doers usually avoid scuffling.

The friendships formed by time-doers vary from casual acquaintanceships with persons who accidentally cell nearby or work together, to close friendship groups who "go all the way" for each other—share material goods, defend each other against others, and maintain silence about each other's activities. These varying friendship patterns are related closely to their criminal identities.

Finally, time-doers try to get out as soon as possible. First they do this by staying out of trouble, "cleaning up their hands." They avoid activities and persons that would put them in danger of receiving disciplinary actions, or "beefs." And in recent years with the increasing emphasis on treatment, they "program." To program is to follow, at least tokenly, a treatment plan which has been outlined by the treatment staff, recommended by the board, or devised by the convict himself. It is generally believed that to be released on parole as early as possible one must "get a program." A program involves attending school, vocational training, group counseling, church, Alcoholics Anonymous, or any other special program that is introduced under the treatment policy of the prison.

All convicts are more apt to choose "doing time," but some approach this style in a slightly different manner. For instance, doing time is characteristic of the thief in prison. He shapes this mode of adaptation and establishes it as a major mode of adaptation in prison. The convict code, which is fashioned from the criminal code, is the foundation for this style. The thief has learned how to do his time long before he comes to prison. Prison, he learns when he takes on the dimensions of the criminal subculture, is part of criminal life, a calculated risk, and when it comes he is ready for it.

> Long before the thief has come to prison, his subculture has defined proper prison conduct as behavior rationally calculated to "do time" in the easiest possible way. This means that he wants a prison life containing the best possible combination of a maximum amount of leisure time and maximum number of privileges. Accordingly, the privileges sought by the thief are different from the privileges sought by the man oriented to prison itself. The thief wants things that will make prison life a little easier—extra food, a maximum amount of recreation time, a good radio, a little peace.[18]

The thief knows how to avoid trouble; he keeps away from "dingbats," "lowriders," "hoosiers," "square johns," and "stool pigeons," and obeys the convict code. He also knows not to buck the authorities; he keeps his record clean and does what is necessary to get out—even programs.

He occasionally forms friendships with other criminals, such as dope fiends, heads, and possibly disorganized criminals, but less often with square johns. Formerly he confined his friendship to other thieves with whom he formed very tight-knit groups. For example Jack Black, a thief in the last century, describes his assimilation into the "Johnson family" in prison:

> Shorty was one of the patricians of the prison, a "box man," doing time for bank burglary. "I'll put you in with the right people, kid. You're folks yourself or you wouldn't have been with Smiler."
>
> I had no friends in the place. But the fact that I had been with Smiler, that I had kept my mouth shut, and that Shorty had come forward to help me, gave me a certain fixed status in the prison that nothing could shake but some act of my own. I was naturally pleased to find myself taken up by the "best people," as Shorty and his friends called themselves, and accepted as one of them.
>
> Shorty now took me into the prison where we found the head trusty who was one of the "best people" himself, a thoroughgoing bum from the road. The term "bum" is not used here in any cheap or disparaging sense. In those days it meant any kind of a traveling thief. It has long since fallen into disuse. The yegg of today was the bum of twenty years ago.
>
> "This party," said Shorty, "is one of the 'Johnson' family." (The bums called themselves "Johnsons" probably because they were so numerous.) "He's good people and I want to get him fixed up for a cell with the right folks." [19]

Clemmer described two *primary* groups out of the fourteen groups he located, and both of these were groups of thieves.[20]

Presently in California prisons thieves' numbers have diminished. This

18. Irwin and Cressey, "Thieves, Convicts, and the Inmate Culture," p. 150.
19. Black, *You Can't Win*, pp. 104–5.
20. Clemmer, *The Prison Community*, pp. 123, 127.

and the general loosening of the convict solidarity have tended to drive the thief into the background of prison life. He generally confines his friendships to one or two others, usually other thieves or criminals who are "all right"; otherwise he withdraws from participation with others. He often feels out of place amid the changes that have come about. One thief looking back upon fifteen years in California prisons states:

As far as I'm concerned their main purpose has been in taking the convict code away from him. But what they fail to do is when they strip him from these rules is replace it with something. They turn these guys into a bunch of snivelers and they write letters on each other and they don't have any rules to live by. (Interview, Folsom Prison, July 1966)

Another thief interviewed also indicated his dislocation in the present prison social world:

The new kinds in prison are wild. They have no respect for rules or other persons. I just want to get out of here and give it all up. I can't take coming back to prison again, not with the kind of convicts they are getting now. (Interview, Soledad Prison, June 1966)

Like the majority of convicts, the dope fiend and the head usually just "do time." When they do, they don't vary greatly from the thief, except that they tend to associate with other dope fiends or heads, although they too will associate with other criminals. They tend to form very close bonds with one, two, or three other dope fiends or heads and maintain a casual friendship with a large circle of dope fiends, heads, and other criminals. Like the thief, the dope fiend and the head tend not to establish ties with squares.

The hustler in doing time differs from the other criminals in that he does not show a propensity to form very tight-knit groups. Hustling values, which emphasize manipulation and invidiousness, seem to prevent this. The hustler maintains a very large group of casual friends. Though this group does not show strong bonds of loyalty and mutual aid, they share many activities such as cards, sports, dominoes, and "jiving"—casual talk.

Square johns do their time quite differently than the criminals. The square john finds life in prison repugnant and tries to isolate himself as much as possible from the convict world. He does not believe in the convict code, but he usually learns to display a token commitment to it for his own safety. A square john indicated his forced obedience to the convict code:

Several times I saw things going on that I didn't like. One time a couple of guys were working over another guy and I wanted to step in, but I couldn't. Had to just keep moving as if I didn't see it. (Interview, Soledad Prison, June 1966)

He usually keeps busy with some job assignment, a hobby, cards, chess, or various forms of group programs, such as drama groups. He forms friendships with one or two other squares and avoids the criminals. But even with other squares there is resistance to forming *close* ties. Square johns are very often sensitive about their "problems," and they are apt to feel repugnance toward themselves and other persons with problems. Besides, the square usually wants to be accepted by conventional people and not by other "stigmatized" outcasts like himself. So, many square johns do their time isolated from other inmates. Malcolm Braly in his novel *On the Yard* has captured the ideal-typical square john in prison:

> Watson had finally spoken. Formerly a mild-mannered and mother-smothered high school teacher, he had killed his two small sons, attempted to kill his wife, cut his own throat, then poisoned himself, all because his wife had refused a reconciliation with the remark, "John, the truth is you bore me."
>
> Watson stood with culture, the Republic, and motherhood, and at least once each meeting he made a point of reaffirming his position before launching into his chronic criticism of the manner in which his own case had been, was and would be handled. ". . . and I've been confined almost two years now, and I see no point in further imprisonment, further therapy, no point whatsoever since there's absolutely no possibility I'll do the same thing again . . ."
>
> "That's right," Red said softly. "He's run out of kids."
>
> And Zeke whispered, "I just wish he'd taken the poison *before* he cut his throat."
>
> Watson ignored the whispering, if he heard it at all, and went on, clearly speaking only to Erlenmeyer. "Surely, Doctor, as a college man yourself you must realize that the opportunities for a meaningful cultural exchange are sorely limited in an institution of this nature. Of course, I attend the General Semantics Club and I'm taking the course Oral McKeon is giving in Oriental religions, but these are such tiny oases in this desert of sweatsuits and domino games, and I can't understand why everyone is just thrown together without reference to their backgrounds, or the nature of their offense. Thieves, dope addicts, even sex maniacs—"
>
> Zeke threw his hands up in mock alarm. "Where'd you see a sex maniac?"
>
> "I don't think it cause for facetiousness," Watson said coldly. "Just yesterday I found occasion to step into the toilet off the big yard and one of the sweepers was standing there masturbating into the urinal."
>
> "That's horrible," Zeke said. "What'd you do?"
>
> "I left, of course."
>
> "Naturally. It violates the basic ideals of Scouting." [21]

The lower-class man, though he doesn't share the square john's repugnance towards criminals or the convict code, usually does not wish to associate closely with thieves, dope fiends, heads, and disorganized criminals. In his life outside he has encountered and avoided these persons for many years and usually keeps on avoiding them inside. He usually seeks a job to occupy himself. His actual stay in prison is typically very short, since he is either released very early and/or he is classified at

21. Malcolm Braly, *On the Yard* (Boston: Little, Brown and Co., 1967), pp. 106–7.

minimum custody and sent to a forestry camp or one of the minimum-custody institutions, where he has increased freedom and privileges.

Jailing. Some convicts who do not retain or who never acquired any commitment to outside social worlds, tend to make a world out of prison.[22] These are the men who

seek positions of power, influence and sources of information, whether these men are called "shots," "politicians," "merchants," "hoods," "toughs," "gorillas," or something else. A job as secretary to the Captain or Warden, for example, gives an aspiring prisoner information and consequent power, and enables him to influence the assignment or regulation of other inmates. In the same way, a job which allows the incumbent to participate in a racket, such as clerk in the kitchen storeroom where he can steal and sell food, is highly desirable to a man oriented to the convict subculture. With a steady income of cigarettes, ordinarily the prisoner's medium of exchange, he may assert a great deal of influence and purchase those things which are symbols of status among persons oriented to the convict subculture. Even if there is not a well-developed medium of exchange, he can barter goods acquired in his position for equally-desirable goods possessed by other convicts. These include information and such things as specially-starched, pressed, and tailored prison clothing, fancy belts, belt buckles or billfolds, special shoes, or any other type of dress which will set him apart and will indicate that he has both the influence to get the goods and the influence necessary to keep them and display them despite prison rules which outlaw doing so. In California, special items of clothing, and clothing that is neatly laundered, are called "bonaroos" (a corruption of *bonnet rouge,* by means of which French prison trustees were once distinguished from the common run of prisoners), and to a lesser degree even the persons who wear such clothing are called "bonaroos." [23]

Just as doing time is the characteristic style of the thief, so "jailing" is the characteristic style of the state-raised youth. This identity terminates on the first or second prison term, or certainly by the time the youth reaches thirty. The state-raised youth must assume a new identity, and the one he most often chooses, the one which his experience has prepared him for, is that of the "convict." The prison world is the only world with which he is familiar. He was raised in a world where "punks" and "queens" have replaced women, "bonaroos" are the only fashionable clothing, and cigarettes are money. This is a world where disputes are settled with a pipe or a knife, and the individual must form tight cliques for protection. His senses are attuned to iron doors banging, locks turning, shakedowns, and long lines of blue-clad convicts. He knows how to survive, in fact prosper, in this world, how to get a cell change and a good work assignment, how to score for nutmeg, cough syrup, or other narcotics. More important, he knows hundreds of youths like himself who grew up in the youth prisons and are now in the adult prisons. For ex-

22. Fifteen per cent of the 116 ex-prisoners were classified as "jailers."
23. Irwin and Cressey, "Thieves, Convicts, and the Inmate Culture," p. 149.

ample, Claude Brown describes a friend who fell into the patterns of jailing:

"Yeah, Sonny. The time I did in Woodburn, the times I did on the Rock, that was college, man. Believe me, it was college. I did four years in Woodburn. And I guess I've done a total of about two years on the Rock in about the last six years. Every time I went there, I learned a little more. When I go to jail now, Sonny, I live, man. I'm right at home. That's the good part about it. If you look at it, Sonny, a cat like me is just cut out to be in jail.

"It could never hurt me, 'cause I never had what the good folks call a home and all that kind of shit to begin with. So when I went to jail, the first time I went away, when I went to Warwick, I made my own home. It was all right. Shit, I learned how to live. Now when I go back to the joint, anywhere I go, I know some people. If I go to any of the jails in New York, or if I go to a slam in Jersey, even, I still run into a lot of cats I know. It's almost like a family."

I said, "Yeah, Reno, it's good that a cat can be so happy in jail. I guess all it takes to be happy in anything is knowin' how to walk with your lot, whatever it is, in life." [24]

The state-raised youth often assumes a role in the prison social system, the system of roles, values, and norms described by Schrag, Sykes, and others. This does not mean that he immediately rises to power in the prison system. Some of the convicts have occupied their positions for many years and cannot tolerate the threat of every new bunch of reform-school graduates. The state-raised youth who has just graduated to adult prison must start at the bottom; but he knows the routine, and in a year or so he occupies a key position himself. One reason he can readily rise is that in youth prison he very often develops skills, such as clerical and maintenance skills, that are valuable to the prison administration.

Many state-raised youths, however, do not tolerate the slow ascent in the prison social system and become "lowriders." They form small cliques and rob cells, hijack other convicts, carry on feuds with other cliques, and engage in various rackets. Though these "outlaws" are feared and hated by all other convicts, their orientation is to the convict world, and they are definitely part of the convict social system.

Dope fiends and hustlers slip into jailing more often than thieves, due mainly to the congruities between their old activities and some of the patterns of jailing. For instance, a central activity of jailing is "wheeling and dealing," the major economic activity of prison. All prison resources—dope, food, books, money, sexual favors, bonaroos, cell changes, jobs, dental and hospital care, hot plates, stingers, cell furnishings, rings, and buckles—are always available for purchase with cigarettes. It is possible to live in varying degrees of luxury, and luxury has a double reward in prison as it does in the outside society: first, there is the reward of consumption itself, and second there is the reward of increased prestige in the prison social system because of the display of opulence.

24. Brown, *Manchild in the Promised Land*, p. 412.

This prison life style requires more cigarettes than can be obtained legally; consequently, one wheels and deals. There are three main forms of wheeling and dealing for cigarettes: (1) gambling (cards, dice and betting on sporting events); (2) selling some commodity or service, which is usually made possible by a particular job assignment; and (3) lending cigarettes for interest—two for three. These activities have a familiar ring to both the hustler and the dope fiend, who have hustled money or dope on the outside. They very often become intricately involved in the prison economic life and in this way necessarily involved in the prison social system. The hustler does this because he feels at home in this routine, because he wants to keep in practice, or because he must present a good front—even in prison. To present a good front one must be a success at wheeling and dealing.

The dope fiend, in addition to having an affinity for wheeling and dealing, may become involved in the prison economic life in securing drugs. There are a variety of drugs available for purchase with cigarettes or money (and money can be purchased with cigarettes). Drugs are expensive, however, and to purchase them with any regularity one either has money smuggled in from the outside or he wheels and deals. And to wheel and deal one must maintain connections for securing drugs, for earning money, and for protection. This enmeshes the individual in the system of prison roles, values, and norms. Though he maintains a basic commitment to his drug subculture which supersedes his commitment to the prison culture and though he tends to form close ties only with other dope fiends, through his wheeling and dealing for drugs he becomes an intricate part of the prison social system.

The head jails more often than the thief. One reason for this is that the head, especially the "weed head" tends to worship luxuries and comforts and is fastidious in his dress. Obtaining small luxuries, comforts, and "bonaroo" clothing usually necessitates enmeshing himself in the "convict" system. Furthermore, the head is often vulnerable to the dynamics of narrow, cliquish, and invidious social systems, such as the "convict" system, because many of the outside head social systems are of this type.

The thief, or any identity for that matter, *may* slowly lose his orientation to the outside community, take on the convict categories, and thereby fall into jailing. This occurs when the individual has spent a great deal of time in prison and/or returned to the outside community and discovered that he no longer fits in the outside world. It is difficult to maintain a real commitment to a social world without firsthand experience with it for long periods of time.

The square john and the lower-class man find the activities of the "convicts" petty, repugnant, or dangerous, and virtually never jail.

Gleaning. With the rapidly growing educational, vocational training, and treatment opportunities, and with the erosion of convict solidarity, an increasing number of convicts choose to radically change their life styles and follow a sometimes carefully devised plan to "better themselves," "improve their mind," or "find themselves" while in prison.[25] One convict describes his motives and plans for changing his life style:

I got tired of losing. I had been losing all my life. I decided that I wanted to win for a while. So I got on a different kick. I knew that I had to learn something so I went to school, got my high school diploma. I cut myself off from my old YA buddies and started hanging around with some intelligent guys who minded their own business. We read a lot, a couple of us paint. We play a little bridge and talk, a lot of time about what we are going to do when we get out. (Interview, Soledad Prison, June 1966)

Gleaning may start on a small scale, perhaps as an attempt to overcome educational or intellectual inferiorities. For instance, Malcolm X, feeling inadequate in talking to certain convicts, starts to read:

It had really begun back in the Charlestown Prison, when Bimbi first made me feel envy of his stock of knowledge. Bimbi had always taken charge of any conversation he was in, and I had tried to emulate him. But every book I picked up had few sentences which didn't contain anywhere from one to nearly all of the words that might as well have been in Chinese. When I just skipped those words, of course, I really ended up with little idea of what the book said. So I have come to the Norfolk Prison Colony still going through only book-reading motions. Pretty soon, I would have quit even these motions, unless I had received the motivation that I did.[26]

The initial, perfunctory steps into gleaning often spring the trap. Gleaning activities have an intrinsic attraction and often instill motivation which was originally lacking. Malcolm X reports how once he began to read, the world of knowledge opened up to him:

No university would ask any student to devour literature as I did when this new world opened to me, of being able to read and *understand*.[27]

In trying to "improve himself," "improve his mind," or "find himself," the convict gleans from every source available in prison. The chief source is books: he reads philosophy, history, art, science, and fiction. Often after getting started he devours a sizable portion of world literature. Malcolm X describes his voracious reading habits:

I read more in my room than in the library itself. An inmate who was known to read a lot could check out more than the permitted maximum number of books. I preferred reading in the total isolation of my own room.

When I had progressed to really serious reading, every night at about ten P.M. I would be outraged with the "lights out." It always seemed to catch me right in the middle of something engrossing.

25. In the sample of 116 ex-prisoners, the records indicated that 19 per cent had followed a gleaning course in prison.

26. *The Autobiography of Malcolm X*, p. 171.

27. Ibid., p. 173.

Fortunately, right outside my door was a corridor light that cast a glow into my room. The glow was enough to read by, once my eyes adjusted to it. So when "lights out" came, I would sit on the floor where I could continue reading in that glow.[28]

Besides this informal education, he often pursues formal education. The convict may complete grammar school and high school in the prison educational facilities. He may enroll in college courses through University of California (which will be paid for by the Department of Corrections), or through other correspondence schools (which he must pay for himself). More recently, he may take courses in various prison college programs.

He learns trades through the vocational training programs or prison job assignments. Sometimes he augments these by studying trade books, correspondence courses, or journals. He studies painting, writing, music, acting, and other creative arts. There are some facilities for these pursuits sponsored by the prison administration, but these are limited. This type of gleaning is done mostly through correspondence, through reading, or through individual efforts in the cell.

He tries to improve himself in other ways. He works on his social skills and his physical appearance—has his tattoos removed, has surgery on physical defects, has dental work done, and builds up his body "pushing iron."

He shys away from former friends or persons with his criminal identity who are not gleaners and forms new associations with other gleaners. These are usually gleaners who have chosen a similar style of gleaning, and with whom he shares many interests and activities, but they may also be those who are generally trying to improve themselves, although they are doing so in different ways.

Gleaning is a style more characteristic of the hustler, the dope fiend, and the state-raised youth than of the thief. When the former glean, though they tend to associate less with their deviant friends who are doing time or jailing, they are not out of the influence of these groups, or free from the influence of their old subculture values. The style of gleaning they choose and the future life for which they prepare themselves must be acceptable to the old reference group and somewhat congruent with their deviant values. The life they prepare for should be prestigious in the eyes of their old associates. It must be "doing good" and cannot be "a slave's life."

The state-raised youth who gleans probably has the greatest difficulty cutting himself off from his former group because the state-raised values emphasize loyalty to one's buddies:

I don't spend much time with my old YA [Youth Authority] partners and when I do we don't get along. They want me to do something that I won't do or they start getting on my back about my plans. One time they were riding me pretty bad and I had to pull them up. (Interview, Soledad Prison, June 1966)

28. Ibid., pp. 173–74.

He also has the greatest difficulty in making any realistic plans for the future. He has limited experience with the outside, and his models of "making it" usually come from the mass media—magazines, books, movies, and TV.

The dope fiend and the head, when they glean, tend to avoid practical fields and choose styles which promise glamor, excitement, or color. Most conventional paths with which they are familiar seem especially dull and repugnant. In exploring ways of making it they must find some way to avoid the humdrum life which they rejected long ago. Many turn to legitimate deviant identities such as "intellectual outsiders," "bohemians," or "mystics." Often they study one of the creative arts, the social sciences, or philosophy with no particular career in mind.

The hustler, who values skills of articulation and maintained a good "front" in his deviant life, often prepares for a field where these skills will serve him, such as preaching or political activism.

The square john and the lower-class man, since they seldom seek to radically change their identity, do not glean in the true sense, but they do often seek to improve themselves. The square john usually does this by attacking his problem. He is satisfied with his reference world—the conventional society—but he recognizes that to return to it successfully he must cope with that flaw in his makeup which led to his incarceration. There are three common ways he attacks this problem: (1) he joins self help groups such as Alcoholics Anonymous, (2) he seeks the help of experts (psychiatrists, psychologists or sociologists) and attends the therapy programs, or (3) he turns to religion.

The lower-class man is usually an older person who does not desire or deem it possible to carve out a radically new style of life. He may, however, see the prison experience as a chance to improve himself by increasing his education and his vocational skills.

The thief tends to be older and his commitment to his identity is usually strong, so it is not likely that he will explore other life styles or identities. This does not mean that he is committed for all time to a life of crime. Certain alternate conclusions to a criminal career are included in the definitions of a proper thief's life. For instance, a thief may retire when he becomes older, has served a great deal of time, or has made a "nice score." When he retires he may work at some well-paying trade or run a small business, and in prison he may prepare himself for either of these acceptable conclusions to a criminal career.

Disorganized Criminal

In the preceding discussion of prison adaptive modes, the "disorganized criminal" was purposely omitted. It is felt that his prison adaptation must be considered separately from the other identities.

The disorganized criminal is human putty in the prison social world.

He may be shaped to fit any category. He has weaker commitments to values or conceptions of self that would prevent him from organizing any course of action in prison. He is the most responsive to prison programs, to differential association, and to other forces which are out of his control. He may become part of the prison social system, do his time, or glean. If they will tolerate him, he may associate with thieves, dope fiends, convicts, squares, heads, or other disorganized criminals. To some extent these associations are formed in a random fashion. He befriends persons with whom he works, cells next to, and encounters regularly through the prison routine. He tends not to seek out particular categories, as is the case with the other identities. He does not feel any restraints in initiating associations, however, as do the square john and the lower-class man.

The friendships he forms are very important to any changes that occur in this person. Since he tends to have a cleaner slate in terms of identity, he is more susceptible to differential association. He often takes on the identity and the prison adaptive mode of the group with which he comes into contact. If he does acquire a new identity, however, such as one of the deviant identities that exist in prison, his commitment to it is still tentative at most. The deviant identities, except for that of the convict, exist in the context of an exterior world, and the more subtle cues, the responses, the meanings which are essential parts of this world cannot be experienced in prison. It is doubtful, therefore, that any durable commitment could be acquired in prison. In the meantime, he may be shaken from this identity, and he may continue to vacillate from social world to social world, or to wander bewildered in a maze of conflicting world views as he has done in the past.

Race and Ethnicity

Another variable which is becoming increasingly important in the formation of cleavages and identity changes in the convict world is that of race and ethnicity. For quite some time in California prisons, hostility and distance between three segments of the populations—white, Negroes and Mexicans—have increased. For several years the Negroes have assumed a more militant and ethnocentric posture, and recently the Mexicans—already ethnocentric and aggressive—have followed with a more organized, militant stance. Correspondingly, there is a growing trend among these two segments to establish, reestablish or enhance racial-ethnic pride and identity. Many "Blacks" and "Chicanos" are supplanting their criminal identity with a racial-ethnic one. This movement started with the Blacks.[29] A black California convict gives his recently acquired views toward whites:

29. This movement was foretold by Malcolm X (see *The Autobiography of Malcolm X*, p. 183).

> All these years, man, I been stealing and coming to the joint. I never stopped to think why I was doing it. I thought that all I wanted was money and stuff. Ya know, man, now I can see why I thought the way I did. I been getting fucked all my life and never realized it. The white man has been telling me that I should want his stuff. But he didn't give me no way to get it. Now I ain't going for his shit anymore. I'm a Black man. I'm going to get out of here and see what I can do for my people. I'm going to do what I have to do to get those white motherfuckers off my people's back. (Interview, San Quentin, March 1968)

Chicanos in prison have maintained considerable insulation from both whites and Blacks—especially Blacks—towards whom they have harbored considerable hostility. They possess a strong ethnic-racial identity which underpins their more specialized felonious one—which has usually been that of a dope fiend or lower-class man. This subcultural identity and actual group unity in prison has been based on their Mexican culture—especially two important dimensions of Mexican culture. The first is their strong commitment to the concept of "machismo"—which is roughly translated manhood. (See the discussion of manhood in the section on the lower-class man in Chapter 1.) The second is their use of Spanish and Calo (Spanish slang) which has separated them from other segments. Besides these two traits there are many other ethnic subcultural characteristics which promote unity among Chicanos. For instance, they tend to be stoic and intolerant of "snitches" and "snivelers" and feel that Anglos and Blacks are more often snitches and snivelers. Furthermore they respect friendship to the extreme, in fact to the extreme of killing or dying for friendship.

Until recently this has meant that Chicanos constituted the most cohesive segment in California prisons. In prison, where they intermingle with whites and Negroes, they have felt considerable distance from these segments and have maintained their identification with Mexican culture. However, there have been and still are some divisions in this broad category. For instance, various neighborhood cliques of Chicanos often carry on violent disputes with each other which last for years. Furthermore, Los Angeles or California cliques wage disputes with El Paso or Texas cliques. Many stabbings and killings have resulted from confrontations between different Chicano groups. Nevertheless, underpinning these different group affiliations and the various criminal identities there has been a strong identification with Mexican culture.

Recently the Chicanos, following the footsteps of the Negroes in prison and the footsteps of certain militant Mexican-American groups outside (e.g., MAPA and the Delano strikers) have started organizing cultural-activist groups in prison (such as Empleo) and shaping a new indentity built upon their Mexican ancestry and their position of disadvantage in the white society. As they move in this direction they are cultivating some friendship with the Negroes, towards whom they now feel more affinity.

This racial-ethnic militance and identification will more than likely become increasingly important in the prison social world. There is already some indication that the identity of the Black National and that of the Chicano is becoming superordinate to the criminal identities of many Negroes and Mexican-Americans or at least is having an impact on their criminal identities.

A dude don't necessarily have to become a Muslim or a Black National now to get with Black Power. He may still be laying to get out there and do some pimping or shoot some dope. But he knows he's a brother and when the shit is down we can count on him. And maybe he is going to carry himself a little differently, you know, like now you see more and more dudes—oh, they're still pimps, but they got naturals now. (Interview, San Quentin, April 1968)

The reassertion or discovery of the racial-ethnic identity is sometimes related to gleaning in prison. Frequently, the leaders of Blacks or Chicanos, for example, Malcolm X and Eldridge Cleaver, have arrived at their subcultural activism and militant stance through gleaning. Often, becoming identified with this movement will precipitate a gleaning course. However, this is not necessarily the case. These two phenomena are not completely overlapping among the Negro and Chicano.

The nationalistic movement is beginning to have a general impact on the total prison world—especially at San Quentin. The Blacks and Chicanos, as they focus on the whites as their oppressors, seem to be excluding white prisoners from this category and are, in fact, developing some sympathy for them as a minority group which itself is being oppressed by the white establishment and the white police. As an indication of this recent change, one convict comments on the present food-serving practices of Muslim convicts:

It used to be that whenever a Muslim was serving something (and this was a lot of the time man, because there's a lot of those dudes in the kitchen), well, you know, you wouldn't expect to get much of a serving. Now, the cats just pile it on to whites and blacks. Like he is giving all the state's stuff away to show his contempt. So I think it is getting better between the suedes and us. (Interview, San Quentin, April 1968)

The Convict Identity

Over and beyond the particular criminal identity or the racial-ethnic identity he acquires or maintains in prison and over and beyond the changes in his direction which are produced by his prison strategy, to some degree the felon acquires the perspective of the "convict."

There are several gradations and levels of this perspective and attendant identity. First is the taken-for-granted perspective, which he acquires in spite of any conscious efforts to avoid it. This perspective is acquired simply by being in prison and engaging in prison routines for months or years. Even square johns who consciously attempt to pass through the prison experience without acquiring any of the beliefs and values of the criminals, do to some extent acquire certain meanings, certain taken-for-granted interpretations and responses which will shape, influence, or distort reality for them after release. (In chapter 6 there will be a discussion of the reentry problems resulting from this taken-for-granted convict perspective.)

Beyond the taken-for-granted perspective which all convicts acquire, most convicts are influenced by a pervasive but rather uncohesive convict "code." To some extent most of them, especially those who identify with a criminal system, are consciously committed to the major dictum of this code—"do your own time." As was pointed out earlier, the basic meaning of this precept is the obligation to tolerate the behavior of others unless it is directly affecting your physical self or your possessions. If another's behavior surpasses these limits, then the problem must be solved by the person himself; that is, *not* by calling for help from the officials.

> The convict code isn't any different than stuff we all learned as kids. You know, nobody likes a stool pigeon. Well, here in the joint you got all kinds of guys living jammed together, two to a cell. You got nuts walking the yard, you got every kind of dingbat in the world here. Well, we got to have some rules among ourselves. The rule is "do your own number." In other words, keep off your neighbors' toes. Like if a guy next to me is making brew in his cell, well, this is none of my business. I got no business running to the man and telling him that Joe Blow is making brew in his cell. Unless Joe Blow is fucking over me, then I can't say nothing. And when he is fucking over me, then I got to stop him myself. If I can't then I deserve to get fucked over. (Interview, San Quentin, May 1968)

Commitment to the convict code or the identity of the convict is to a high degree a lifetime commitment to do your own time; that is, to live and let live, and when you feel that someone is not letting you live, to either take it, leave, or stop him yourself, but never call for help from official agencies of control.

At another level, the convict perspective consists of a more cohesive and sophisticated value and belief system. This is the perspective of the elite of the convict world—the "regular." A "regular" (or, as he has been variously called, "people," "folks," "solid," a "right guy," or "all right") possesses many of the traits of the thief's culture. He can be counted on when needed by other regulars. He is also not a "hoosier"; that is, he has some finesse, is capable, is levelheaded, has "guts" and "timing." The following description of a simple bungled transaction exemplifies this trait:

Man, you should have seen the hoosier when the play came down. I thought that that motherfucker was all right. He surprised me. He had the stuff and was about to hand it to me when a sergeant and another bull came through the door from the outside. Well, there wasn't nothing to worry about. Is all he had to do was go on like there was nothin' unusual and hand me the stuff and they would have never suspected nothing. But he got so fucking nervous and started fumbling around. You know, he handed me the sack and then pulled it back until they got hip that some play was taking place. Well you know what happened. The play was ranked and we both ended up in the slammer. (Field notes, San Quentin, February 1968)

The final level of the perspective of the convict is that of the "old con." This is a degree of identification reached after serving a great deal of time, so much time that all outside-based identities have dissipated and the only meaningful world is that of the prison. The old con has become totally immersed in the prison world. This identification is often the result of years of jailing, but it can result from merely serving too much time. It was mentioned previously that even thieves after spending many years may fall into jailing, even though time-doing is their usual pattern. After serving a very long sentence or several long sentences with no extended period between, any criminal will tend to take on the identity of the "old con."

The old con tends to carve out a narrow but orderly existence in prison. He has learned to secure many luxuries and learned to be satisfied with the prison forms of pleasure—e.g., homosexual activities, cards, dominoes, handball, hobbies, and reading. He usually obtains jobs which afford him considerable privileges and leisure time. He often knows many of the prison administrators—the warden, the associate wardens, the captain, and the lieutenants, whom he has known since they were officers and lesser officials.

Often he becomes less active in the prison social world. He retires and becomes relatively docile or apathetic. At times he grows petty and treacherous. There is some feeling that old cons can't be trusted because their "head has become soft" or they have "lost their guts," and are potential "stool pigeons."

The convict identity is very important to the future career of the felon. In the first instance, the acquiring of the taken-for-granted perspective will at least obstruct the releasee's attempts to reorient himself on the outside. More important, the other levels of the identity, if they have been acquired, will continue to influence choices for years afterward. The convict perspective, though it may become submerged after extended outside experiences, will remain operative in its latency state and will often obtrude into civilian life contexts.

The identity of the old con—the perspective, the values and beliefs, and other personality attributes which are acquired after the years of doing time, such as advanced age, adjustment to prison routines, and complete loss of skills required to carry on the normal activities of civilians—will usually make living on the outside impossible. The old con is very often suited for nothing except dereliction on the outside or death in prison.

4

LOOKING OUTSIDE

THE "STREETS" FROM INSIDE

Since the vast majority of convicts expect to return to the "streets," and they share their plans for this eventuality, the outside is an important dimension in the prison meaning world. Release and renewal of life on the outside are the dominant concerns of time-doers and gleaners. Even jailers, although they tend to make prison life their central concern, are cognizant that they will return to the outside community. At the level of public discourse, the outside is "where it's at"—where pleasures, activities, and commodities which are absent in prison exist in abundance. It is disgraceful, even if it is true, to admit that one prefers prison. Only lifers may openly turn their backs on the outside. All others must appear to desire release intensely.

The discussions and the plans, therefore, about his future on the outside are very important to the extended career of the criminal felon. He learns prison meanings and concepts—a convict perspective of the "streets"—which will influence his behavior for years to come. In particular he learns three involved concepts which serve as guides for his planning about the future and his behavior after release. These are "making it," "doing all right," and "the old bag." These concepts and the broader prison perspective of the outside world assume importance for him and remain important because of his relationship to a general prison reference world and, in particular, a significant, smaller reference group of fellow prisoners.

Public and Private Reference Worlds

The planning and discussions about the future take place at two different levels. One is that of the general prison community, or at least a large segment of it, the "yard." At this level, the conversations about the future are cliché-ridden and have a humorous slant. The meanings and values they reflect are very close to the dominant prison meanings and values.

I'm goin' a get myself a lunch pail, a plastic lunch pail the parole officer can see through and see I got a lunch inside. I'm goin a make that slave every day. (Field notes, San Quentin, December 1966)

Ya, baby, I'm gonna play it cool out there, wait for the one little score, get myself a boat, a sail boat, and then split, leave this shitty state. They'll have to come and get me in the West Indies or South America. I'm gonna write ——— [a board member], gonna send him a picture of me on my boat, laying back, a big drink in my fist, some native chick on my side. I'm gonna tell that motherfucker to come down here to Rio and get me. (Field notes, San Quentin, November 1966)

More serious and more realistic planning takes place among small groups of close friends or associates. In these private discussions, plans are worked out more specifically and in greater detail. These plans are still to a degree compatible with the dominant prison values. However, due to their greater specificity and to the fact that they are made among persons who are familiar with each other's particular postures towards crime, the prison, and the future, they may depart somewhat from the stock central prison value and belief systems.

These two reference groups will remain very important to the individual after he leaves prison because of an important prison activity which he participates in or witnesses. After a convict departs, his friends and acquaintances attempt to follow his progress on the outside. This strong interest in departees exists because prisoners experience the outside world through their friends who venture into it, test certain strategies and methods for living outside through these departees, and have a sincere interest in knowing how their friends do after they leave prison. Therefore, after someone is released, his friends still in prison speculate on his progress. They glean information about departees from various sources—family members, friends who visit or correspond with them, and especially returning felons. Any news, true or false, about a departed convict circulates rapidly among his friends and acquaintances. Furthermore, from the stories brought back of encounters between ex-prisoners, the convict learns to anticipate chance or arranged meetings with prison friends. The dominant theme in these, he knows, is a mutual exchange of information on how each is doing on the outside. Claude Brown reports on such an encounter:

He said, "Hey Sonny, how you doin?" But he was kind of cold.

"Oh, I'm doin' fine, man."

"Yeh, I haven't seen you around lately, man. I've been asking about you, and nobody seems to know where you cut out to."

"Well, I left town, man."

"Yeh, I heard. Is there anything to that rumor, man, about you goin' to school?"

"Yeh, Reno, it's something different, something to do."

Reno threw up both hands, as if to say, "Wow, what a change!" He sort of backed away from me. Then he smiled and said, "Sonny, I always knew you had somethin' like that in you, man. I'm glad that you went on and did it." [1]

1. Claude Brown, *Manchild in the Promised Land* (New York: The Macmillan Company, 1965), pp. 409–10.

A major effect of all this is that the convict serving a sentence becomes cognizant of and sensitive to the fact that the eyes of the yard and his friends will be on him for some years to come. He will be judged by these two prison reference worlds, by a set of expectations which are part of the general criminal perspective in the prison, and by a set of particular standards that emerges in his interaction through the years with close friends.[2]

Making It

In discussions of the future on the outside, "making it" means mainly staying out of prison:

This time I'll do anything to make it. I mean it, man. I'll collect garbage. I'll do anything the man tells me. He says shit and I squat. Ain't no way I'm gonna do something that'll bring me back to this place. Man, I've had it. (Field notes, San Quentin, May 1967)

Making it has three major aspects: (1) becoming financially viable, (2) coping with the parole "system," and (3) keeping out of the old bag. Though criminal and semicriminal methods for earning a living are thought to be feasible by some inmates, generally it is believed that to make it one must "straighten up his hand"—that is, one must refrain from most illegal activities and find some legal source of income. Convicts surrounded by failures in crime tend to be skeptical of their own and others' chances of succeeding in some illegal enterprise. Making it occupationally implies a certain amount of stoicism, discipline, and tenacity. To make it while having few or no vocational skills, after acquiring the stigma of an ex-convict, and after being away from the occupational world for a length of time (perhaps never having been part of it), requires, it is generally believed, considerable fortitude and perhaps a little luck. Because of this belief, achieving economic viability is seen to be challenging and rewarding in itself.

As important as achieving economic viability to making it is coping with the parole "system." This system is regarded as an obstacle because:

They've set the whole system up to make you fail. They want you to come back. They let you out of here on a yoyo. You're out there a little while then they pull the string, zap, you're back. They got a good thing going here, man, can't you see it, they don't want to lose you. (Interview, San Quentin, July 1966)

The prison population is generously sprinkled with living proof of this

2. This situation, in which a cohort of peers is passing through a temporary status and spending considerable time in discussions of the future, is similar to that experienced by most servicemen and students. In each of these cases, it is typical that a particularly significant reference group forms in the perspective of the persons involved, and that this reference group remains important to those involved for years to come, more important, perhaps, than any group of *others*.

belief; that is, men who claim that they were returned to prison though they were making it in other senses—they were earning a living and keeping out of the old bag (their old deviant routine). They contend that they were brought back "behind some chicken-shit beef" or that they would have made it, but the "man" wouldn't get off their backs and he "drove" them to "fuck up." So to make it, one must put forth a large effort to avoid technical violations and to tolerate the harassments and restrictions of the parole agent. In the novel *The Riot,* a convict expresses this attitude toward the "system":

> "You heard what he said!" Kelly cried. "It's the goddamn parole system! Five times I been out on parole and every time I get out there, I gotta put up with some snooty, know-it-all college kid tellin' me how to live." He began mimicking in falsetto: "You're not to live with a woman, Mr. Kelly. You've been frequentin' barrooms, Mr. Kelly. You haven't been givin' me an itemized list of your spendin's, Mr. Kelly." His voice shifted to a snarl. "You've been driving a car. You've been seen with ex-inmates. You've been doin' this. You've been doing that. If you don't behave, I'll send you back!" He paused, breathless, glaring around the room. "I don't know anybody but ex-cons out there. How'm I gonna meet people? I'm not suppos'ta drink, drive, or screw. What else is there?" [3]

The Old Bag

Keeping out of the old bag is seen to be a major obstacle to making it. The old bag in this context is a former life routine involving a great many felonious acts which have a high probability of detection, arrest, and conviction. For instance, getting "strung out"—becoming addicted to opiates—is returning to the old bag in the truest sense. The addict must be in possession of drugs, traffic in drugs, and/or commit theft regularly. Any one of these can and usually does lead to rearrest.

Though the old bag, when looked back upon, may have considerable glamor, excitement, and fascination, it more often smacks of desperation, self-destruction, and physical danger. Most deviants do not regret their past criminal actions, however; but they often regret the stupidity and carelessness of their particular criminal careers. Though they do not necessarily plan to refrain from all criminality, they often plan to avoid the particular desperate cycle they were trapped in.

> Ya, man! He kept telling me how he was gonna stay out of the old bag. No more stuff for him. He had two narcotics beefs and they weren't going to get him on no dope beef again. Pornography was going to be his game. "Nobody comes to the joint for pornography." He kept talking that pornography shit until he had me believing it. When they brought him back with a new sales beef I kept on him for several weeks, reminding him about pornography. (Field notes, San Quentin, March 1967)

3. Frank Elli, *The Riot* (New York: Coward-McCann, Inc., 1966), pp. 171–72.

Keeping out of the old bag, though it doesn't necessarily mean total abstinence from crime or felony commission, always entails a reduction of felonies and perhaps the avoidance of certain types of felonies—such as those which carry a stiff penalty and have a high risk of arrest and conviction. Besides this it often means avoidance of certain persons who are involved in desperate and careless felonious routines and places—such as the Tenderloin or Mission districts in San Francisco—where *many* ex-felons are engaged in these routines.

For ex-criminals who are entertaining noncriminal plans for the future, keeping out of the old bag often implies complete avoidance of criminal or felonious behavior. Among these persons the feeling usually exists that one slip can result in a precipitous descent into a full criminal routine.

I heard that Jimmy is out there popping his fingers, smoking grass and asking where it's at. He's forgot about his plans. He won't make it. He'll be back in the full bag and then we'll see him at the front door in white pajamas. (Field notes, San Quentin, October 1967)

This belief in his own strong proclivity towards deviance is an important aspect in the thought processes of the criminal. He believes that statistically the chances are strong that he will return to deviance. For instance, most drug addicts have accepted as factual the widely circulated statistic that 94 per cent of drug addicts return to drug use after release from prison or after treatment. The majority interviewed stated that at least 70 per cent of those released eventually return to prison. In his own case, the prisoner often takes the view that any difficulty or unusual circumstances might divert him towards the old bag, and that once pointed in that direction it is difficult to change course. He often has sufficient examples of this type of fall in his own preprison biography to substantiate this belief.

Doing All Right

Besides making it—that is merely staying out of prison—convicts look forward to the gratification of their desires and the fulfillment of their goals. In the vernacular, they want to "do all right." They feel they have been denied a multitude of small pleasures and several major ones—especially sexual pleasures. In endless "trips," they discuss how they are going to catch up in the enjoyment of these. This pleasure-seeking or fulfillment side of future planning has two aspects: (1) immediate satisfaction of a multitude of denied pleasures and (2) long term fulfillment of goals and desires.

Immediately upon release, the plans are typically to enjoy many of the ordinary, taken-for-granted pleasures of the outside world: walks on the city streets, long-denied delicacies—hot dogs, malts, bacon and eggs, and a steak—and unlimited forbidden recreations—an art movie, a nudie movie, a ride in a car, or a picnic at the beach.

More important than these simple pleasures is sexual intercourse. The convict's sexual urges, long denied, are strong. Retelling past sexual exploits and planning future sexual activities are the most frequent topics in "tripping." From both a heightened sexual urge and from group expectations which are generated in months of discussions of future sexual activity, the convict anticipates sexual satisfaction at the earliest possible time after release. Properly, this should be on the first day or within the first few days. There is no excuse for extended delay in this matter.

If you're out there with all those pussies running around, ain't no excuse for a man not grabbing himself one in the first day or so. (Field notes, San Quentin, January 1966)

Among immediate friends or to himself the individual convict may privately admit that the likelihood for immediate gratification of this desire is small unless he is returning to his wife or girl friend. Publicly, however, this is not admissible.

Sexual prowess and one's masculinity are at stake, and in prison these are very sensitive matters for at least two reasons. First, in the monosexual milieu, homosexual acts, though their frequency is probably exaggerated, are a prevalent form of sexual expression, and this gives rise to considerable insecurity regarding one's heterosexuality.[4] Abstention from homosexual activities or participation only as the aggressor ("jocker") does not exonerate one from frequent challenges to his manhood. With few exceptions, all persons, by direct invitation to participate in homosexual acts and accusations of having participated, and by malicious or humorous derogation, have their masculinity questioned from time to time. The following personal accounts of prison experiences exemplify this activity:

Old guys, they called them wolves, they saw me looking at this stuff and thought I might be a gal-boy. One came up and propositioned me. I didn't like that none at all. I said, "If any of the stuff goes on with me in on it I'll do the fucking myself. I been a man all my life." I doubled up my fists to show him I meant it.[5]

"Tico, we're more than cousins, kid, we're brothers. Just handle yourself right, don't make fast friends, and act cool. Don't play and joke too much, and

4. It is hard to estimate accurately the extent of participation in homosexual acts in prison. It is my belief that most people, even the convicts themselves, tend to overestimate the degree of actual participation. Ninety-one per cent of sixty-seven parolees answered that they had never engaged in even one homosexual act. The reliability of this figure is hard to judge.

5. Haywood Patterson and Earl Conrad, *Scotsboro Boy* (New York: Garden City Press, 1952), p. 79.

baby don't, just don't accept candy or smokes from stranger cons. You might end up paying for it with your ass."

He kept on looking at the concrete walk and his face grew red and the corners of his mouth got a little white. "Piri, I've been hit on already," he said.

I thought, *My God, he's got a jailhouse gorilla reception already.* "Yeah," I prompted, "and . . ."

"Well, I got friendly with this guy named Rube."

Rube was a muscle-bound degenerate whose sole ambition in life was to cop young kids' behinds. "Yeah," I said, "and so . . ."

"Well, this cat has come through with smokes and food and candy and, well, he's a spic like me and he talked about the street outside and about guys we know outside and he helped me out with favors, you know, real friendly." [6]

The second source of sensitivity about one's manhood in prison is his doubt of his prowess as a seducer. In the prison milieu, as in the lower-class milieu, the prestigious male is the Don Juan, the successful seducer of women. In the absence of females, however, with no opportunity to measure one's masculine appeal, and where all claims about past accomplishments are suspect and one has aged and fallen out of step, uncertainty about one's appeal to the opposite sex is likely to grow. Eldridge Cleaver comments on this kind of doubt:

Take the point of being attractive to women. You can easily see how a man can lose his arrogance or certainty on that point while in prison! When he's in the free world, he gets constant feedback on how he looks from the number of female heads he turns when he walks down the street. In prison he gets only hate-stares and sour frowns. Years and years of bitter looks.[7]

The convict, therefore, is apt to be anxious about his masculinity in regard to homosexuality-heterosexuality and his prowess as a seducer.

In long-range planning, doing all right emphasizes various types of pleasure-seeking and goal fulfillment. With some inmates the emphasis is on material or monetary success:

I want to get a car, some clothes, an apartment, maybe a house. You know, man, all the things I would have had if I hadn't come to prison. I want to get a good job, so I can get myself on my feet. After I get started then I might want a lot of other things like a stereo, some furniture. There are a lot of things, you know, little luxuries that I'm going to get after I get going out there. I know it is going to take time, but I'm gonna go slow first, but someday I'm gonna be living good. (Interview, Soledad Prison, June 1966)

With others it is on recreation:

There are a lot of things out there that I never learned how to do. I don't know if I like to go to ball games. I never bowled and played golf. I might like these things, man. I'm gonna spend a lot of time just experimenting. I know

6. Piri Thomas, *Down These Mean Streets* (New York: Alfred A. Knopf, Inc., 1967), pp. 265–67.

7. Eldridge Cleaver, *Soul on Ice* (New York: McGraw-Hill, Inc., 1968), p. 16.

I've been missing a lot of things, even before, so I'm gonna spend a lot of time just catching up on these things. (Interview, San Quentin, June 1966)

Or artistic pursuits:

I got this painting thing. I got to see if I can do something with my art. I've been working at it for the last three years in prison and when I get out I'm gonna see if I can get down with it. Maybe nothing will happen. Maybe I'll never get good enough so I can sell the first painting, but I'm gonna have to give it a whirl. (Interview, Soledad Prison, June 1966)

As with the planning for immediate gratification, an essential ingredient of doing all right in future planning is the sexual dimension:

I'm not going anywhere without a woman beside me. I want a chick along side me in the car, when I go to the show. I want to be able to reach over and pat her leg any time I get ready. This is all I'm going to do, around the house, out driving around, going places, is be with my chick. Ya know, man, I might not talk to any men for four or five years. (Interview, Soledad Prison, June 1966)

I want to get me a good old lady, you know, some little girl that knows what's happening, not some square broad. I don't want one of those hustling broads either. If I get a good old lady, not some dog, not a bitch, then I'll be all right. (Field notes, San Quentin, March 1967)

STYLES OF DOING ALL RIGHT

In the continuous public and private discussions of future plans and goals, several fairly cohesive styles reappear. These are openly discussed and embraced by criminals because they are compatible with the perspective shared by the criminal segment of the prison population. In general, these styles exhibit some or all of the attributes necessary for a prestigious life from this viewpoint, and they do not have two forbidden or undignified attributes. For instance, to be considered "all right" they must have some of the following attributes: (1) sexual possibilities—that is, offer abundant opportunities for sexual fulfillment; (2) relative financial richness; (3) excitement, color, or glamor; (4) "sharpness"—some association with illegal or marginally legal financial enterprises (e.g., auto sales); and (5) autonomy.[8] They should not possess (1) "slave" traits—laborious, unskilled, menial, dirty, monotonous and subservient work; or (2) policeman traits. This latter is an unforgivable betrayal of the criminal world.

He asked me, "Sonny, what you doin, man?"

8. These last three dimensions (excitement, color or glamor, and sharpness and autonomy) are related to three categories (excitement, smartness, and autonomy) of the lower-class milieu described by Walter Miller in "Lower-Class Culture as a Generating Milieu of Gang Delinquency," *Journal of Social Issues* (1958).

"I told you, man, knocking about in school."

"Yeah, but what you studyin', man? You must be into somethin' down there."

"I haven't made up my mind yet what I'm gonna get into."

"Well, do me one favor, man."

"What's that?"

"Now, baby don't go down there and come back the Man. That'd be some real wicked shit. All the stuff we been through together, if you became the Man and busted me or any of the cats around the neighborhood, that shit would really hurt, man."

"Yeah, I guess it would, Reno," I laughed. I said, "Yeah, imagine me becoming the Man. Even I wouldn't know how to take it." [9]

These styles of doing all right constitute a bazaar of ideas from which individuals may pick and choose. They are styles which are displayed for public inspection and evaluation. Individuals may try one on and display it in the public arena. At the same time while they are receiving the evaluations at the public level, among their close associates or in their own mind they may experiment with this or other styles in a more serious manner. These levels of speculation remain somewhat independent. For instance, the strength of commitment, which can be tenuous at all levels, is usually different at each level, and in fact the styles speculated upon can vary at different levels.

It should be emphasized that the individual is not necessarily strongly committed to the styles he tries or that he is limited to only these styles. The importance of this public planning process and the existence of this fountain of living patterns is that it is a source of standards which will be internalized and which will be used by others to evaluate his progress on the outside after release, and to a lesser extent, as a source of potential future styles.

There is some variation in the type of planning that takes place among particular individuals according to their criminal identities, their mode of adaptation to prison, and the stage of their prison sentence. These factors will be considered later in the chapter. First, let us examine some of the most frequently discussed prestigious outside living styles.

Conventional Styles

The swinger. In many cases the criminal plans to "straighten up his hand"; that is, to live a life relatively free from criminal activities. There are several conventional approaches to this, of which the most common is the working-class rounder or swinger. In this approach an individual earns a living—necessarily a good wage—at some labor or trade and then devotes his leisure to seeking "action." His action-seeking activities will include women, cars, clothes, drinking, bars, night clubs, dancing, parties, drug use (especially marijuana, barbiturates, and amphetamines), sports,

9. Claude Brown, *Manchild in the Promised Land,* p. 410.

and trips to action spots (Las Vegas, Reno, Tijuana, and Old Mexico). This life has most of the abovementioned aspects valued on the yard. Additionally, since there is considerable overlap with the styles of the lower-class youth and some criminals, it permits continued contact with former peers from his deviant and prison life. Therefore, this life as it is conceived does not require any radical transformations; it merely necessitates two things: a good salary and avoidance of the old bag—the former self-defeating or legally vulnerable activities.

Settling down. A conventional style which privately is probably the most popular, though not as popular on the public level, is that of "settling down":

> Ya, man, did ya hear about ________. He's making that slave everyday, got himself an old lady, a couple of rug rats and is staying home. You know, I hear he digs it. I think it's beautiful. This is the first time he stayed out over six months in the last twelve years. Maybe he's gonna make it this time. I'm all for him. (Field notes, San Quentin, July 1967)

Like the swinger style, settling down requires a job with reasonably good pay. It further requires "a good old lady—not some dog [unattractive female] or some bitch." After having these two, the "gig" and the old lady, the person lives a "normal" life.

According to strictly conventional patterns, however, it is not exactly a normal life that is conceived. There are several important departures from conventionality. The first is the old lady. The average "square broad" appears to be too puritanical and too conventional. On the other hand, hustlers or rounders are too promiscuous, irresponsible, and undependable. The woman desired must have the right combination of hipness and squareness.

Second, there often are plans for controlled deviance in this style:

> Man, all I want to do is smoke a little weed.
>
> I'm gonna stay home most of the time and get high, listen to music, watch TV and ball the old lady. What's wrong with that? They won't bring me back for that, will they? (Field notes, San Quentin, July 1967)

The playboy. Others aspire to greater financial affluence and/or economic independence. They plan to obtain their own business, perhaps a small bar, which will earn a good living and give them independence or to obtain some larger business which promises greater wealth. They may even plan to enter the business world as a white-collar executive. For the first few years on the outside, the individual with these aspirations usually intends to commit a major portion of his time and efforts to his business career. In the small remaining portion of time and in the future years he usually aims at participation in the central American dream life, that of the consuming, pleasure-seeking "playboy."

This life as it is conveyed in the movies, TV, and magazines has many highly valued dimensions of doing all right. Primarily it presents abundant opportunities for contact with glamorous and promiscuous women and opulent living. Furthermore, it appears very "sharp"; that is, the financial rewards seem disproportionate to the amount of work involved, and there is considerable opportunity for semilegal theft.

The rich old lady. A highly praised future style, though one which few convicts consider seriously, is the "rich old lady" plan. Here, one captures a wealthy woman and lives the playboy life. This is remotely possible, it is believed, because the masculine and virile ex-convict is fascinating to "high-class broads." A more realistic variation of this (and one that is speculated upon seriously by many) is the plan to marry a career woman. This seems feasible because

> there're a lot of those broads out there, schoolteachers, librarians, secretaries, gals who ain't looking too good. I don't mean they're dogs, they're just not winners. You know, man, maybe they had an old man and lost him and now they're in their thirties laying to grab some healthy guy who'll fuck the shit out of them. And these gals are making good bread, I mean they're scraping in $800 or $900 a month and got a little savings account. (Field notes, San Quentin, October 1966)

At this juncture—after marrying the career woman—this plan may take various directions. Perhaps the convict plans to loaf and live on her earnings and savings or perhaps use her money for a small business or school:

> Did ya hear about T? Ya, man, he is doing good. After he left CRC last time, a guy down there—one of the counselors—took an interest in 'im. Got 'im a job and got 'im in school. He met this chick—a psychiatrist or something and got married. Now I hear she's no raving beauty and she's in her thirties, but she makes good bread and she's intelligent as hell. Now she's putting T through school. Bought him a car and they got a house. Ya, he's doing all right. (Field notes, San Quentin, November 1967)

Transformation styles. There is a class of conventional plans involving some basic changes in the orientation of the individual which will be called transformation styles. Usually they center around the pursuit of a vocation which requires considerable preparation; e.g., a B.A. or other schooling. More important, these styles entail a shift in particular values and goals or perhaps a general shift of orientation. For instance, a vocation is not pursued so much for monetary gain, as in the case with the playboy executive style, as for the satisfaction of the work itself. In general, an important theme of this plan is a search for a life or for work which has more "meaning," "satisfaction," "self-respect," or "dignity." Some of the particular occupational careers which are sought and which are thought to offer some of these dimensions are engineering, accounting, architecture, journalism, business administration, teaching, and, currently, "new careers." [10]

Although in the yard there is general ignorance of the actual content of most transformation styles, the sketchy conception that does exist is favorable. The vocations aspired to seem fairly sharp; that is, the salary is good and you use your intelligence rather than your muscles. In many respects they appear to be similar to the playboy executive style. The yard, however, is still ambivalent on the new social-work careers. They smack somewhat of do-gooderism, which is not esteemed. On the plus side, however, is the fact that they are a way of making it without "slaving."

Marginal Styles

"Kinky" occupations. Many speculate upon marginal styles; that is, routines involving patterns which are on the margin between legality and illegality or which, though not strictly illegal, are unconventional. These are especially appealing because they: (1) offer semilegal, and therefore "sharp," money-making methods; (2) are consistent with anticonventional, deviant views of oneself; and/or (3) offer an alternative mode of continued resistance and antagonism toward "them"—the system, the establishment, the police, or the middle class.

Some of the marginal styles are centered around occupations which may be marginally illegal, such as automobile, book, or furnace sales; or occupations such as bartending, bellhopping, and cabdriving, which, though not illegal in themselves, open up many possibilities for participation in illegal or semi-illegal activities. The leisure activities of these occupationally marginal styles are much like those of the rounder, or, if the financial rewards are greater, the playboy executive.

Artist styles. Other marginal styles are not founded upon occupations, but some other unconventional or deviant pattern or set of patterns; e.g., writer, painter, musician, and bohemian student-intellectual styles. These "outsider" styles, which are appealing to a limited segment of the yard, offer continued association with other deviants, freedom from slaving, and often, considerable excitement, action, or glamor. The artist, writer, and musician careers offer the additional incentive of possible public recognition. Furthermore, these three are especially appealing because,

10. A new area in social work, called "new careers" in several government-funded programs, has recently opened up for minority-group members. This field, which does not require any formal training, takes two major forms: (1) a number of positions with government-sponsored urban development programs and community-action agencies funded mainly by the War on Poverty program, and (2) membership in private self-help groups, such as Synanon and Seven Steps, which are organized, administered, and staffed primarily by ex-deviants and which are involved in the rehabilitation, reconstruction, or redirection of criminals.

although they usually promise meager financial rewards, they involve "meaningful" and "creative" activities.

Student-intellectual style. The student-intellectual or professional-student style does not promise future rewards in terms of money or recognition. It is, however, more available since it does not require talent or a sacrifice of time to develop a skill. Furthermore, since it usually only calls for a simple "gig" which affords a living with a minimum time sacrifice, it offers freedom from economic competition. The important aspects of this routine are the pursuit of culture and knowledge. The intellectual-student spends his nonworking hours—the major portion of his time—at school, public or school libraries, museums, art galleries, lectures, plays, concerts, operas, coffeehouses, and bohemian-intellectual bars.

Bohemian style. The full bohemian style has the positive attributes of drug use, antiestablishment and antisquare posture, sexual promiscuity, work rejection, and independence. However, it has two negative aspects—dirtiness and impecuniousness. Furthermore, among white criminals, it appears to involve too much racial mixing between the sexes.

Expatriation style. An extremely popular marginal plan is expatriation. Here the convict plans to achieve freedom from the system, the Department of Corrections, the conventional society, the police, and the repressive legal system, by leaving the country. The most common version of this is to build or buy a boat—usually a sailboat—and then live on this boat while traveling the Caribbean or the South Pacific. Sometimes the individual plans to obtain funds for this plan with a "caper" or two or to continue financing himself while traveling by illegal activities, such as smuggling. However, illegal activities are not essential, and very often the convict plans to earn enough money to buy or build a boat through a legitimate job and then support himself by chartering the boat.

Besides merely discussing this plan, many inmates make extensive preparations for its execution. They study navigation, boat design, and boatbuilding, and peruse travel literature. All of these are enjoyable activities behind bars and, coupled with the dreams of ocean sailing, they lend extraordinary appeal to this plan.

Other convicts seeking this type of freedom speculate on migrating to a foreign country, and they also make extensive preparations. For instance, they study the language of the country they plan to enter, its history and contemporary social conditions, and explore possible means of support once there.

Controlled-addiction style. A marginal style unique to dope fiends is the controlled-addiction plan:

This guy in my cellblock has been telling me about methadone. He says that he preferred it to stuff. He says he used more when he first started using it than he did after he got hooked. Man, I just gotta find something that I can handle out there. I know I'm kidding myself if I think I'm not goin' to use anymore. I have to find something I can use that doesn't have me running down the streets with a pistol in my hand. That heroin is awful, man. You could own the factory and in a couple of weeks you'd be down the corner trying to get Manuel Rodriguez to score for you. There just isn't enough heroin to keep a habit going. (Field notes, San Quentin, June 1967)

In the plan for controlled addiction, since drugs fulfill most of his needs, the dope fiend envisions living a comparatively sedate and conventional life. It is generally believed among dope fiends that if they had a secure supply of drugs, they would be content with a relatively slow-paced, simple existence. They believe that they would be able to work and then avoid "trouble" and "heat" in the remaining hours. This secure addict life is filled out by the avoidance of crowds, staying home, going to movies, and other simple, relatively unexciting pleasures, but pleasures which, when enhanced with drugs, are quite satisfying. Of course the major obstacle in this plan is the absence of a secure, consistent, and safe drug source. Because of this, *controlled addiction* is often coupled with *expatriation*. There are several countries, such as England, Mexico, Morocco, Tangiers, where addicts believe that drugs may be easily obtained legally or semilegally, e.g., through doctors. This, however, raises another obstacle which has not been adequately solved, that is, a source of income in a foreign country.

Revolutionary style. Finally an emerging marginal style which appeals to a small but growing segment of the criminal prison population is that of the revolutionary. In the past this mode was almost exclusively political extremism. Recently, since World War II, a new form of racial revolutionism has emerged among the Negroes:

This is probably as big a single worry as the American prison system has today —the way the Muslim teachings, circulated among all Negroes in the country, are converting new Muslims among black men in prison, and black men in prison in far greater numbers than their proportion in the population.[11]

Though presently the Muslim movement seems to be declining in California prisons, there are other Negro revolutionist groups on the ascent —especially the Black Panthers.

In the revolutionary style, the criminal usually plans to affiliate himself with a particular organization, such as the Muslims, the W. E. B. Du Bois Club, the Socialist or Nazi Party, and submerge himself in the revolutionary social activities of these organizations. Many—following Malcolm X —plan to make a full career of revolutionary activities by achieving positions of leadership in these organizations.

11. *The Autobiography of Malcolm X* (New York: Grove Press, Inc., 1964), p. 183.

The revolutionary styles are poorly accepted among the general criminal population. They irritate a deep and sensitive conservative nerve in most convicts. Though the criminal, especially the white criminal, is deviant and in many respects antiestablishment, he usually feels that he is an "American." When America is under criticism from without or from malcontents within—from communists, socialists or militant Negroes—he shifts from his deviant identity to a more deeply founded conservative American identity and becomes the defender of certain sacred American traditions and institutions, especially private property, racial discrimination, and capitalism.

However, though most convicts are hostile toward revolutionaries, they do not feel the repugnance toward them that they do, for example, toward "snitches" and "punks." The revolutionary career, therefore, is tenable. Furthermore, these careers have positive attributes to balance the disapproval. They are antiestablishment and antiauthority, and they offer ideologies which transfer responsibility for the criminal's position of disgrace and disadvantage from himself to the enemy—the establishment or the "white devils."

Criminal Styles

The "big-score" plan. The most typical criminal style is the "one big score" plan. Since the individual's downfall—his arrest and conviction—is seen to stem from the desperate life round (the old bag) which included frequent and highly visible felonies, a successful criminal plan is one which has very infrequent and carefully planned and executed "capers." The one big score plan has two versions: (1) the big score for the purpose of entering another life (e.g., a business, education, or departure from the United States), or (2) the occasional big score, once or twice a year, as a continued style of existence. In both versions, the plan is to go slow, play it "cool," plan carefully, keep up a good front (especially for the parole officer), avoid association with "assholes," "snitches," and any other people who "draw a lot a heat," or places where there is a lot of heat, and to work completely alone or only with one or two others who are trusted.

Narcotics sales. Another plan is to accumulate a large sum of money or make a steady large income through narcotics sales:

The way I got it figured is I'll take two or three hundred, get some stuff across the border—I know a lot of dudes dealing in Mexico—get rid of it in L.A. through the connections I got there. Make another trip. I'll have someone make these runs for me. I'm gonna be real careful, not deal with anyone I don't know real well. Only deal in ounces, you know. Stay away from stool pigeons. I know enough guys I can deal through, so I won't have to take any chances. The only thing I gotta watch is getting strung out. I can't start using myself. But I know this and I know if I get hooked, I can't make it, I gotta come back. If I'm real careful I can make ten or twenty grand in a minute. I know, I've done it before. Only I was strung out, I shot it as fast as I made it. I couldn't keep hold of any bread. (Field notes, San Quentin, June 1967)

"Hustles." A third type of criminal plan is to enter some enterprise, a "hustle" which, though illegal, is not penalized heavily or detected and prosecuted frequently. Booking bets and pimping have been the two most common of these in the past, but presently manufacturing and selling pornography is a frequent plan. In this plan, the full life round usually entails many of the characteristics of the "rounder" or "hustling" life; that is, association with other deviants, women, drugs, drinking, parties, cars, clothes, and action-seeking.

The "escapade." Finally there is the plan for the "escapade," a plan which is common among state-raised youths, particularly those who jail in prison:

Ya, baby, I'm laying to get out there and shoot me some of that good shit. I got a partner who's waiting for me. He's gonna have some stuff for me when I hit the bricks. We got some capers planned, he's just waiting for me to get out. I'm gonna hang that parole on the fence and make it. I figure I'll lay around and get high for a few days, rip off some pussy—my partner's got some little hot cocked bitches waiting—then we'll pull some scores and leave the state. (Interview, San Quentin, July 1966)

VARIATIONS IN THE PLANNING PATTERN

In the foregoing we have been discussing the collective planning process and ignoring regularities according to identities and modes of adaptation to prison. As mentioned earlier, discussions of the future which take place continuously may be viewed as a bazaar of ideas from which individuals may pick and choose. Their choices are influenced, to some extent, by meanings acquired prior to prison and nurtured by their associations in prison and by the meanings related to their mode of adapting to prison; but more importantly, their choices are influenced by certain dimensions inherent in each phase of their sentence.

Fish Stage

In the fish stage—while the prisoners are still in the Guidance Center for testing and orientation to prison or adjusting to the prison where they will begin their prison sentence—they are still mentally close to the outside. They may be planning their prison life, but they do so with the outside as a reference world.[12] At this beginning stage, with the "streets"

12. Stanton Wheeler found that there was less conformity to prison moral codes at

still on their mind, many plan to take advantage of the months or years in prison to acquire polish in their criminal techniques, to solve "problems," or to acquire new skills and knowledge so that upon release they can begin life again where they left off. This is especially true of dope fiends, thieves, hustlers, and heads. State-raised youths and disorganized criminals are more likely to forget the outside immediately and immerse or reimmerse themselves in the prison world; i.e., they begin to jail.[13]

Middle Stage

For most, the outside world fades in a few months. Their prison program, leisure activities, studies, shows, and TV fill out their time. The streets becomes a less and less important reference world. Looking outside continues, however. In this phase there is considerable random speculation about the future. Individuals try on future styles, test them for fit, and then pass on to the investigation of others. This is done usually in more intimate conversations with close friends. Others' comments and plans, and public discussions of the outside, serve as a source of ideas, evaluations, and standards.

There is considerable freedom to speculate at this stage due to certain characteristics inherent in the prisoner status. The convict, like the teenager, is suspended in a temporary status and is barred from participation in the status towards which he is moving, the free adult-civilian status. He may engage in artificial and/or preparatory activities which bear a similarity to future activities of the free adult-civilian status—e.g., some prison jobs and prison training assignments. However, he is acutely aware that these are very different from the actual activities on the outside.

Furthermore, like the teenager, he is free from many of the responsibilities of the free adult-civilian. His necessities are taken care of. His routine within certain limits is planned for him. With these responsibilities *and* the opportunity to engage in adult-civilian activities removed, he has unusual freedom to speculate and vacillate on his future plans.

Besides the freedom to speculate offered by this situation, there is an absence of factors which promote commitment to a particular life routine. For instance, with no opportunity to actually engage in the life round of a particular adult-civilian style, the convict does not enjoy any of the successes, fulfillments, and pleasures of this life, and he does not build a

---

the beginning and end of the individual's sentence. This supports the contention made here that orientation to the outside is still somewhat operative in the "fish" stage. See "Social Organization and Inmate Values in Correctional Communities," *Proceedings, American Correctional Association* (1959), pp. 189–98.

13. Peter G. Garabedian did not find the U-shape curve in the orientation to the outside in the case of "outlaws" and "politicians," two types which tend to fall into my state-raised, disorganized criminal, and jailer categories. See "Social Roles and the Process of Socialization in the Prison Community," *Social Problems* (Fall 1963), pp. 139–52.

reference world, a new perspective, and a group of significant "others" through interaction with persons involved in this life round. Furthermore, other convicts who are generally skeptical and envious of others' future plans will not reinforce commitment by accepting his plans and by shifting their views of him in light of the new plans. Instead, they undermine commitment by persistent efforts to discourage him and to convince him that it is useless to try to change or to make any elaborate plans. Consequently, it is difficult for a convict to sustain an interest in any one style, and typically, throughout the middle stage of his prison career, he speculates widely.

Jailers. Although this speculation among criminals proceeds with considerable randomness, there is a small degree of regularity in the styles speculated upon by persons with similar identities and similar adaptive modes. For instance, among those who jail—more often state-raised youths and disorganized criminals—little planning takes place. Most of the "tripping" concerns events which have occurred in this or former prison sentences. Thoughts about the future on the outside appear in the form of clichés involving wild criminal and pleasure-seeking escapades that will be undertaken upon release. When they occasionally speculate more seriously and more elaborately, being poor criminals, they usually pick a conventional style, most often the settling down or wage-earning rounder style.

Time-doers. Time-doers alternate between criminal, marginal, and conventional styles. The thief, to whom monetary gain is a central value, usually skips from the big-score plan, which is his main forte, to a marginally deviant occupational style, such as car sales, and to a conventional small business plan. The hustler, who also values monetary gain, but who has leaned toward "sharp" crime as opposed to "heavy" crime, more often swings from a criminal hustle, such as pimping, to a marginal occupation, such as sales or bartending, or to a white collar, playboy, conventional style.

The head, who has a less pecuniary and less competitive posture, will often speculate on smaller-scale "hustles," such as small-scale marijuana sales. In choosing marginal styles, since he is apt to have a philosophical and/or esthetic leaning, he tends towards the "outsider" marginal styles —more often that of the artist, writer, student-intellectual, or bohemian. In conventional styles, he often speculates on a variation of the wage-earner, "rounder" style. In his case, he plans to get a simple "gig," some employment which preferably entails a minimum of "hassle," and then fill out his life with the pursuit of exotic pleasures. He plans excursions (while under the influence of marijuana or other hypnotic drugs) to public places, parks, museums; attendance at psychedelic events—shows, dances or "happenings" which feature a barrage of sight and sound; or visits to natural settings, such as beaches and mountains; or the pursuit of drug-heightened sexual orgies with "freaks," women who abandonedly engage in a wide variety of sexual activities.

Dope fiends who have a long background in drug traffic and hustling tend toward the big drug score or hustling when they embrace criminal plans. In speculating on marginal styles, since they are likely to have either a hustler or a bohemian, artist, or intellectual pre-drug history, they may choose either the occupational or outsider styles. In choosing a conventional style, the dope fiend is influenced by his distaste for monotony and drudgery and, therefore, tends to avoid settling down. He is likely to pick any of the remaining conventional styles, possibly with a slight leaning toward the "white-collar" playboy style.

Gleaners. In this middle stage of the sentence, gleaners are usually more diffused in their planning. They delay final specification until later and follow a general "self-improvement" program. They are usually aiming for some style of transformation, but at this stage, they often know too little about the content of or avenues to this life. Moreover, they often begin working toward some professional or white-collar field, but in the education process, they experience a value shift and become diverted toward an outsider style—very often that of the student-intellectual.

Among gleaners there is a slight tendency for hustlers to choose transformation styles and for heads and dope fiends to opt for outsider styles. This is because of the value placed on monetary gain by the former and the tendency of the latter to be interested in esthetics and philosophy.

Getting Short

In the final stage of their sentences, criminals tend to decrease speculating on various styles and to focus on one specific life style. At this stage, with release approaching and the possibility of rearrest drawing near, there is a shift toward conventional styles.[14] However, an important consideration looms here which often upsets consideration of the future and restricts the individual to planning at the immediate level; that is, restricts him to the level of "making it." This is the task of setting up a program. In order to be released, the convict must be accepted by a particular parole regional office, and he must have employment or at least, in his parole agent's estimation, very good prospects for obtaining immediate employment after release. The latter is an obstacle for many convicts approaching release, and often results in their changing the location of

14. This corresponds to some degree to the shift that Wheeler discovered at the end of the prison sentence. He found that inmates shifted toward the staff interpretation of moral issues. I contend here that they also shift toward conventional future plans, and that their conscious desire to avoid reimprisonment at this point in time may explain both shifts. See "Social Organization and Inmate Values in Correctional Communities."

their parole, changing their employment plans, and therefore changing or, temporarily at least, forgetting future plans made before they were "short" and were faced with setting up a program.

Besides coping with these specific difficulties, setting up a program necessitates a shift of attention from speculative future concerns to immediate and more mundane details. This shift often causes the convict to drop, forget, or change future plans he had settled upon during the middle stage of his sentence.

The intensity of this disruption varies somewhat according to the adaptive mode of the individual. For instance, those who jailed, who for the most part did not plan a future life with much detail or content, do not experience much disruption in their plans. They have lost their orientation to the outside and often all their contacts with actual persons on the outside. Therefore, it is both difficult for them to become highly motivated to set up a program and to succeed in setting up one if they do try. They often make no effort and depend completely on the parole agency to make their release arrangements. For the most part they continue to speak of wild escapades. Those who do plan to live a conventional life, since they are usually ignorant of the actual content of conventional styles, usually talk vaguely of going to work and/or settling down. As release approaches, they concentrate more on making it and they tend to take a "wait and see" attitude toward the future.

Time-doers usually have a clearer picture of the content of the style they intend to pursue, because it is more often a style they had considerable contact with or actually participated in. However, they too may become immersed in setting up a program and have their plans temporarily sidetracked or permanently changed.

The gleaner, as release approaches, is in somewhat the same position as the convict who jails; i.e., he is planning to enter social worlds of which he has little or no first-hand knowledge. The gleaner, however, is strongly committed to "making it" and eventually "doing good." Sensing the potential distraction of setting up a program, and experiencing anxiety about the uncertainties of his future life style, he often struggles to cope with these potential diversions with detailed plans. For instance, he makes budgets for his projected income, schedules of daily activities, lists of necessities he intends to purchase, and schedules for purchasing them. However, his plans are often so crystalline and fragile that they shatter when disturbed.

NONCRIMINALS

The foregoing discussion purposely excluded square johns and lower-class men, since persons committed to these identities do not usually enter into public discussions of the future, and styles from their perspective are not found among plans discussed publicly. Generally, these persons are content with the general outline of their life and are not so prone to speculate on the future. They may plan to change aspects of this life—e.g., increase vocational skills, increase earning prowess, alter material circumstances, or change personality characteristics, especially those believed to be related to their problem. But they usually maintain their basic orientation to life, their square john or lower-class-man identity. What planning they do usually takes place in private with close friends, most often persons with the same identity. Generally, their planning is more intelligent. They know more about the social world to which they are returning and tend not to speculate on various styles. This is one of the factors explaining the lower recidivist rates of these two classes of inmates.

The square john has an important passive relationship to the planning process in prison. He serves as one of the major sources of information on conventional styles. In prison there are square johns from most segments of the conventional world; for example, professional people, businessmen, entertainers, and skilled workers. Criminals—especially gleaners—who speculate on some unfamiliar conventional style often consult various square johns to obtain first-hand information about these occupations and their concomitant social worlds. Some square johns whose particular life style or occupation is particularly esteemed among gleaners, such as actors or professors, are often cast into leadership roles of formal or informal groups—acting clubs, speaking clubs, and informal intellectual groups.

5

REENTRY

The impact of release is often dramatic. After months of anticipation, planning, and dreaming, the felon leaves the confined, routinized, slow-paced setting of the prison and steps into the "streets" as an adult-citizen. The problems of the first weeks are usually staggering and sometimes insurmountable. Becoming accustomed to the outside world, coping with parole, finding a good job—perhaps finding any job—and getting started toward a gratifying life style are at least difficult and for many impossible.

When released, the convict can be seen to be proceeding along a narrow and precarious route, beset with difficult obstacles. If the obstacles are too difficult, if satisfaction and fulfillment not forthcoming, and/or his commitment to straightening up his hand is too weak, he will be diverted from the straight path toward systematic deviance. He himself believes in the route's precariousness and the high probability of his failure, and this intensifies its precariousness. Many of the obstacles are, however, both very real and very difficult.

The reentry problems have been divided here, somewhat arbitrarily, into three areas which will be treated in separate chapters. The first area includes the problems that arise immediately upon release—problems which arise mainly because the ex-felon is suddenly transplanted from one setting to another. These problems, which are experienced to some extent by all returnees (ex-servicemen, Peace Corps returnees, releasees from prisoner of war camps, etc.), are related to "getting settled down" and "getting on your feet." What is implied by these two phrases is that before serious enterprises can be undertaken, before plans can be put into action, or before any real satisfaction in life can be expected one must withstand some immediate disorienting experiences and become a functioning and viable civilian who at least has good clothing and a place to live.

The second group of problems is encountered after one is on his feet (that is, one has become reoriented and, with some degree of success, a functioning citizen) and now seeks to do more than just "get by." These can be viewed as the obstacles to "doing good" or obstacles to achieving a satisfying life style. Although the ex-convict to some extent shares this class of experiences with other returnees, the intensity of the experiences and some of their dimensions are uniquely his.

Finally, the last of the three problem areas includes those which arise because the ex-felon is under the supervision of the parole agency, which legally may impose restraints upon him, alter his life routine, and without any new legal action return him to prison.[1] To examine how the parolee copes with the parole agency, a careful analysis must be made of the parolee's relationship with the parole agent and of some of the important aspects of the parole system. This aspect will be treated in a separate chapter, although many of the problems are interrelated with those of the other two areas.

AWARENESS OF THE REENTRY PROBLEM

Before examining the separate aspects of the reentry experience itself, I would like to contrast briefly the awareness of the problem relative to other types of releasees with the ignorance of it relative to parolees and to explore some of the reasons for this ignorance in order to emphasize the importance of a better understanding of reentry in the case of the parolee.

The first systematic attention to the special problems incurred by a population returning to its former social setting was directed toward English veterans of World War II who were being repatriated from war prisons or being discharged from overseas duty.[2] Some attention was paid to the similar situation in America.[3] Recently, the reentry problems of the Peace Corps returnees have been causing considerable concern.[4]

In all these instances the adjustment problems are seen to be complex, involving extreme personal stress, psychological "symptoms," and problems of "resocialization," as well as the more obvious adjustment problems, such as locating employment.

1. Virtually all California felons are released on parole; in 1966, the figure was 94 per cent. Consequently, in the ensuing chapters, the terms parolee, releasee, and ex-felon are used almost interchangeably.

2. See, for example, A. T. M. Wilson, "The Serviceman Comes Home," *Pilot Papers,* Volume I, No. 2 (April 1946); A. Curle, "Transitional Communities and Social Reconnection: A Follow-up Study of the Civil Resettlement of British Prisoners of War," *Human Relations,* Vol. I, Part 1 (1947); P. H. Newman, "The Prisoner-of-War Mentality: Its Effect after Repatriation," *British Medical Journal* (1946); S. Davidson, "Notes on a Group of Ex-prisoners of War," *Bulletin of the Menninger Clinic,* No. 10 (1946); M. Jones, "Rehabilitation of Forces Neurosis Patients to Civilian Life," *British Medical Journal,* I (1946); and G. C. Pether, "The Returned Prisoner of War," *Lancet,* I (1945).

3. Roy Grinker and John Spiegel, *Men Under Stress* (New York: McGraw-Hill, Inc., 1945); George Pratt, *Soldier to Civilian* (New York: McGraw-Hill, Inc., 1944); Donald Becker, "The Veteran: Problem and Challenge," *Social Forces* (October 1946).

4. Julius Horwitz, "The Peace Corpsman Returns to Darkest America," *The New York Times Magazine* (October 24, 1965); Richard Stolley, "The Reentry Crisis," *Life Magazine* (March 9, 1965), pp. 98–100; "Culture Shock: Adjusting to Life Back Home," *Newsweek* (March 15, 1965), p. 30.

In the case of the felon being released on parole, however, there seems to be little or no awareness of many facets of the impact of reentry.[5] A publication of the California Department of Corrections handed out to each man before release does have the following statements:

> You are going to get out. "The free world! The streets! The ever-loving bricks!" What do you expect? "The sky to split? Heavenly music to waft in four directions? Wide Open Arms to Greet Every Entrance?"
>
> It Ain't
> Like That!!
> It Ain't
> Like That
> At All!!!
>
> The world has been rocking on all the time you've been in. Usually, few people actually know that you have been away.
>
> No one is going to do all your planning for you. Chances are pretty good that you'll have to start from scratch in building a social life—any life.
>
> Loneliness is one of the greatest problems facing a parolee. It may help if you give this a little thought before you jump out there. It won't be easy. Don't expect to swim in milk and honey.[6]

Generally, however, there is little indication either from the literature or from interviews of persons involved in dealing with parolees of the existence of any awareness of the broader aspects of the reentry problem. This general blindness seems to be related to formal and informal societal conceptions of the ex-convict. For instance, from one perspective the ex-convict is seen to be an erratic person—he is "emotionally disturbed," "sociopathic," "potentially dangerous," or "dependent." Therefore, any unusual behavior or any "symptoms," such as the actions that have been reported by "normal" returnees in other instances, would be attributed to the personality propensities of the ex-convict and not to the transitional experiences. From another perspective the ex-convict is seen as a person of low moral worth who is being granted the special privilege of early release provided he agrees to live up to certain minimum standards of behavior—the special parole regulations. He should be thankful for this privilege and should find no difficulty, if he has regained some worthiness, in responding by conducting himself properly. Failure to do so stems from his thanklessness and/or unworthiness. Finally, the legally restricted parole status of the ex-convict often obscures the true picture of the important experiences in the parolee's first days. In this status he is

5. The one exception to this is the recent article by Elliot Studt, "The Reentry of the Offender into the Community," U.S. Department of Health, Education, and Welfare, No. 9002 (1967). Studt emphasizes reentry as status passage and describes the difficulties encountered because of unpreparedness to occupy outside social roles. The emphasis in the following chapters will not be on the social *roles*, but on other interactional dimensions, such as perspectives, identities, and meaning worlds.

6. *How to Live Like Millions*, California Department of Corrections Publication No. 272 (38135), p. 8.

subject to special restrictions and is in contact with an agency which is supervising him and affording him certain kinds of help. Actions of the parolees which stem partly or wholly from other aspects of the reentry impact are often interpreted by observers, and the parolee himself, as reactions to the strains inherent in this status. For instance, any erratic behavior—any appearances of disorganization, frustration, irritability, or depression, or any of the behavior patterns which have been frequently observed to accompany other instances of reentry—can in the parolee's situation be attributed to his inability to adjust to the formal and informal expectations (some of which are ambiguous and conflicting) inherent in the parole status, to a personal conflict with the parole agent, or to difficulties which were incurred because of the parole status becoming known, such as employment difficulties or difficulties in establishing social ties. All of these can and often do contribute to the total range of problems that the parolee faces in reentering. Often, however, they are given undue weight, and they screen the more profound dimensions of the initial reentry problem.

The parole agent is often incapable of understanding the full scope of reentry because of characteristics of his position. (The parole agent's position, his tasks and his relationship with the parolee will be examined more fully in another chapter. Presently only a brief mention of some of these characteristics will be made.) The agent must police and help—"work with"—the parolee. He stands between potentially hostile segments of the citizenry and the parolee; he must give assurances to the former that he is doing his best to see that a potentially dangerous person is under control and must attempt to force the latter to adhere to a system of rules and regulations which can be very restrictive and obstructive to his efforts to adjust. Because of these often conflicting demands and the parole agent's heavy case load and limited time, the task of surveillance is seldom accomplished to anyone's satisfaction.

In helping or "working with" the parolee, the agent must "set up a program." Setting up a program entails finding the parolee employment and housing—if the parolee does not have these himself—and placing him in special department programs such as a nalline or out-patient clinic, parole school, and group counseling. Some aspects of working with many parolees are difficult and never cease. Parolees are one of the least employable segments of American society. Many of them are unskilled, or members of racial minorities, and have virtually no work record. On top of this they are ex-convicts. For these persons the agent must find jobs or supply leads and exhort them to pursue these leads. Besides jobs the agent must see that the parolee, who has often exhausted his financial resources, has a place to sleep and money for food until he obtains work and receives a paycheck. Again he has limited resources to do this. There is a department fund from which he may draw money for meal tickets, hotel rent, and some spending money, but this fund is far from unlimited and is often exhausted toward the end of the fiscal year. This facet of "working with" the parolee can be frustrating and time-consuming for the agent.

Besides these two primary tasks, the agent has to fulfill many procedural duties. He must visit each man a specified number of times, make regular progress reports on each parolee, and write special violation or emergency reports in the event the parolee is arrested, absconds, or repeatedly breaks the conditions of his parole. Needless to say, the most troublesome parolees, who may be the parolees who are having the most difficulty with the reentry impact, greatly increase the parole agent's work load.

Because of the heavy burden of his duties and his position relative to potentially hostile segments of society, the parole agent tends to be limited in his ability to conceive of the full scope of the parolee's adjustment problems. He tends, because of the enormity of the parolee's problems which are related to his assigned task, to be aware only of those which bear directly on his duties and which are conceivable from the perspective underlying the official definition of his position. As he sees it, the problems that the parolee faces in leaving the institution and settling in the outside community are (1) maintaining financial support of himself and his dependents, which means finding and holding regular employment, any employment; (2) avoiding "trouble"—staying away from bad associates, locations which the parole agent feels are "trouble" areas, and situations which may cause "trouble," such as some common-law relationships; (3) cooperating with the parole agent—maintaining an attitude of respect, being available for interviews, taking the agent's advice, and coming to him with any major problems (but not too often, for then he becomes a burden); (4) obeying society's laws and the special conditions of parole. From the agent's viewpoint these interrelated problems, which alone present difficulty enough, constitute the totality of the parolee's adaptive problems. If he approaches an acceptable solution of these he will remain outside of prison and have a good relationship with the parole agent. This should satisfy the parolee. If he fails in the early stages of his parole, then the parole agent tends to see his failure in terms of the conceptions mentioned above: the parolee is an erratic person, morally unworthy, or incapable of adapting to the strains of the parole status. It is seldom that any weight is given to the reentry impact itself.

Of course there are exceptions to this. For instance, one agent counseling a member of my sample who had just served ten years in Folsom recognized that the man was "shook up" upon release. He told the man, who had been given a few hundred dollars by his mother, to go to his place of residence, which was ten miles outside of the center of San Francisco in a very small suburban community, and relax for a few weeks. He advised him to come to the city a couple of times a week and refamiliarize himself with the pace of things before trying to plunge into a full, adult-civilian routine. But this small glimmer of understanding is rare and even in this case could only be indulged because of the financial status of the parolee. In the majority of the cases of reentry I studied, there was a complete lack of understanding on the part of the parole agent of the reentry impact, and where there was some understanding the exigencies of the parole agent's tasks prevented the agent from giving special consideration to the parolee in view of this understanding.

GETTING SETTLED DOWN

Two important and related themes appeared in interviews of convicts about to be released on parole. First there was considerable optimism in their plans and expectations, and most revealed the belief that their chances were average or better to live outside without being brought back. It seems that at this point in their prison career, at its termination, they had acquired considerable real or feigned optimism. Most of them expressed the belief that making it is up to the individual, and now that they had decided to try to make it their chances were very good. Most who come back, they believed, don't want to make it. Only four of the sample expressed doubts about their chances of making it.[7]

The second theme was a widely expressed concern for "getting out and getting settled down." Whatever their long-range plans, the great majority indicated an immediate desire to "get their feet on the ground," to "get into a groove of some kind." Most indicated an awareness that they would be starting from scratch, from the bottom, that "the streets" would be strange at first and that before they could begin real progress toward any goals there would be a period during which they must familiarize themselves with the outside world, meet a lot of immediate exigencies, and build up a stock of material necessities—clothes, toiletries, furnishings, etc.:

> I am going to move very slowly at first. I'm going to look twice to see if the light is green before crossing the street. I'm not going to look for a job right away. After this 7½ years I just want to get my feet into the earth again. I have a friend who is giving me a place to stay. He has some kids and some animals. I just want to relax and learn about these things again. Then I am going to get a job, any job, a dishwashing job. I don't care what work I do, because it is going to be the leisure time that counts. I'm going to find out what I want to do with my leisure time. (Taped interview, San Quentin, June 1966)

> I wanna get out and get to work. Then I wanna see my kids. As soon as I sees the parole officer I'm goin'a see my kids. I'm goin'a get a little room at first

7. In a recent study of parolees undertaken by social welfare students, this pre-release optimism was also detected. See Lanny Berry, *et al.*, "Social Experiences of Newly Released Parolees" (unpublished master's thesis, University of California, 1966), p. 68.

and then in a coupl'a weeks I'm goin'a look for an apartment with some extra rooms. Then I'm goin'a take it easy for awhile, get my hair fixed. I ain't goin'a look for no woman for awhile. I'm goin'a have to see about my driver's license and I wanna look around for a little car. I'm goin'a need a car to visit my kids, some of them are over in Oakland. I like the job I got, but I would like a little more money. I need some rent money, some furniture and some money for a car. (Taped interview, Soledad Prison, July 1966)

First I just want to get a forty hour a week job. I don't care what it pays, if I just have a check coming in every week. Then I can plan on something. I can start working towards something. If I don't have no job, or if I just work one or two hours here and a couple of hours there, like last time, then I can't look ahead to nothing and I probably won't make it. (Taped interview, Soledad Prison, July 1966)

The ex-convict's attempts to settle down and to get his feet on the ground are, however, often thwarted by a barrage of disorganizing events which occur in the first days or weeks on the outside. In spite of his optimism, preparedness, and awareness of the experiences in store for him, the disorganizing impact on the personality of moving from one meaning world into another, the desperation that emerges when he is faced with untold demands for which he is ill prepared, and the extreme loneliness that he is likely to feel often prevent him from ever achieving equilibrium or direction on the outside. Often a sincere plan to "make it" in a relatively conventional style is never actualized because of the reentry impact. Many parolees careen and ricochet through the first weeks and finally in desperation jump parole, commit acts which will return them to prison, or retreat into their former deviant world. Many others, though they do not have their plans destroyed and do not immediately fail on parole because of the experiences which accompany their return to the outside community, have their plans, their perspectives, and their views of self altered. At the very least, reentry involves strains which are painful and which deserve attention.

In exploring this phase of the reentry phenomenon, the ex-convict as an individual or a type will not be considered. Identities and modes of adaptation to the prison milieu will be suspended for the time being and reentry will be examined as a general phenomenon experienced by all parolees. Other instances of reentry or similar phenomena will also be examined in order to produce wider understanding of this transitional experience.

Withstanding the Initial Impact

The ex-convict moves from a state of incarceration where the pace is slow and routinized, the events are monotonous but familiar, into a chaotic and foreign outside world. The cars, buses, people, buildings, roads, stores, lights, noises, and animals are things he hasn't experienced at firsthand for quite some time. The most ordinary transactions of the civilian have dropped from his repertoire of automatic maneuvers. Getting on a streetcar, ordering something at a hot dog stand, entering a theater are strange. Talking to people whose accent, style of speech, gestures, and vocabulary are slightly different is difficult. The entire stimulus world—the sights, sounds, and smells—is strange.

Because of this strangeness, the initial confrontation with the "streets" is apt to be painful and certainly is accompanied by some disappointment, anxiety, and depression.

I don't know, man, I was just depressed the first few days. It was nothing that I could put my finger on. (Field notes, San Francisco, September 1966)

The thing I remember was how lonely I was out there the first few weeks. (Interview, San Quentin, January 1967)

I mean, I was shook, baby. Things were moving too fast, everybody rushing somewhere. And they all seemed so cold, they had this up tight look. (Interview, San Quentin, July 1967)

My dad picked me up at the prison and we spent the day driving up to San Francisco. It was night by the time we got to the city, 'cause we stopped and ate and looked at the ocean on the way. Well he dropped me off at my brother's where I was going to stay and left. My dad and my brother don't particularly dig each other. It was late and my brother was in bed. He had this couch set up for me. It was right under a window and this apartment was up about five stories or so. Well, it was one of these drippy nights in San Francisco. The bay was pretty close and a fog horn was blasting out every minute or so. I laid down and tried to go to sleep. Man, it was weird. I was thinking, so this is the big day that I had waited so long for. Man, I was depressed and nervous. The whole thing was unreal. (Interview, San Francisco, June 1968)

These experiences are not unique to the return of the felon or unique to the reentry phenomenon. Travelers to foreign places usually experience similar feelings.[8] Often when one returns home after a short absence, there is an immediate reaction of disappointment, self-doubt, and meaninglessness.[9] The reports of other returnees reveal similar experiences.

Three components of the initial impact. The released felon, as is the case with other persons who suddenly find themselves in a strange world, is disoriented by the new physical surroundings and social settings in different ways. First, the strangeness of the sensory experience unsettles him in a very subtle manner. He is usually proceeding to an urban center upon release, and the intensity and the quality of the new stimulus world can be overpowering. There is more noise and different types of

8. For a literate description by a traveler of this experience see H. M. Tomlinson, *The Face of the Earth* (New York: Dell Publishing Co., 1960), p. 34.

9. A character in Thomas Wolfe's *The Web and the Rock* (New York: Dell Publishing Co., 1960) gives us a good example of this situation (p. 350).

noise. There are many more lights and colors, and there is a great deal more rapid motion:

> The first thing I noticed was how fast everything moves outside. In prison everybody even walks slow. Outside everyone's in a hurry. (Field notes, San Francisco, September 1966)

> The lights at night kind of got me. (Interview, San Quentin, January 1967)

> The first time I started across the street, I remember, I was watching a car coming and I couldn't judge his speed very good. I couldn't tell if he was going to hit me or not. It was weird. (Interview, San Francisco, June 1968)

> Riding in the car was like riding in a boat. It was rolling back and forth. I got sick right away. (Interview, San Francisco, June 1968)

Usually the discomfort and the resultant disorientation is not explicitly identified and traced to its sources. The returnee often feels an uneasiness which he can't identify or he feels a sense of "unrealness"; that is, a feeling that he is not really experiencing this but is witnessing it as an observer or he is dreaming it.

Second, he is disorganized because of his lack of interpretive knowledge of the everyday, taken-for-granted outside world. Alfred Schutz in discussing the situation of the stranger approaching a foreign social world describes a type of knowledge of everyday activity that strangers do not possess:

> Any member born or reared within the group accepts the ready-made standardized scheme of the cultural pattern handed down to him by ancestors, teachers and authorities as an unquestioned and unquestionable guide in all the situations which normally occur within the social world. This knowledge correlated to the cultural pattern carries its evidence in itself—or, rather, it is taken for granted in the absence of evidence to the contrary. It is a knowledge of trustworthy *recipes* for interpreting the social world. . . .[10]

The ex-convict to some extent reenters the outside world as a stranger. He has been away and has forgotten many of the cultural patterns, and in the passage of time changes in these patterns have occurred. He too finds that immediate interpretive recipes which smooth social functioning (and without which every encounter becomes a strained, embarrassing, and difficult trial) have been lost to him and will have to be learned again:

> They were talking different and doing different things. I felt like a fool. (Interview, San Francisco, July 1966)

> The clerk asked me what I wanted and for a minute I couldn't answer her. It was like I didn't understand her. (Interview, San Francisco, June 1968)

10. "The Stranger: An Essay in Social Psychology," *American Journal of Sociology* (May 1944), p. 501.

Third, he is ill-prepared to function smoothly in interaction with outsiders in the outside world because he has lost the vast repertoire of taken-for-granted, automatic responses and actions. These are what Schutz calls "recipes for handling things and men in order to obtain the best results in every situation with a minimum of effort by avoiding undesirable consequences."[11] Here again the ex-convict is like the stranger. He has lost the ability to perform many ordinary civilian skills which have no use in the prison world and, therefore, are not practiced. For instance, he has not made change, boarded streetcars and buses, paid fares, or bought movie tickets or items across a store counter. He had done these things before prison, but during the prison experience he lost his ability to perform these actions in the unthinking, spontaneous manner in which citizens perform them and expect others to perform them:

On about the second day I'm out I get on this trolley and start fumbling in my pocket for money. There're a lot a people behind me trying to get on, but I can't figure out how much to put in the box. You know what, man, I don't know how to find out how much to put in the box. The driver's getting salty and I don't want to ask him cause I'm embarrassed, so you know what I do? I back off the fucking thing and walk fifteen blocks. (Interview, San Francisco, July 1966)

There is a process of escalation in actual interactional settings when it is discovered that one does not have these interpretative and behavior recipes. As soon as others who automatically assume that the stranger possesses the taken-for-granted knowledge and responses discover that he doesn't, they too become self-conscious, move from the level of taken-for-granted interpretations and responses, and start doubting the reliability of their own recipes and patterns.[12] The doubt and self-consciousness is fed back and forth, further disorganizing each member of the setting, especially the stranger who is aware that he is responsible for getting this confrontation off its firm foundation of the taken-for-granted social patterns. During several hours spent with a parolee on his first day outside, I witnessed the difficulty the simple act of purchasing a coke at a hot dog stand can present the unprepared "stranger." He went to the window and a young waitress brusquely asked him for his order. He was not able to reply immediately and when he did, his voice was not sure, his pronunciation not clear. The waitress, who appeared unsettled, didn't understand the order even though I did with ease. The second time she

11. Ibid., p. 501.

12. Harold Garfinkel has conducted experiments in which students purposely encountered unprepared persons and refused to take for granted that which normally is. The unprepared persons usually indicated some disorganization, and the interaction could not be continued while the student persisted in doubting the taken-for-granted basis of the interaction. ("Studies of the Routine Grounds of Everyday Activities," *Social Problems* (Winter 1964), pp. 225–50.

understood it and went to fill his order. When she returned, handed it to him and quoted the price, he was still unsettled. He did not have the money ready. After a brief hesitation, during which the waitress waited quietly but nervously, he started searching his pockets for money. He was especially slow at getting the money out of his pocket and could not rapidly pick either the right change or a larger sum to cover it which most people would do in this situation. He seemed to have to carefully consider these somewhat strange objects, cogitate on their relative value, weigh this against the price quoted, and then find some combination of them which would be equal to or more than that price. He admitted afterwards that he had been very unnerved by this experience and had been having similar difficult experiences since his release.

Impact on the self. How do these disorganizing experiences which all releasees seem to experience lead to the feelings of self-doubt, self-estrangement, and meaninglessness which they report? We must take a hard look at the relationship between these disorganizing experiences and the nature of self-conceptions and perspective to understand the reactions. Our conceptions of self—the definitions, values, beliefs, and meanings which constitute the design we recognize and act upon as our "self"—are interwoven into a fabric of a total world perspective—our meaning world. The patterns and designs of this world exist only in the interweavings of all the component strains; the self as a cohesive design exists only in the interweavings of meanings pertaining directly to the self and meanings of the world in general. But the fabric is never completed. Like Penelope's tapestry, it is constantly being unraveled and then rewoven daily in ongoing interactional settings. Our meanings of self and the world are being tested, supported, or reshaped within a situation in interaction with others who are engaged in the same process. In order for there to be a continuity of design in the fabric of perspective, there has to be some degree of continuity of familiarity in the setting. A radical change, a shift in setting, where the objects and meanings of the new setting are unfamiliar, interrupts the weaving—the maintenance of the patterns and designs. Not only does the world seem strange; the self loses its distinctiveness. Not only does the person find the new setting strange and unpredictable, and not only does he experience anxiety and disappointment from his inability to function normally in this strange setting, but he loses a grip on his profounder meanings, his values, goals, conceptions of himself.

In this situation, planned, purposeful action becomes extremely difficult. Such action requires a definite sense of self, a relatively clear idea of one's relation to other things, and some sense of one's direction or goals. All of these tend to become unraveled in a radical shift of settings.

Variations in the initial impact. Although all released felons experience this facet of the reentry problem to some degree, most endure it and reorient themselves and continue to act with some continuity and stability relative to their former definitions, conceptions, and plans. The intensity of this shock varies from ex-convict to ex-convict. For instance, returning to a familiar setting helps to reduce the duration of the initial impact. I interviewed one parolee after he had been out for one week, who said that he had been slightly "shook up," but was over it now. His appearance and behavior supported this claim. This parolee had moved back into his parents' home, into his old room. The clothes he left were waiting for him; they only needed some minor alterations. His wife and child, although they had not gone back together, were visiting him and the family almost nightly. He had succeeded in securing a desirable job. The familiarity of the setting, coupled with the removal of other obstacles, helped this person to quickly reestablish some continuity with a familiar world. For him the initial reentry impact was minimal. For others, especially those who are coming to a strange city where they have no friends, possibly no secure job, the disjointed experience is tremendous. I spent several hours on several occasions in the first week of another parolee. This person was born and raised in Colorado and lived in San Jose when he was sent to prison. This was his first stay in San Francisco, and he had no job upon release. During the prerelease interview he had impressed me as a person with exceptional control over his actions. He had definite plans and stated that he was determined not to do anything which would deter him from following them. On the outside, however, he admitted that he was extremely "shook." For the first four or five days he couldn't eat a meal; he tried several times but after several bites found he could not force any more food down his throat. When he finished his daily routine of job hunting, he couldn't stay in his room, so he walked the city for hours, sometimes late into the night. He reported having a great deal of trouble talking to people, even though he had fancied himself as outgoing and glib. He felt foolish when he tried to buy something in a store because he seemed to have difficulty taking the money out of his pocket and finding the correct amount of change. During these transactions he reports that "the saleslady was looking at me like I was some kind of idiot." This individual, in spite of the intensity of his reactions, maintained his self-control. He went through this period with detachment and amusement. He seemed to be operating on two levels. On one level he had lost grip of himself, of his reactions, his body and his feelings; but on the other level he was witnessing himself reacting in this abnormal fashion.[13] He said that he knew that he would eventually settle down "once I get a job and get a routine."

Others do not take this experience with such aloofness. One parolee with a long background of alcoholism told me in a prerelease interview

13. Bruno Bettelheim describes a similar type of detachment from himself in his adjustment to a concentration camp in "Individual and Mass Behavior," *Journal of Abnormal Psychology* (October 1943), p. 431.

that he had found a solution to his alcohol problem and would not be troubled with it this time on the outside. He further disclosed relatively specific immediate plans. A man in his forties who had finally overcome his "inferiority complex," he was going to report immediately to the union where there was a job waiting for him, join an Alcoholics Anonymous group and participate religiously, join one or two social clubs so that he might meet a woman his age whom he would marry and then begin "living a normal life." He was released by an oversight of the parole agent on July 3, a Sunday before the Fourth of July. It would be two days before he could report to the union or the parole agent. He wandered the streets of San Francisco feeling "nervous," "depressed," "scared," and "lonely." He walked into a Market Street bar and plunged into a two-day "drunk." He sobered up enough on Tuesday to report to the parole agent, fearful that he would be locked up immediately for violating the conditions of his parole by drinking. The parole agent was not too severe with him and after a "bawling out" directed him to report to the union. The parolee, in somewhat better spirits, but still hung over, left the parole office, cashed the check the agent had given him—the remainder of his $60—and launched another "drunk." He made his way to skid row, a milieu he was well acquainted with from his former years of drinking. A week passed and his funds were depleted. He sobered up and contacted his parole agent, who placed him in city jail for four days to "dry out." The agent picked him up from the jail and after a conference with the district parole supervisor took him to the union where he secured a job. He had no money for rent and the agent would not advance him any, but he found a room in a Salvation Army hotel for derelict seamen. He lasted two more weeks, during which time he worked and remained sober. But then he quit his job and absconded. Although alcohol seems to be an important factor in this man's failure, the initial shock of reentry certainly was instrumental in preventing him from reestablishing some self-organization so that he might start executing the plans he had made in prison. When I reminded him of these plans on four different occasions during his chaotic first month, he variously shrugged them off, desperately assured me that he was going to begin following them, or didn't respond.

Meeting the Exigencies of Living as a Civilian

The ex-convict faces problems in simply meeting the bare requisites of civilian life which are much more acute than the same class of problems of other returnees. In the case of prisoner-of-war repatriates, war veterans, and Peace Corps returnees, there is some indication of special employment difficulties. For instance, Peace Corps returnees have reported that employers were not eager to hire them upon return; in fact, their Peace Corps experience might have been detrimental to their employment potential.[14] In these cases, however, they are usually speaking about their employability at the professional or executive level, not simply finding a "job"—any job. And after finding job difficulties many of the Peace Corps members found grants, fellowships, and teaching assistantships open to them if they returned to higher education (and so far 60 per cent have).[15] The problem of the parolee is often finding any job or at least a job which pays a living wage. In this as in other facets of meeting the exigencies of the life of the citizen, the parolee faces special and extreme problems for which he is usually extremely unprepared.

At the time of this study, the parolee was released with one change of sports clothes—a low-priced sports coat, two sports shirts, a pair of slacks, two pairs of dress socks, and plain-toed black or brown shoes—and three sets of khaki, blue or white work clothes, a pair of work shoes, and two changes of underclothing. Theoretically he is allowed a flexible sum of money to pay his expenses until he draws his first paycheck. However, this always turned out to be $60, $20 of which he receives when he leaves the institution and the rest when he reports to the parole office. Many parolees have some supplementary funds (56 per cent of the seventy interviewed after a year stated they had extra money, but 70 per cent still had less than $100) from prison jobs that paid up to 10 cents an hour, from friends or other sources—pensions, bonds, or their own savings. The parolee, if his job requires, may request special funds to buy tools. Other than this, he is given transportation to the city where he is to be supervised on parole.

Employment. The initial and probably the biggest obstacle in this problem area is obtaining employment. In order to be released on parole in California, the convict must have financial support—employment, support from his family, friends, or from other sources—or have a good possibility of securing immediate employment through a union, the California State Employment Service, or a private employment agency. One of these alternatives must be approved by the parolee's prospective parole agent. To meet this requirement of release, the parolee does one of the following:

1. He obtains his job (on guarantee of support) while in the institution by contacting friends or relatives who locate employment for him, former employers, unions, or by corresponding directly with prospective employers. The latter is probably the least successful. Unless the parolee has some sought-after skill, it is very unlikely that employers will hire him without an interview. Only two in the sample of forty-one secured jobs by writing directly to employers—one with a fruit-packing company which does seasonal hiring and the other with a

14. Stolley, "The Reentry Crisis," p. 105.
15. Ibid., p. 104.

shoe-manufacturing company. Ten persons found jobs through their family, friends, or former employers.

2. If the prospective parolee is in contact with friends or relatives and wants to be sure of not being "overdue," he will sometimes have them set up a "shuck" job. Although they cannot find someone who will actually hire the parolee, they often have a friend who will make a fictitious offer of employment. In this case, by prior agreement with friends, relatives, or with the convict himself, some potential employer, possibly a relative or friend, promises to hire the man upon release with no intention of doing so. This is done merely to fulfill the requirement that he have a job to be released. Once released the parolee reports to the agent that he was not hired because of some unforeseen change in the employer's situation, or possibly the parolee will keep up the fiction and use the job as a "front" while remaining unemployed unbeknownst to the agent.

3. If the person cannot find his own job, real or fictitious, then he must rely on the parole agent to find him a job or to approve his release without a job. The latter is becoming the most common pattern. Sixty-one per cent of seventy parolees were released without immediate employment. If a person has support—for instance, if he is to live in the home of a relative or friend who will guarantee support until the parolee finds a job—the agent will usually approve his release with no job. The emerging pattern, however, is to release the parolee to some organization which guarantees placing him on some job within a reasonable length of time. The agent usually has contact with several unions, such as the culinary unions, which, unless the general employment situation is tight, will agree to place some parolees. Frequently the parolee is released to the California State Employment Service. In the last three years this agency has become officially active in parolee placement. Presently most state employment offices have a special counselor who is assigned to parolees. These counselors work closely with the parole agents. One agent expresses the present attitude toward placement in this way:

> The state has a huge bureaucracy primarily devoted to finding people jobs. Why shouldn't they find these guys jobs instead of me. My job's watching these guys—I'm not trained to find them jobs. Let the people who are trained do it and I will do what I am trained for. That way the taxpayers get the most for their money. (Interview, San Francisco District Parole Office, October 1966)

However, the California State Employment Service is not very effective in placing parolees. Only two of the seventy parolees stated that they received their first job through the CSES, and only seven stated that they received and help during the year from the CSES.

Although the emerging pattern is to release a person without a job when he has not found a job himself, some agents prefer that he be employed and are active in locating jobs for them. Four of seventy parolees were initially placed by their agents. One of these persons had completed a training course in sheet metal work in prison, was taken out for an interview before his release date, and then when the employer agreed to hire him was released early. The agent in this case had picked the parolee especially for this job because he wanted to "open up" a particular company to parolees. This agent, as is the case with some others, is actively placing parolees on desirable jobs. Other agents prefer to tap another resource for releasing men. This practice was more prevalent in the past when the department requirement on men having a job was more stringent. Some agents have contacts with industries or small businesses which use parolees as a source of cheap labor, for example, car washes, Goodwill Industries, and many small restaurants. These jobs usually have extremely low pay and/or undesirable working conditions. The agent cultivates these contacts because they serve as a last resort. He is able to place his least employable parolees through them. Often the agent receives other types of cooperation from such employers. They will keep him informed of the activities of the parolee and in this way the agent is able to increase his surveillance over him. The employers are served by having a source of cheap labor over which they have extra controls. The parolee is in the disadvantageous position of having few or no job resources, and often he is required to stay on the job by the agent.

The problem of earning a living doesn't end for the parolee upon release. Many of the jobs do not work out, are undesirable, or were fictitious, and many parolees have no jobs. Sometimes, the parolee and the agent must cope with the employment difficulties throughout the parolee's supervision. In the sample of seventy, 30 per cent were not employed at the end of the first year or when they had been returned to prison, and 54 per cent stated that they had a hard time finding, or never could find, a good job. The difficulties that many parolees have in securing desirable —and desirable by the most modest criteria—employment cannot be overemphasized. As previously mentioned, the parolee is one of the hardest to employ in our society. He is often low-skilled or has no skill, and he carries the stigma of the ex-felon and often the stigma of race. In spite of the highly publicized emphasis on trade training in California prisons, few men learn an employable trade during their sentences there. For instance, out of seventy, only 40 per cent received trade training in prison and only 27 per cent of the 40 per cent received two or more years' training. In a study conducted by a Regional Office within the Parole Division it was found that only 36 per cent of all parolees had received trade training in prison and that only 34 per cent of the 36 per cent were working in a field related to their training.[16] Interviews with employment counselors in the CSES revealed that the only training programs which they unanimously believed were suitably geared to the outside employment situation and gave adequate training were nursing, welding (there was one dissent here), sheet metal, auto mechanics, auto body and fender repair, and cabinet making.[17] The inmates interviewed before release reported that it is difficult to get into these programs. At San Quentin, which has a population ranging from 3,500 to 4,000, 316 men can participate in the trade-training programs at one time. Furthermore, there are special restrictions on some classes of convicts; e.g., older men and narcotics offenders are restricted from most programs. The fact is that most of the persons who enter the California prisons with no employable skill are leaving them in the same way.

Residence. Upon release, residence is a problem for some. A temporary residence will be found for all parolees who do not have an offer of residence with their families, friends, or in halfway houses. The agent, however, usually sends them to one of three or four low-priced hotels in the skid-row areas of the city. Some of these are very undesirable living places. They are used principally by winos and destitute pensioners. They are dirty and depressing. One parolee stated in a prerelease interview:

The parole office put me in some hotel that had a bunch of winos in the lobby. I had to sneak in the back door because I didn't want anyone to see me walking in the place. This time I'm not goin'a let him stick me back in one of those places. (Taped interview, Soledad Prison, July 1966)[18]

The picture is not always so grim. Some hotels regularly used by the agency are not undesirable, and most agents allow the parolee to find his own room if he desires. Many of the parolees, with the aid of friends, other parolees, or organizations (such as the Seven Step organization in San Francisco) succeed in finding fairly desirable and cheap hotel lodgings.

Residence becomes a bigger concern if the parolee doesn't find a job immediately and does not have extra money to pay his rent beyond the first week. The $60 budget offered by the agency lasts him about one week. Then he is more or less on his own. The agency will supply rent slips for one of several hotels in the Bay Area for another week, almost all

16. "Caseload Inventory–Region III," 12, 31, 1967, California Department of Corrections Document (1967). On file in "Parole Action Study" files, Center for Study of Law and Society, University of California.

17. Wendy Harris, an interviewer hired by the Parole Action Study, conducted these interviews of employment counselors.

18. When this man was released on parole after this interview in July 1966, his parole agent placed him in a hotel on Third Street in San Francisco's skid-row section. This time the parolee "jumped" parole in the first week.

of which are skid-row hotels. From then on the parolee must find some other way to pay his rent. Sometimes the agent will refer him to charity organizations, such as the Salvation Army; but often by this time the parolee has given up, absconded, or returned to systematic deviance. This may mean he has turned to illegal means of making money or to other deviants for assistance—for lodging, money, and companionship.

Clothing. Clothing becomes a growing concern after the first few days. The prison-issued clothes, especially the shirt, need to be washed or cleaned and pressed. If the parolee has no job and needs to present himself in a neat fashion for job interviews, this problem is acute. Many parolees either salvage some of their old clothes (which are usually conspicuously out of style) or use some of their extra funds for this purpose. But if the parolee does not have the extra resources, as was true of more than half of the sample of seventy, he is faced with a frustrating problem. After a few days, it becomes difficult for him to keep himself appearing neat and clean. This is likely to occur at a time when other worries are mounting and when the feelings of loneliness and self-estrangement are at their height.

The clothing problem does not go away in the first week or so. In order for a person to live the simplest social life, a minimum of clothes far beyond that which is issued to the parolee is required. In the first weeks or months many frustrating situations emerge and many activities are closed to the parolee because he does not have adequate clothing.

Transportation. Transportation can also be a serious obstacle to settling into a routine. For the majority of parolees it will be some time after release before they find it possible to own an automobile. They must have special permission to drive, automobile liability and property damage insurance (which is very expensive for a parolee who is in a high-risk category), and permission to own an auto. In the first weeks or months of their parole, they must depend on public transportation or friends or they must walk. Most of them are unfamiliar with the public transportation system and their first attempts to use it are difficult and at times embarrassing. Using public transportation for going back and forth to work is at times troublesome. For instance, one parolee in my sample who lives in San Francisco secured a job in Marin County. To get to work he caught the bus at 6:30 A.M. and arrived home after 6:00 P.M. For those who do not secure work in the first few weeks and who run out of funds, the 15- or 25-cent bus fare becomes a very large sum. Walking then supplants riding.

"Taking care of business." Beyond these more obvious and specific exigencies there are more subtle activities at which the parolee is particularly inept and which interfere with his progress toward settling into a groove, these will be referred to as "taking caring of business." For instance, the

ability to schedule one's time is lost in the slow-paced, routinized prison life. The convict is accustomed to having his life regulated by an assortment of bells, horns, whistles, and commands. Once outside he must relearn to parcel out his day for himself, but this is a skill that has many obscure contours and requires unnoticed resources (for instance an alarm clock) and a period of practice. For no other reason than being out of the habit of taking care of business, the parolee tends to forget appointments or times of appointments, to disobey minor laws—especially traffic and parking laws—to forget to pay fines, bills, and to meet many small citizen obligations which are so routine to the average citizen that their performance is seldom even noticed and never considered problematic. But beyond simply forgetting these small civilian responsibilities, the parolee often has an "obstinate" posture toward the petty details and the petty rules of civilian life.

His failure to take care of business is usually attributed by "normal" citizen-observers—such as parole agents, who do not understand the full complexities of these acquired skills—to his "laziness," his lack of desire to succeed on parole, his lack of moral worth, or his psychological inadequacies.

There is a snowballing tendency in the problems in this area. A failure to meet one of them usually compounds the difficulties in meeting others. For instance, if the person does not have a job upon release or loses his job before he can earn money to buy some clothes, pay his rent, and form a base of security, as time passes and his funds diminish it becomes increasingly hard for him to find new employment. His clothes become dirty and wrinkled. He sometimes cannot afford to use the public transportation system and he wears out the poorly made prison-issued shoes walking to look for work.

Agency Response

The response of the parole agency in the meantime is often unsympathetic and ineffectual. As the parolee accelerates down this spiral into desperation, he becomes a headache to the parole agent. Not only is he failing to obey the parole rules by not maintaining employment and conducting himself as a good citizen, he is increasingly seeking or threatening to seek aid from the parole agent—aid which the parole agent has limited resources to supply. For instance, the parole agent's job connections are few and soon exhausted, his financial resources likewise. He can advance money for hotel rent and meal tickets, but the agent is discouraged from doing this beyond the first week. There is a general feeling among agents and supervisors that a parolee, if given the chance, will abuse this service. The parolee, theoretically, may borrow cash sums, but in actuality loans are infrequently made. Twenty-two per cent of the seventy requested a loan and 14 per cent received one. (One agent stated that he hadn't made a loan in five years.) One reason for this may be that the agent must lend the money to the parolee out of his pocket and then be reimbursed by the state the next month. This imposition on the agent, coupled with the general agency opinion that parolees would sponge off the agency if they were allowed to borrow frequently, results in infrequent loans.

One parolee in my sample, whose job did not materialize because of the 1966 slump in building trades, worked sporadically for several months at odd-tile setting, painting, and construction jobs which he contracted on his own. He was not earning enough money to pay his bare expenses and was broke a considerable portion of the time. There was no governmental financial aid available for this man—he was not eligible for welfare or unemployment benefits. He did receive several cash loans from friends, but this source was limited. On one occasion he made a trip from Hayward where he resided to the parole agency in Oakland—a distance of twenty miles—using his last money for bus fare. He asked the agent for a small loan for additional carfare and phone calls. The agent refused, telling him that the fund was exhausted.

The parole agent very often tries to wash his hands of these troublesome cases who threaten to take up a great deal of his efforts and who constantly beseech aid which he does not have adequate resources to give. These nuisance cases—those who are having extreme difficulty in meeting the exigencies of life and who are caught in a snowballing descent toward disaster—are a major disconcerting factor in his employment duties, a factor he must learn to cope with. Some simply ignore the problem. Others increase their efforts to solve this problem by attempting to locate jobs for the men and find other resources for aid. I believe, however, that many agents cope with this threat to their peace of mind by taking on attitudes and beliefs that attribute the parolee's difficulties to the parolee's own weaknesses. He hasn't found a job or held a job because he is lazy, didn't try hard enough, doesn't want a job, is really hanging around with other criminals and doesn't want to work, has no intentions of working, and is really participating or planning to participate in some deviant activities and is just "shucking" the parole agent in telling him that he is trying to find work. Of course, from the perspective of the parole agent, these accusations are somewhat valid in the case of some parolees. In many cases, however, they are false, and the agent uses them as screens to shield him from the disturbing plight of many parolees.

BUFFERING AGENCIES

Recently, several organizations have emerged which serve to mitigate the reentry impact. In 1961 a nonprofit, nonsectarian private organization of Bay Area citizens, the Allied Fellowship Service, opened a halfway house in Oakland for released parolees. A second halfway house was opened in 1962 in San Mateo, also by a private, nonsectarian group. The American Friends Service Committee followed with a halfway house in San Francisco in 1965. The total capacity of these three houses, all of which are large family residences taken over by the various organizations, is about fifty parolees at any one time. More recently the Department of Corrections took over a three-story government building in Oakland, moved their parole offices into the ground floors, and remodeled the top two floors into a halfway house. This house, because of a special regulation imposed by the Oakland city government, is only open to former residents of Oakland and can house fifty-four. These halfway houses, however, will only accommodate a small percentage of parolees who come to the Bay Area in any given period, and entrance to two of them is restricted to various classes of parolees; in the Department of Corrections house, for example, one has to be a former resident of Oakland, and in the American Friends Service house the parolee has to be accepted by an administrative board which evaluates such factors as the parolee's suitability for this type of living, his suitability for the neighborhood in which the house is located, and his employment potential. For those parolees these houses do serve, many of the problems of reentry are circumvented. The house setting, the association with other recently released parolees who are experiencing similar problems and who share past experiences, the reasonably priced room and board (payment of which can be forestalled until the parolee is employed), and a place to go to sit and watch TV help ease some of the pain of the first weeks on the outside.

However, many men in the halfway houses express some dissatisfaction with this living arrangement. Sometimes they state that they would like to get out and get going toward finding some groove, some routine in the community. They feel that the halfway house, although it has certain advantages, is a temporary crutch, and while in this setting they are still anxious about truly "making it" outside—that is, getting completely out on their own in the community with no support. Many complain that residing in the halfway house is still living in a situation with too much supervision, since all the houses necessarily impose rules over and beyond the parole rules and society's laws. They often express other dissatisfactions with the halfway house. Some don't like associating closely with some of the other parolees. One parolee, who had money stolen from his room at one house, said that there were too many petty thieves and bums at the house. Others express dislike for the interracial situation, since the halfway houses are carefully nondiscriminatory and the men are often in a closer association with other races than was true in prison.

Seven Steps, a growing organization founded by an ex-convict, Bill Sands, and staffed primarily by ex-convicts, some of whom are on parole, is another buffering institution.[19] The Seven Steps program starts inside the walls for persons who are to be released from San Quentin (the program will soon be expanded to include other prisons). Six weeks before release, members start attending weekly meetings at which parolees, ex-convicts who are off parole, and other community members, many of them professional people interested in parolee problems, deliver short "pep talks," testimonials, and short autobiographies on how they "made it." The program is replete with slogans and is similar to Alcoholics Anonymous. Its "Seven Steps to Freedom" is patterned directly after the AA pledge. It attempts, especially in its prerelease orientation, to commit the individual to the organization, securing pledges that he will continue to participate in the program when released, which entails attending its functions and offering assistance to other ex-convicts and the organization itself.

Concretely, Seven Steps does the following things for persons released from San Quentin: It picks up members and other persons released that day at the gate at San Quentin and drives them to the city where they may catch a bus or train to the location of their parole program, or it takes them to Seven Steps Headquarters, formerly on Market Street, now on Mission Street in downtown San Francisco. Here they are introduced to other Seven Steps parolees or ex's who are at the headquarters, which consists of an administrative office, a smaller office, and, in the Market Street headquarters, a large lounging room with chairs, couches, a TV, phonograph, coffee maker, and ice box usually stocked with soft drinks. The parolees, if they need it, are given information on jobs and residence. As yet, however, the Seven Steps has only been moderately successful in cultivating employment and residence leads.

The experience of parolees who had some contact with Seven Steps seems to indicate that the most important service this program offered was a stopping off place for the first two or three weeks, a place to go during the day and sit and perhaps get into a conversation with somebody "who speaks your language." This in itself is a big help because an important problem for most parolees in the first weeks is that they have nothing to do after they have looked for a job or finished working, and have no money, no friends, no spot to go to just pass time in relatively congenial surroundings. But although they agreed that it gave them a place to go that was free and somewhat congenial, most expressed disappointment not with the actual administrators but with the class of ex-convicts that stayed with the program and therefore tended to control its informal activities. They stated that "social misfits," "gunsels," and "punks" stayed with the program mainly because they couldn't find any other place to go.

The family is the most frequently used buffering agency. In a sample

19. Bill Sands, *My Shadow Runs Fast* (Englewood Cliffs, N. J.: Prentice-Hall, Inc., 1964).

of forty-one parolees, thirteen moved into the homes of relatives (eleven into the homes of parents, brothers, or sisters; one into his wife's home, one into his uncle's home) and five others were given some aid—financial aid and/or aid in finding jobs and residence—by the family.[20]

The family is most consistently a help in meeting the exigencies of becoming a civilian. It can provide, if only temporarily, a residence and food. It often serves as an important source for employment. Four parolees in my sample of forty-three were employed by their families and four others obtained jobs with the help of family members. Further, the family usually helps take care of many other concrete problems, such as additional clothing, toilet articles, tools, and transportation. It also may help the parolee considerably in attempts to take care of business. Family members can help to resocialize him into the numerous commonplace but subtle and difficult citizen skills, such as scheduling his time, paying his bills, meeting his small obligations, etc.

Still, the family's ability to buffer other problems is problematical. In withstanding the initial shock there are many factors operating in the family setting which could either mitigate or intensify these problems. The absence or presence of conflict within the family, conflict between the parolee and his family, the compatibility of the parolee's and the family's commitments, the total character of the family's and parolee's past history together will have an important bearing on the solution of problems. One parolee in my sample returned to the home of his mother and stepfather after serving five years. Their quarreling and bickering shocked him and added to the initial impact of reentry. He became disgusted and depressed. After also having job difficulties, he jumped his parole. Another parolee came out to the home and employment of his aunt and uncle. The former relationship between the parolee and his aunt had been far from harmonious. In the first week conflict grew between them. She reported that he failed to get up the first morning for work and made too many toll phone calls to friends. One morning when she was driving him to work he brought his dirty work clothes in a loose bundle and she admonished him for not putting them in a paper bag. An argument over this ensued and the aunt stopped the car and ordered him out. This parolee was suddenly left with neither money, job, nor residence. In fact, his aunt refused to return the parolee's clothes for several weeks, further hindering his adaptive efforts. So, instead of serving as a dampener of the initial shock, the family sometimes intensifies the impact and blocks the parolee's progress toward settling into a groove. In many instances the family may be the major force driving the man back into systematic deviance.

Furthermore, the parolee is a potential unsettling force in the family. This has been recognized and described in the case of returning service-

20. Two interviewers, Wendy Harris and Suzanne Mount, supplied the greater proportion of the information on the seventeen families referred to here.

men and repatriated war prisoners.[21] The parolee disturbs the ongoing flow of the family's life; not only does he find them strange and foreign, they also find him this way. Even for families with a harmonious past relationship, reintegration is difficult for both sides, and if the past has been filled with conflict and difficulties, reintegration is a tumultuous problem if it occurs at all. Of the seventeen parolees who had some significant relationship with their families, there is indication that in the cases of thirteen there were serious difficulties, and seven of these were serious enough that the parolee's course was disrupted by family conflict.

The parole agency generally tries to take full advantage of all these buffering agencies. For those parolees for whom they have the full responsibility of "setting up a program," they often try to place them in halfway houses and then their main task is completed. Though their feelings toward Seven Steps is mixed (many agents express concern over the fact that ex-convicts are congregating and associating in unsupervised settings, and many of the public statements of Seven Steps members have irritated them),[22] they still make occasional use of the Seven Steps program.

In the case of the family, the parole agents seem to feel that if a man has his family going for him, he has a better chance. If the family offers the parolee a place to live and board, the agent will usually okay his release program, even though he has no job and there is indication that the relationship between the family and the parolee had been detrimental in the past. By placing the man with his family, one of his biggest worries has been taken care of; that is, being sure that the parolee has a place to eat and sleep at least for the difficult first weeks or months. Unless his attention is drawn by some extraordinary event or information that the parolee is having difficulties with his family, the agent tends not to look too closely at the family setting. This corresponds to the general societal attitude of keeping out of family affairs, but is added to in this case by the agent's desire not to upset the situation, since if he does he may be faced with new problems which will require some difficult action on his part.

21. See Curle, "Transitional Communities and Social Reconnection," pp. 50–51; and Wilson, "The Serviceman Comes Home," pp. 12–14.

22. In one meeting, a guest parole agent brought up the question of what a parolee should do if he sees a law being broken. Almost unanimously, the Seven Steps members present declared that they would not call the police. The most they would do would be to try to stop the crime, especially if it involved injury to a person.

6

DOING GOOD

The ex-convict, once he has withstood the initial impact and has achieved some degree of viability, sets out to seek gratification and perhaps to fulfill plans made in prison. The problem of "making it" will consume his attention and efforts for some length of time. But unless the individual has already failed at this level and has been diverted back to the old bag, absconded, or been returned to prison, he will achieve some degree of stability and viability on the outside and then not be satisfied with merely "making it." Reaching the next level of experience on the outside (that is, doing good), involves surmounting a new and more difficult series of obstacles.

BECOMING IMMERSED IN A NEW MEANING WORLD

The returning felon must find a group of people with whom he shares a meaning world in order to start enjoying life on the outside. What is suggested here is some deeper immersion in the social world of a particular group or collectivity than is required merely to interact with them. It is one thing to have the type of knowledge, described by Schutz, about the group being approached to be able to understand their acts, behavior, and to act appropriately;[1] but to interact with others in a manner which is satisfying and "meaningful," there must be considerably more overlap in the dimensions of their meaning worlds. They must "speak each others' language" in the fullest sense of this phrase.

In order for this to occur there must be a fairly *recent* extended experience with each other or experiences within similar situations with similar meanings. A common occurrence which illustrates the importance of recent shared experience for meaningful interaction is the chance meeting of two former friends. After the first few exchanges of news there invariably follows a difficult pause when both parties suddenly realize that they have nothing to talk about. The conversation lags; it is useless to try to continue. So with difficulty they part, both feeling uncomfortable and

1. "The Stranger: An Essay in Social Psychology," *American Journal of Sociology* (May 1944).

disappointed in their inability to generate some of their lost rapport. What happened is that the old basis of their rapport, the shared meaning world, has disappeared through time. The things in which each are presently interested mean nothing to the other, and there is no chance that in these few minutes the former meaning basis can be restored or a new basis can be built. In truth, although they were friends, they are now strangers. If there are exceptions to this pattern, then it is usually because in the interim both have been engaging in similar activities, and they do have a fresh shared meaning world. Most returnees experience this inability to relate to their former friends and family:

> To make the situation more difficult he found that war experiences of his few surviving men friends were quite unlike his own. And curiously enough his cousin who had been in the gunners at the front knew nothing about the Russian advance in Lembert. So the ex-prisoner felt cut off from his race and generation, an object of pity, or even of indifference or contempt.[2]

> His [Peace Corps volunteer's] friends and relatives seem not to be too clear on where he had been or what he did there or why it was important. They don't appear to be much interested in the rest of the world. And the volunteer in turn cannot get excited about the things that stir them: new cars, color TV sets.
>
> Returning joyful to old friends, they discover that they have nothing much to talk about. "I came back more serious, I suppose, and much more concerned about things like peace and civil rights," says Joseph Mullins of Griffin, Ga. In Philadelphia, Frank Guido looked up the companions he had known, "but all we had in common was the past."
>
> "I can't talk to people anymore," says John Bond, who served in Ethiopia. "I think they are boring, and I'm sure they think I'm the same." At cocktail parties Kathryn Hannan finds herself tongue-tied. "I'm not in tune with all the conversational status symbols anymore—where you went to school, whether you ski, how you spend your weekends," she says. "It's ritual, and I haven't learned it yet." [3]

After the other problems—withstanding the initial impact and meeting the exigencies of civilian life—begin to fade this problem of locating a world of meaning often confronts the ex-convict. The categories—the beliefs, goals, desires, values—that made up his meaning world inside are beginning to decay now that he is away from the experiences and the interaction network that supported them, and he hasn't formed a basis of meaning within a social world on the outside. Strangely, nothing he does seems to bring enjoyment:

> At least inside I had my goals, my plans. Now that I am out none of these seem to mean anything to me. I don't have anything to look forward to, nothing excites me. (Field notes, nalline clinic, October 1966)

2. G. K. Pether, *Soldier to Civilian* (New York: McGraw-Hill, Inc., 1944), p. 572.
3. Richard Stolley, "The Reentry Crisis," *Life Magazine* (March 19, 1965), pp. 98, 102, 104.

His interaction with civilians is not only unsatisfying; it can be very aggravating.

You wanna know what your first big shock is? Them citizens, man! Those motherfuckers are somethin' else! Man, what a disappointment! Those are the motherfuckers you've got to cut it with, and you find out they're a bunch of turds! I was living in one of them lanai type apartments . . . everybody knows everybody else. So it didn't take me long to get on the inside of everybody living there. Man, you think these guys on the yard are bad? You ain't seen nothin till you've seen them citizens in action; wait'll you see them people fuckin each other around. What a bunch of petty, treacherous motherfuckers! And I'm talkin about their personal, friendship dealings; I ain't talkin about business deals and all that shit! At first, I thought it was me, I thought maybe this joint had my thinking fucked up; so I tried to figure them out . . . and I did! I found out they're a bunch of two-faced, hypocritical motherfuckers! I'm telling you; I'd rather be miserable-assed me, than get stuck off in the same bag as them citizens! Man, those people are fucked up! You'll see what I mean when you get out there. (Interview, San Quentin, January 1968)

Another parolee reported to me that even though he was back among friends, back with his family, around people he knew formerly or new friends, he felt lonely most of the time. The prison experience is not only a gap in time when the shared meanings with old friends fade, but it is a time when the individual becomes immersed solidly in the prison meaning world. So besides finding that he no longer shares much with his old associations and that it is difficult to really "get something going" with new activities and new people, he longs for his old activities and interaction with his friends from prison.[4]

Some parolees, usually those with fewer inroads into outside social worlds and who, therefore, are experiencing this aspect of reentry, as well as other aspects, more intensely, solve the problem of their loneliness by interacting primarily with other ex-felons—often persons they knew in prison. Frequently a group of parolees who have been released in the same time period begin to "hang around" together at some locale—a bar or cafe. Members of these groups are usually engaging in some illegal activities, and therefore the groups do not last too long. Some of the members are arrested and sent back to prison. Others slowly establish themselves in other social worlds and drift away from the group.

Many parolees who do not interact primarily with other ex-felons still enjoy some interaction with friends from prison. Although their major participation is in other social worlds, they accidentally or intentionally meet their old prison friends and "cut up old capers." These moments afford them a chance to escape other social settings, such as work, school, or the family, in which they haven't become completely immersed. But as time passes, unless they are still active in deviant worlds, they become

4. See, for example, Claude Brown, *Manchild in the Promised Land* (New York: The Macmillan Company, 1965), pp. 103–4, 119–20.

immersed in the new settings and the old meaning worlds fade. The meetings with old buddies become more strained and the visits become less satisfying.

Many ex-prisoners in the height of their loneliness (though it is usually not possible for them to admit such thoughts) actually long for the prison setting. The memory of the undesirable aspects of prison fades, and life among their friends, the familiar prison activities, the freedom from the worries they are now facing become more and more appealing. Many failures result from the ex-convict's conscious desire to be back in the familiar meaning world of the prison. One parolee on his eighth month on the outside stated:

> Sure I miss the place. I had a lot of good friends there. I actually hated to leave. I knew that I wouldn't see most of these guys again. And I had a lot of good things going there. I had my house fixed up. I had my job, I was getting used to the food, was going to school. And I had some goofy friends, we used to do a lot of wild things together. Except for broads, I didn't mind the joint at all. (Interview, parolee's residence, November 1966)

FINDING A GOOD JOB

In most conventional schemes of doing good, a "good" job is an absolute necessity. The difficulty, however, that the ex-convict faces in finding employment, any employment, was mentioned in the last chapter. This cannot be emphasized too much. In Glaser's study of parolees, he discovered that the median monthly income of his sample after three months out of prison was only $207.00.[5] In my own sample, the average reported monthly income at the end of the year or when returned to prison during the year was $334.00. This is not "doing good." The inmate, it must be remembered, does not have lowered aspirations. He feels that a portion of his life was taken from him and he desires to catch up. Although the opportunities for him are reduced, his aspirations are high. As Glaser states it:

> Prisoners have expectations of extremely rapid occupational advancement during the years immediately following their release, expectations which are unrealistic in the light of their limited work experience and lack of vocational skills.[6]

Lack of Vocational Skills

Glaser emphasized lack of skill and work experience as the major obstacle in finding a good job. My own findings corroborate this. Thirty per cent of those interviewed a year after release stated that lack of skill was a

5. Daniel Glaser, *The Effectiveness of a Prison and Parole System* (Indianapolis: The Bobbs-Merrill Company, Inc., 1964), p. 360.
6. *Ibid.*, p. 358.

major problem in finding a good job. It is clear that the majority of California felons are released with no trade training in prison and no employable skill.[7] On the basis of work experience and trade training alone, ex-convicts are certainly one of the least employable segments in the United States.

They are also ill-prepared for employment in a less obvious way. The routine of seeking and applying for work is one at which ex-prisoners are especially inept. In order to obtain a good job, which very often is a job with a large corporation or a government agency, one must fill out an application, be interviewed, and take special tests. Most ex-convicts find these very difficult, in fact, painful. Filling out an application, for instance, is something with which they have had little or no practice. Furthermore, most applications are slanted toward the middle-class applicant, and this makes it especially difficult for the ex-convict and lower-class person. These applications invariably request a listing of all former employment, and sometimes an accounting of periods of unemployment, and there are often only five or six spaces allotted for this. Clearly this is structured for a person with an orderly past employment record. The ex-convict often has no work record or has had so many jobs he can't recall all of them. His attempt to supply this information can be frustrating and intimidating. In a sense, the act of filling out such an application for an ex-criminal, or for that matter most lower-class persons, is a formal act of laying oneself open to the close scrutiny of conventional judges. This scrutiny usually makes the ex-convict feel embarrassed or guilty. One parolee reported to me his feelings about job hunting and filling out applications:

> Man, I just never've been able to go through that job-hunting scene. I don't know how to ask for a job. I feel shitty standing there asking some broad about a job. Then she hits me with a long application and I'm really in trouble. I just can't fill out one of them. Most of the questions I can't answer because they haven't got anything to do with me or my life or I can't remember. They just weren't written for a guy like me. They were written for some guy who went to work right out of high school and only held two jobs before this one. I get to that part about former employment and I got to pass. Last place I just wrote across that space that I would explain all that when they talked to me. (Interview, parolee's residence, November 1966)

STIGMA

Stigma and employment difficulties go hand in hand. The arrest record and ex-convict status is definitely a major obstacle to obtaining

7. A recent unpublished study conducted by a regional office of the California Parole Agency discovered that only 36 per cent of parolees had received any trade training, and that only 34 per cent of these were working in a field related to their training, possibly indicating that the training was not adequate.

a "good" job. In my sample, 50 per cent stated that they had difficulty in finding a good job because of their ex-convict status. Thirty-nine per cent said they actually failed to obtain or lost a job because of this.

This discrimination in employment, however, is not universal and is changing rapidly in some areas of the employment field. In union employment, for instance, there seems to be little or no discrimination against the ex-convict; in fact, in many unions the reverse is true. They are sometimes sent out on jobs faster and sent to better jobs when the dispatcher knows that they have been recently released. This might be explained by the sympathy union organizations feel towards criminals and ex-convicts because of a past affinity to criminals in the history of union organizations. There are, however, some instances of bias against ex-convicts in some unions, particularly toward some classes of ex's. For example, the baker's union and butcher's union in San Francisco do not admit ex-felons with a drug record.

Until very recently employment in government agencies was universally closed to ex-convicts. Now, however, this is changing and there is an increasing tendency for these agencies to hire ex-convicts. In particular, some California state agencies have, upon special consideration, been hiring ex-convicts. In fact, the California Department of Corrections during a period of several years hired several ex-convicts to fill prison positions, mainly at Vacaville Prison. Furthermore, there is a class of new government agencies which hires many members of minority groups and some ex-convicts. These are the agencies involved in the War on Poverty and urban projects which are supported by the Office of Economic Opportunity and similar federal appropriations or grants. As yet, in the total picture, the jobs offered by these agencies and the few breakthroughs in other government agencies are insignificant. None of a sample of 116 parolees were working with a government agency or government-sponsored agency.

It is still fairly accurate to say that jobs with large private business corporations and jobs with government agencies are almost closed to the ex-convict.[8] These classes of jobs constitute the great majority of "good" jobs. What is left for the ex-convict are jobs with small businesses which are more flexible in their policies, jobs through unions, and jobs with some large companies, such as high-pressure sales companies, which have found ex-convicts especially suited for this type of sales work.

This problem of stigma as an obstacle to finding a good job becomes

8. Alfred Himelson, in a study of employment and bonding of men with criminal records in California, found that 77 per cent of manufacturing firms and 94 per cent of finance, real estate, and insurance firms "would not hire," "would not hire under certain conditions," or "would hire rarely or seldom." Eighty-four per cent stated that bonding companies would not bond employees who had a record of convictions for burglary. ("Risk and Rehabilitation: A Study of the Fidelity Bonding of Former Offenders" [Xerox manuscript, 1966].)

more complex when we introduce two new dimensions. First is the difference between subjectively experienced job discrimination and actual discrimination. In many instances, because of the past history of extreme discrimination against him, the ex-convict feels that many doors are still closed which are actually open or partially open. He sees the situation as one in which there is no opportunity and, therefore, does not try to obtain many kinds of jobs. For him, stigma in hiring is still operating very strongly, much more strongly than actually may be the case.

Secondly, the visibility of his stigma, or rather the lack of visibility, is an important dimension in his vocational efforts. For the most part, the ex-convict is discreditable rather than discredited.[9] Except for a few who have made their past membership in deviant worlds highly visible through habitual gestures, tattoos, and speech mannerisms, most ex-convicts can "pass" with ease in most informal situations and in some formal, i.e., employment, situations.[10] Technically, the agent is required to have the parolee inform his employers that he is a parolee; in fact, some agents do not follow through on this or they allow the parolee a period of time to become established before requiring him to do so. The major difficulty in passing in the employment situation is that the information which can discredit him is available to all employers in the form of police records, and most large employers routinely obtain these police records for new employees.

This presents the ex-convict with a difficult problem. When he applies for a job and fills out an application, most of which have one question related to the applicant's record, he may choose to falsify this application in hopes that they will not check the police record or if they do, sufficient time will have passed for him to earn a good work record with the company or win the confidence of one or more of the company officials. On the other hand, he may be taking a chance of being automatically fired for falsifying the employment application. So he may choose to answer honestly and take the chance of never being able to prove himself on the job. There is no agreement on the most successful course here. Both, to my knowledge, have been tried with success *and* failure.

Informal Stigma

Stigma in other areas of his life, in informal relationships, is of little importance to *criminal* ex-convicts. In the first place, in informal settings, with the exception of the highly visible ex-convicts mentioned earlier, they find it easy to pass if they desire to do so. Furthermore, though in the general society the felon status is a discrediting attribute, among

9. This distinction is made by Irving Goffman in *Stigma* (Englewood Cliffs, N. J.: Prentice-Hall, Inc., 1963), pp. 41–42.

10. Again, this is a concept borrowed from Goffman's discussion of stigma (*Stigma*, pp. 73–91).

deviants it is of no importance or at times may even be a prestige-winning attribute. When deviants strongly committed to a deviant identity are in interaction with conventional persons who, if they knew of the stigma, would treat the person differently than they treat normal individuals like themselves, the deviants rarely feel discredited. Sixty-five per cent of sixty-four parolees answered that they had never felt ashamed or uncomfortable in a social setting because of their ex-convict status. The deviant identity and concomitant world view insulates them from the contempt, disgust, condescension, or patronization of others. In his discussion of stigma, Goffman mentions this possibility:

Also, it seems possible for an individual to fail to live up to what we effectively demand of him, and yet be relatively untouched by this failure; insulated by his alienation, protected by identity beliefs of his own, he feels that he is a full-fledged normal human being, and that we are the ones who are not quite human. He bears a stigma but does not seem to be impressed or repentant about doing so. This possibility is celebrated in exemplary tales about Mennonites, Gypsies, *shameless scoundrels,* and very Orthodox Jews. [Emphasis mine][11]

This is only true, however, of the committed deviant. Square johns and ex-criminals who are considering transforming their identities are sensitive to the expectations of other reference groups. The following table demonstrates the relationship between deviant *vs.* square john identities, and the experience of stigmatization in informal settings:

	Per Cent Felt Stigma	*Per Cent Felt No Stigma*	*Number*
Square Johns	50	50	10
Criminals	27	73	49
Total			59

An effect of the stigmatization experienced by those ex-deviants who desire to move out from under the protective umbrella of a deviant perspective is to encourage the brethren to remain under its protection. Consequently, stigma is perhaps an important force in maintaining commitment to deviant social worlds.[12]

ACHIEVING SEXUAL GOALS

An integral part of doing good is living a life rich in sexual experiences. This, however, is difficult to achieve for most ex-convicts, at least for a few months after release. It is particularly difficult for ex-

11. Ibid., p. 6.

12. See Edwin Lemert, *Human Deviance, Social Problems and Social Control* (Englewood Cliffs, N. J.: Prentice-Hall, Inc., 1967), p. 42, for a discussion of stigma and commitment to deviance.

criminals who are trying to avoid their former deviant world and explore a new style, especially if this new style is entirely different from their former deviant one and, therefore, somewhat foreign to them. As mentioned earlier, an important appeal of the old bag is that it promises relief from a sexually barren life, either through actual sexual activities with female associates of the familiar deviant world or through the deviant activities, such as hustling and drug use, which can substitute for or inhibit sexual urges.

In the *ideal* postprison sexual career, the new releasee must give vent to his denied sexual urges at a very early date, preferably the first or second day after he is released. After he gets settled down he should either "get a good old lady" who isn't a "dog"—that is, physically unattractive—or have numerous attractive girlfriends with whom he is sexually intimate.

As it turns out, however, both of these are difficult to achieve, especially in a manner which meets the expectations of the prison reference world. In the period immediately after release the felon is particularly handicapped. The average time of the earliest sexual experience *reported*—which must be considered below the actual time—was one week. As emphasized in the last chapter, the new releasee is financially and emotionally ill-prepared to socialize with people in general and the female sex in particular. Often he has no civilian clothes and only $60.00. He is unaccustomed to talking to female civilians. Furthermore, he might be experiencing the disorganizing effects upon the self which accompany reentry. As the weeks, and perhaps months, pass he usually remains in a position of disadvantage. Normally it will be several months before he is financially, socially, and emotionally equipped to enter most American seduction arenas.

Convicts who are not returning to a wife or girlfriend are not fully aware of the difficulty they will encounter in making their initial sexual contact and then achieving some satisfying *relationship* with a female or females. They have forgotten that although there is a favorable proportion of females to males in the society in general, the majority of the female segment is probably unacceptable by their own standards of age, beauty, and physical charm. Their conception of what the average female "on the streets" is like has been distorted, and their standards upgraded, in their isolation from women. This is because the sample of female images that are available to them through the mass media are skewed toward glamor and beauty. Moreover, the convict becomes highly sensitive to physical appearance because one of his few contacts with femininity and one of his most important sexual activities is looking at magazine pin-ups and motion-picture actresses.[13]

The convicts' expectations in this area are highly unrealistic. Actually,

13. Eldridge Cleaver comments on his pin-up and its importance to him in *Soul on Ice* (New York: McGraw-Hill, Inc., 1968), p. 7.

most women will fall into the category of "dogs" who are not acceptable for serious or permanent relationships. This anathema—the dog—is not exclusive to convict culture but exists in the American culture in general and in the lower working-class culture in particular. For instance, Paddy Chayefsky exploited this theme in his play about the working class bachelor, *Marty*.[14] A convict comments on the type of "ol' lady" he is going to seek:

I'm goin' to get me an ol' lady right away. I want some chick that I can hold a conversation with, though. I don't mean some intelligent chick who's a dog. I ain't goin' fuck with no dogs. (Interview, San Quentin, October 1966)

Furthermore, our society has a serious vacuum. There are few *public* courtship institutions. Outside school, work settings, and informal social gatherings among friends, such as house parties, there is no respectable spot for a woman to meet men. All other meeting places are "pick-up" spots and in these the girl is at a disadvantage. It is implicit that meetings and dates that originate in pick-up spots should lead to early sexual unions and, therefore, the girl who goes to these places and allows herself to be picked up has her reputation tarnished. There is a tendency for "nice" girls and many desirable girls to avoid these pick-up locations.[15] This results in an even greater shortage of desirable girls who are available to those who do not have inroads to the few respectable meeting places.

In the one social world which does offer the opportunity to make contact with desirable females in public places, such as bars and night clubs —the swinger or playboy scene—the newly released ex-convict is still in a position of extreme disadvantage. The female "swingers" of this world are in short supply and are in a position to pick and choose carefully. Usually these girls earn their prestige within a particular crowd indirectly through the position of their boyfriend. Usually it is their boyfriend's material wealth, "hipness" as revealed in current fashions of dress and vernacular, and prestige within a particular crowd which wins the female prestige. All these take time to acquire. For example, a recent releasee remarks on his problems in picking up a girl:

I been goin' down to this little bar close to the center. But I ain't got no front. You know, man, no car, no clothes. I get into a conversation with some little chick, but she puts me down right away. She don't want to look down inside me to see what I got goin'. All these chicks have nice jobs, new cars, nice clothes, and big egos. A sucker wearing a joint suit, no apartment, no car ain't got a chance. (Interview, Oakland, August 1966)

The ex-convict, trying to avoid his deviant ties, is likely to be working

14. *Television Plays* (New York: Simon and Schuster, 1955). See especially pp. 169–71.

15. John Clellam Holmes suggests that this is changing and a new, sexually equal girl is emerging in the U.S. (*Playboy* [January 1968], pp. 181–82, 186, 214–16).

in an all-male setting, is not likely to be going to school, and for quite some time is not likely to have friends invite him to private parties. For the most part, until he becomes accepted in a new social world, he will be left with the less desirable unattached females—divorcees in their thirties, young boarding house "plain Jane" rural migrants, or other "dogs"—who make themselves available in pick-up spots. These are acceptable for one-night stands only. In the period immediately after release, however, because of lack of funds, automobile, clothes, and minimum social skills, even these types are somewhat unavailable to him.

Malcolm Braly, an ex-convict from San Quentin, in a novel *On the Yard,* artfully describes the plight of two different releasees in regard to sexual experiences. We turn here to a fictional account because of the sensitiveness of the subject. Men rarely speak honestly of their sexual achievements, and a good novelist's description is usually more accurate than an actual account:

Finally Chilly found himself free again at twenty-four, a two time loser with almost seven straight years of reform school, county jail and prison behind him. . . . He moved into a medium-sized hotel on Powell Street and started looking for a woman. There were a large number of single women in downtown San Francisco, but he didn't know how to make a beginning, and confiding his need to some third person who might have arranged to have it serviced was too much like admitting a weakness. The need itself was a weakness, the inability to gratify it an aggravation. To go it alone was to risk rejection, or to expose his ignorance, and he was uncertain of his capacity to weather either of these situations calmly. He was aware of the charge he had accumulated, and he was afraid he might blow it.

Finally, after several weeks a woman had picked him up, and inevitably it was an older woman. Chilly guessed her to be in her middle forties and from the beginning she made him inexplicably uneasy. . . .

When he next made parole, he quickly discovered that his cosmetic ears cut no ice. The bitches, as he put it, still wouldn't let him score on their drawers, but continued to deal way around him as if they sensed some violent far-out freakishness thrashing around in his hectic yellow eyes.

He decided he couldn't make it without wheels so he hot-wired a new Buick convertible and finally managed to pick up a girl in the Greyhound Bus depot. She'd just arrived nonstop from Macon, Georgia, with one change of clothes in a paper bag.

"This your machine?" she asked, smoothing the Buick's leather seat.

"Sure. You like it?"

"It's most elegant."

She was so mortally homely Red figured she'd come near scaring a dog off a gut wagon, and she was built like a sack of flour, heavy, shapeless and white, so he drove straight up into the hills, parked and reached for her. She was already slipping down the leather seat.

"You got something in mind, California?"

Red experienced a momentary uncertainty, staring down at the girl's shadowed face. She was stretched flat now, her legs slewed off to the side and her scuffed black shoes rested on the floor-boards.

"Maybe," he said.

"Some of them old things back home would be halfway to Kingdom Come already."

He brushed up her cotton dress, and clambered awkwardly over her as she adjusted her underwear, and began to push uncertainly at her general softness until she shifted skillfully beneath him, and he plunged wildly, pounding his head against the car door.[16]

The extent of the ill-preparedness and, therefore, the possibility for sexual frustration, is related to the distance one plans to maintain from his former life style and social world. For instance, gleaners who have planned radically different lives for themselves have the most difficulty in forming sexual unions. Persons who plan to avoid their former life patterns often begin life on the outside in a strange locale, or at least in a strange social space. They are approaching the new social worlds with the intention of acquiring a new perspective, a new taken-for-granted world. But the subtleties of the courtship game in the new social world are obscure dimensions and learned only after considerable experience.

This obstacle, lack of sexual opportunities, is less important to square johns and lower-class men. Both are more likely to be returning to a familiar milieu and don't have an old bag, that is, a social world, to avoid—only "problems" or "trouble" to avoid. Both are more likely to be returning to a wife or some network of social relations which offers the opportunity to promote sexual unions.

NOT DOING TOO GOOD

Doing good according to the ex-convict's own expectations and the expectations of the prison social world is at least very difficult and for many impossible. After making it (that is, surmounting the reentry crisis), meeting the exigencies of the citizen, most ex-convicts do not move on to doing good. They do not find a good job, do not become immersed in a new social world which interjects "meaning" into their lives to any satisfying degree and they do not achieve a desirable and acceptable relationship with a woman or women.

Failure to Get Started

Many who had planned to pursue a conventional career never arrive at doing good because they don't move beyond making it. Just meeting the exigencies of life overwhelms them. Perhaps their age and lack of

16. *On the Yard* (Boston: Little, Brown and Company, 1967), pp. 229–30, 5–6.

skill brings them continuing employment difficulties. Often they have accepted some steady employment which pays a very low salary, such as busing or washing dishes. These jobs prove to be dead-ends. They offer no chance for advancement and take up all the ex-convicts' time, energy, and spirit, preventing them from exploring other job opportunities. Often minor health problems and drinking habits prevent them from maintaining steady employment and force them to seek only menial jobs which one may change regularly. Furthermore, if they are still on parole, they are very likely having considerable trouble with their parole agent, who is usually very concerned about parolees who continue to have employment troubles. The parole agent often has them visiting the office frequently, and he makes frequent visits to their residence and job, threatens them with suspension, and perhaps places them in city jail from time to time to "dry out," to scare them, or to give them time to reorient themselves.[17]

A Rut

Often they solve the problems of getting on their feet, but in doing so fall into a rut from which they cannot ascend. They get by on a job which does not pay well, but while just getting by they become engaged in a full routine of activities which consume the major portion of their lives. They hang around a neighborhood working-class or skid-row bar or a pool room. They cultivate a circle of friends who are also living this style of life. They become involved in going to work, returning to their small hotel room, cooking their meals, eating in cheap skid-row cafeterias, doing their laundry, and perhaps if their finances permit, drinking at night.[18]

Dreams Collapse

Others make initial strides or considerable progress toward their goals, but as they draw closer to their planned destination they are disappointed because it is beset with complications and problems they hadn't anticipated, it is quite different than they supposed, or it doesn't exist at all. For instance, the working-class swinger or the playboy style have built-in complications and frustrations. The relationships between participants in these scenes are usually quite competitive and invidious. Relationships with females are rarely harmonious or extremely satisfying. In the lower-class swinger style there are certain routines, such as the weekend

17. In informal interviews, three agents admitted using this tactic in handling difficult alcoholic parolees. This happened to one out of a group of ten parolees I observed in their first week on parole.

18. For a good description of an ex-convict in this type of rut, see John Barlow Martin, *My Life in Crime* (New York: Signet Books, 1953), pp. 151–85.

amphetamine, barbiturate, liquor, and sex binges, which are physically debilitating and mentally depressing.

The "settling-down family scene" also has its own disappointments. The wife or old lady, who originally seemed charming and beautiful, often loses her charm and beauty. Debts mount, petty differences between husband and wife emerge, and the pleasant experiences between the two become rarer. Their sexual life becomes dull and the male partner (or sometimes both) seeks other sexual partners. Often, after the passage of time, the family scene degenerates into an ugly, bickering, nagging routine, a far cry from that visualized from prison.

Transformation styles also can prove quite disappointing. Sometimes when an ex-felon actually succeeds in completing some training, overcomes employment obstacles, and secures a "white-collar" job, he discovers that the excitement or the interest he had anticipated is not there. Most of the work is mundane, routine, and dull. Life at that level, life among the middle class, is also replete with petty concerns and complications and is quite invidious and mundane.

Facing Disappointment

These disappointments appear to be much like those encountered by most people, disappointments they take in stride. The same disappointments, however, are different for the ex-convict because of his prison experience. The ex-convict has high hopes and has set high standards. He has the "catch up" ethic. This ethic is enforced by a severely critical body of judges—the yard. Furthermore, he is an ex-deviant. This gives him an alternative—the old bag. Also, he knows that prison isn't unendurable, and here perhaps is the chief difference between him and the average citizen which makes the disappointments they each experience so different. As time passes the bad memories of prison fade and it becomes less and less threatening and, in fact, more and more appealing as an alternative to disappointment.

When this final disappointment—failure to reach the level of "doing good"—is recognized and consciously accepted, the ex-convict is at a critical turning point. At this time he either reorganizes his thinking about the future and alters his plans, perhaps scaling down his aspirations and reconciles himself to a generally less satisfying life than he had hoped for, or he veers back to the old bag.

There are two career points when this realization is more likely to occur which may be seen as critical stages in the ex-convict's postprison career. The first is after the ex-convict has succeeded in making it and enough time has passed for him to realize that he is caught at that level. He can see that he is not progressing beyond making it. Of course, the exact time that this occurs varies from individual to individual and with the difficulties experienced in making it, but it seems most likely to occur from four to five months after release. The second critical period is after the ex-felon is discharged from parole or has been on parole for several years and virtually all parole restrictions have been lifted. Many parolees have been attributing their failure to rise above making it to the handicap of being on parole. When this restriction is removed, they sometimes are forced to face the fact that even without this restriction they will not move on to the cherished level of "doing good." [19]

Return to the Old Bag

When the return to deviance occurs it varies in speed and form among the different identities. For instance, state-raised youths and disorganized criminals, especially those who jailed during prison, often gravitate to locations in the city (such as Market Street, the Tenderloin, or the Mission districts in San Francisco) where they meet other desperate, careless, unsophisticated deviants. Here they live chaotic lives infused with drug use and petty criminal activities. They "hang around" local bars and all-night coffee shops, such as Compton's Cafeteria in the Tenderloin. The carelessness and visibility of their illegal activities guarantees their return to prison, an eventuality to which they are reconciled and, in fact, seem to look forward.

The dope fiend's return to deviance is less visible. Presently most dope fiends are involved in the nalline program. They report weekly or biweekly to a clinic where they sit from one to two hours in the company of other dope fiends (many of whom they know) and wait for their shot of nalline and subsequent eye-dilation check. If they have used an opiate within forty-eight to twenty-four hours before the test, it will be detected.

The nalline program is central to the dope fiend's return to deviance. First it is a source of pressure toward the old bag, because at the clinic he is weekly confronted with the dope-fiend reference world. It is here, more than any other place, that the standards of doing good in terms of the prison dope-fiend world are invoked. The thirty or forty other dope fiends present at the clinic stand as judges who evaluate others' progress or lack of progress. The prison standards of doing good are impossible to forget when the dope fiend is forced to appear each week for judgment.

Second, the clinic is a source of enticement into drug addiction. The "bag man" (drug connection) is at the clinic or available through others at the clinic. There are many who have returned to drugs who come to

19. I have no concrete data to support this contention. Many parole agents, however, have related to me cases of parolees committing "senseless" crimes after successfully completing their parole. The agents stated the belief that this was a crucial turning point in th ex-convict's postprison career.

the clinic and relate how they are able to use and "beat" the nalline test. When he is ready to return to drugs he usually joins those dope fiends (one parolee estimated to me that this is 50 to 70 per cent of the dope fiends in the nalline program) who leave the clinic and proceed to "score" and "fix." Immediately after clinic is an appropriate and satisfying time to use drugs because he has been set up psychologically for a fix by the act of receiving a shot of nalline, which has put him through the ritual of the fix with one important component withheld—the "high." In fact, the nalline has done the opposite; it usually makes him irritable or depressed. Moreover, if he uses immediately after the test, he has six days before the next test to "clean up."

The dope fiend slipping back into the old bag often begins a routine of fixing after the day of his clinic appearance and then "cleaning up" for two or three days before. He may go for months following this pattern. He can continue to live a relatively normal existence while using drugs because having to use drugs intermittently prevents him from becoming addicted and, therefore, having to increase his dosages. The nalline clinic, while it has helped to induce and entice him into drug use, serves as a control on his habit. One addict stated:

> I never enjoyed stuff more in my life. I use for two or three days after clinic and then stop a couple days before. I been goin' like this for months, man, it's great. This is the first time I haven't got strung out in my life. I don't get so fucked up I can't work and I ain't got no habit so I don't need so much stuff that I can't buy it with the bread I'm earning. Or, man, if I ain't got no bread I can pass that day. (Statement, Nalline Clinic, San Francisco City Hall, October 1966)

Often, however, he slips from this routine. He uses too close to his day to appear at the clinic, so he doesn't appear. He makes an excuse to the parole agent, but this arouses the agent's suspicions, and he won't be allowed to do this regularly. After missing one or two appearances, he either jumps parole or is given a surprise test by his agent and is caught. If he jumps parole he tries to remain hidden. He stays indoors as much as possible and avoids "hot" locales except when he has to score, but he must "hustle" to support his drug use. He shoplifts, pimps, sells drugs or, "taps tills," and thus remains highly vulnerable to arrest.

If he is arrested without a new criminal charge or if the parole agent detects his drug use before he becomes immersed fully in the old bag, he may be sent to the Narcotics Treatment Control Unit at San Quentin or Chino for "dry out" and counseling. After a period of up to ninety days, upon the approval of the Adult Authority, he is returned to parole supervision. Often the cycle begins again. Sometimes he is returned to the NTCU two or three times but, eventually, if he continues to return to drug use, he will be arrested on a new charge and returned to prison or returned for a technical violation.

The head, although the pattern here is not so distinct, may not gravitate toward such a precarious and legally vulnerable routine. If his narcotics use is restricted to marijuana smoking, a return to its use does not constitute a drastic change in his routine. He usually establishes contacts with other heads from whom he obtains marijuana and perhaps with whom he shares a wide range of social activities. Other than this his life may remain orderly. He continues to work and shows no physical deterioration and confronts no problems from his use of marijuana, except the danger of being arrested for possession or sales of marijuana (as mentioned in chapter 1, all persons who use drugs and especially heads are guilty of sales as it is legally defined). Perhaps the most important change in his routine and his general posture is that his commitment to certain plans and goals becomes loosened and he becomes a less motivated, less active person.

Many heads, however, turn to the use of drugs which have a more profound physiological impact and result in more drastic behavior changes. For instance, the use of "speed" (methamphetamine) produces hyperactivity and, after continued use, severe reality distortion and paranoia symptoms. One's behavior becomes increasingly bizarre and erratic and the "speed" head is usually detected after the commission of a minor but highly visible crime. For example, one parolee in my sample after being out three months was arrested after he tried to pass a forged prescription. He had been turned down by two druggists and the third called the police. When they arrived he was walking slowly away from the drugstore and made no attempt to avoid arrest.

The thief's return to deviance is usually more careful and less obvious. He reestablishes contact with former partners or new partners from his prison peers. He begins to plan and execute "scores." Sometimes he does this with considerable caution and planning and maintains a carefully constructed "front"—a "shuck" job, a dual residence, and a generally conventional-appearing routine. He is sometimes able to avoid arrest, at least for some length of time. More often, however, he is rearrested for a new felony, usually burglary or armed robbery. The prison experience, instead of preparing him for crime, has made him a less efficient criminal. He is out of practice and out of date in criminal activities. His parole status makes him more vulnerable to arrest because (1) his presence is known to the police who use the parole agency as a source of information about possible law violators, (2) the parole agent in his contacts with the parolee—in particular his unannounced visits—is a constant threat to his secrecy, (3) if he comes under suspicion he does not have the usual constitutional guarantees against illegal search and seizure, and (4) if he severs relations with the parole agency and absconds, he is vulnerable to immediate arrest and subsequent investigation which may lead to the detection of new crimes.

Double Disappointment

The return to deviance is not always permanent. After turning away from the disappointments and failures of the straight path, toward the promise of fulfillment in the old bag, the deviant routine itself may prove to be a bigger disappointment. The financial and sexual rewards in most old bags are not abundant; they are, in fact, very skimpy. To make big money, in fact, just to earn a living at some hustle or at stealing is for most dope fiends, hustlers, and thieves, difficult, time-consuming, physically debilitating, and mentally depressing. There are many desperate and monotonous periods when finances are low or absent, when there is no place to sleep, no food, and nothing to do but hang around a pool hall, a bar, coffee shop, or street corner, waiting for something to come by, something to do, or some way to make money. The threat of going back to prison looms larger and larger and adds to the depression. Finally the deviant routine often has a profound impact on one's health and, therefore, his spirits. The use of alcohol, heroin, and methamphetamines especially undermine one's health and lead to periods of depression. Consequently for many, the return to deviance turns out to be worse than the unsatisfying conventional life they were attempting to pursue. At times, therefore, an ex-convict after returning to the old bag for a period will reattempt to straighten up his hand. This, of course, is difficult. Descent into the deviance has contingencies. He has usually made public pronouncements about his return to deviance and these must be retracted. He has possibly incurred financial, health, addiction, or alcohol problems which make the return to the conventional life difficult. If this is the case either extreme resolve or considerable outside aid is necessary. Sometimes the family is a source of this aid, less often the parole agency. It has happened that the agency, by placing a man in jail or the NTCU program for a dry out, does make it possible for him to straighten up his hand once more.

7

THE PAROLEE-AGENT SYSTEM

LEARNING THE SYSTEM

FROM THE PRISON

The expectant parolee becomes "socialized" into the parole social system throughout his prison experience.[1] He constructs a sketchy conception of the status and the structure of demands that can accrue to his forthcoming position from other convicts who have recently been on parole and who relate their experiences on parole and offer their interpretations of the parole system. Even if he has been on parole before there will have been changes since he was out with which he must become familiar.

As his release approaches the process of socialization becomes intense. He becomes active in setting up a program for himself on the outside—getting a job, a place to live, trying to locate other resources, money, a car, his driver's license, etc. Often his only resource for accomplishing this is the parole agency. In making his release plans, he is forced to give more consideration to the demands which will be made of him because of his parole status. His program must be approved by the particular district agency office in the locale where he plans to reside. From the prison a case summary, which discloses the parolee's planned residence and employment, is sent to the regional and the district office, where he is assigned to a particular parole agent. Then through relatives, friends or perhaps only the correctional counselor who handles prerelease cases at the prison, the parolee begins to communicate with his prospective agent. He learns who it is to be and makes inquiries in the yard about this agent. He learns that he is a "dog" or that he is "all right" from men who were under his supervision or had some indirect contact with him. The prospective parolee usually doesn't take these characterizations as conclusive, since he knows that parole violators usually impart an unduly grim description of parole and parole agents. Besides, he has learned from various stories that the agent-parolee relationship is a particularized one. The agent, it often seems, approaches each parolee differently.

1. The vast majority of convicts in California are released at least once on parole, so parole is an important phase in the career of the felon. In 1964, for example, of the 4,611 first releases, 92.4 per cent were released on parole, while only 7.6 per cent were discharged from prison. (Figures obtained from the Research Division, California Department of Corrections.)

In the last two months the prospective parolee comes into fairly intense interaction with the parole system. He attends preparole classes led by a person who is somewhat familiar with parole. The problems of parole are discussed. Often convicts who have had previous experience with parole dominate the discussion, since they speak with the authority of actual experience. Usually, since they are parole failures, they speak strongly against the parole system. On the other hand, agents from the field visit preparole classes and bring with them persons who have been on parole for some months or have been discharged from parole. They impart a less derogatory version of the parole routine and counterbalance the descriptions of the parole failures.

In preparole classes the "Conditions of Parole," the causes of parole failures ("violations"), and the opportunities for "making it" are the major topics. The parolee is given a seventeen-page pamphlet, "How to Live Like Millions," which gives general advice for the newly released and lists the conditions of parole and a brief interpretation of each.[2]

After Release

Upon release, as the first condition of parole, the parolee reports to the district office, for the "initial interview" with his parole agent. At this time he is further apprised of the conditions of parole. The agent reveals to him the particular program which has been approved for him. If he did not have a place of residence and job planned for himself, then the agent will inform him of the residence that he has tentatively established and the job or the routine for obtaining employment that the agent has planned—e.g., daily reporting to the California Department of Employment. At this interview the agent informs the parolee of the frequency and the types of agency contacts that he, the parolee, must fulfill. He also will inform him of special programs that he must participate in if these have been recommended by the Adult Authority or if the agent or supervisor feel they are called for. There are numerous special programs which are constantly being introduced, altered, and dropped by the parole division. Presently, a parolee can be assigned to (1) an out-patient clinic—usually on the recommendation of the Adult Authority following recommendations by the prison psychiatric staff—which offers group and individual psychotherapy on a weekly basis; (2) the nalline program—if there is a record of narcotics use other than marijuana—which involves a weekly or biweekly visit to the clinic located in a city building where the parolee receives a shot of nalline which will detect opiate use and is inspected for hypodermic needle marks by a physician; and (3) group counseling conducted weekly or monthly by the parole agent.

2. For a complete list of the conditions of parole, see the Appendix.

The actual contacts that the parolee makes with the agent after the initial interview vary with the type of supervision—"conventional" or "work unit"—and the classification within these types of supervision—A, B, or C. Usually the maximum number of personal contacts is one per week, but an agent may on his own discretion require more. Besides this, the agent is expected to make collateral visits—a phone or personal contact with someone other than the parolee about the parolee. In the beginning weeks when the parolee is getting settled in a job and residence, has financial difficulties, desires permission to drive, to leave the county, or to buy a car, he himself is apt to initiate frequent contacts with the agent, usually at the parole office. Furthermore, in the first month or so he can expect a surprise visit or two at his home or job. He may also come into contact with his agent at the regular group-counseling meetings and, if he is assigned to the nalline program, at the nalline clinic since two agents, in rotation, are present at each clinic.

Unless the parolee is having difficulties—employment difficulties or arrests—or has brought his agent's disapproval and closer surveillance in ways which will be discussed later, he can expect as time passes to have fewer and fewer contacts with the agent. The intensity of his supervision as it is formally structured may be reduced at regular intervals if the supervisor and agent agree. For instance, after three months of Conventional A supervision—which calls for two personal contacts per month, one of which must be in the field, and two collateral contacts—it may be reduced to Conventional B—which requires one personal and one collateral contact per quarter. After three years this may be reduced to Conventional C—which requires one personal field visit and one collateral contact every six months. Other than this, by the fifth of each month, the parolee sends in or delivers his monthly report, which gives information on residence, employment, income, savings, indebtedness, operation of motor vehicles, and his availability for interviews.

In the first few weeks, or perhaps months, the relationship between the agent and the parolee takes shape. Each sizes up the other and forms some conception of the other's orientation and performance in the parole system. The parolee "runs tests" on the agent—that is, he reveals bits of information about himself, his activities, his plans, or his wishes to see how the agent reacts. For instance, he mentions that he would like to move in with a girl or that he encountered a friend—an ex-convict—and waits for the agent's reaction. In this way, he forms a conception of his informal status. The agent likewise probes into the parolee's performance on parole. He checks to see if the verbal declarations of performance match the parolee's actual performance. He does this through collateral contacts with friends or relatives, through informal inquiries with police officers or other agents who might have accidental contact with the parolee, and through parolees who will supply information on other parolees.

THE PAROLEE STATUS

The parolee, in the first weeks or months, becomes cognizant of two characteristics of his parolee status. First, from his standpoint there are two levels of expectations. There is a set of expectations which originate from somewhere above—the formal expectations. These are contained in the conditions of parole, the expectations of the Adult Authority, and the administrators who make the rules. However, there is an informal status which is more important to him. This is constituted by the particular expectations of his parole agent and perhaps, if he has ever been pulled into interaction with a supervisor, those of the agent's superior. From various informal cues, possibly elicited in the tests he runs on the agent or perhaps from explicit definitions supplied by the agent, the parolee becomes familiar with the agent's orientation to parole work in general and to him in particular. The parolee learns that the agent has great discretion and can impose special conditions and restrictions and afford special liberties, all of which may narrow the limits set by the parole conditions or widen them considerably.

The second status aspect of which he becomes aware is that it is impossible or at best extremely difficult to live strictly within the limits set by the conditions of parole—the formal parole status. This proves difficult for various reasons: (1) In order to become viable, to meet the bare citizen exigencies it is often necessary to break some of the conditions. For instance, condition IX states that the parolee must have written permission from the parole agent before he may drive a motor vehicle. Before the agent can grant this permission, however, the parolee must show that he has a valid driver's license and bodily injury and public-damage insurance coverage (which is expensive for parolees since they are placed in a high-risk category). Often the parolee, before he can afford the insurance, must drive to maintain employment. One parolee in my sample lived in Martinez and obtained a job in Oakland, a distance of approximately 30 miles. His brother-in-law loaned him a car for transportation. When the agent discovered that the parolee was driving, he told him to get insurance right away. The parolee told him that he could not afford it that month, but would get it the next month, which he did. But for about six weeks he was in violation of the conditions of parole. Forty-seven per cent of those interviewed admitted that they drove a car before receiving written permission to drive.

Second, in some instances it is, in all practicality, impossible to live according to the conditions of parole. For instance, condition II states that the parolee must have permission to leave the county of residence. The San Francisco Bay Area is in many ways one large sprawling community which covers six counties—San Francisco, Marin, Contra Costa,

Alameda, San Mateo, and Santa Clara. A parolee may reside, work, and have his social activities in different counties. Usually when this is the case he receives blanket permission to travel within the Bay Area. In other cases this is not true. One parolee in my sample resided and worked in San Jose. His family and friends were all in his hometown San Francisco. He was told by his agent to get permission each time he wanted to travel to San Francisco, which he did each weekend and sometimes during the week. The parolee soon found that it was difficult to contact the agent for permission because the agent was seldom in the parole office, and after office hours, when the parolee usually decided to go to San Francisco, the agent could not be reached. The agent had told him that he could be contacted through the police department after office hours. The parolee tried this, but he wasn't able to locate anyone in the police department who knew the agent or had any idea how to get in contact with him. The parolee, with unusual persistence, told the agent of his unsuccessful attempts to reach him, and the agent responded that he hadn't talked to the right people in the police department. The parolee dropped the matter at this point, believing that the agent didn't intend to be contacted and didn't want to openly admit this. It is clear from the parolee's standpoint that it was impossible at times to get in touch with the agent and to fulfill the conditions as the agent had defined them.

Condition III states that it is necessary for the parolee to maintain gainful employment. For many parolees who are unskilled, members of racial minorities, older, or have no work history, maintaining employment is next to impossible, especially in times of high unemployment. The belief that "a man may find a job if he is willing to work" is part of the perspective from which the conditions of parole were written, but it is far from the reality experienced by many lower-class persons and ex-deviants.

Finally, most parolees carry a deviant identity into the parole setting. They were lower-working-class men, dope fiends, thieves, etc., before going to prison. The arrest, sentencing, and prison experience, it was shown, often served to both strengthen the commitment to one or another deviant identity and overlay it with the identity of the "con." The conditions of parole to these "ex-deviants" are not only difficult, but are virtually impossible to maintain, given their perspectives. This is especially true in cases where they return to a milieu in which deviant perspectives prevail. For instance, condition V states that the parolee "shall not use alcoholic beverages or liquors to an excess." Parolees who return to a lower-working-class milieu are often back in close interaction with wives, relatives, and friends who periodically "drink to an excess." Drinking in this milieu has a different meaning than it does from the perspective underlying the parole conditions.

Condition VIII states that the parolee "must avoid association with former inmates of penal institutions unless specifically approved by your parole agent, and you must avoid association with individuals of bad reputation." This as it is written is impossible to follow for a sizable proportion of parolees. Sixty per cent of those interviewed after a year indicated that they had violated this condition. Parolees, even the most conventionally oriented, make close friends in prison whom they usually plan to meet on the outside—if only for one or two short visits. More often, convicts make some lasting friendships which they intend to maintain. Furthermore, parolees often discover that other parolees are one of the best resources for finding jobs and residences and for supplying money, tools, and transportation which the recently released parolee desperately needs. Other parolees who are passing or have passed through similar difficulties and who are closer in all ways to the individual's problems are more willing and at times more able to extend help.

Beyond these more or less planned incidents of association, it would be virtually impossible for some parolees not to associate with ex-inmates or persons with bad reputations unless they went to live in a new city or perhaps a new state. These are persons who have been raised in locations such as the Negro or Mexican-American lower-class neighborhoods —the "ghettos"—where many of one's friends and relatives are either ex-convicts or persons who by conventional criteria are "individuals of bad reputation"; that is, they have long arrest records. One elderly Negro parolee who had returned to Folsom Prison to speak to a preparole class commented on "association":

> What do they mean don't associate with ex's and guys with bad reputations? I don't know nobody who hasn't done time or been arrested many times. Where I was raised and live now, in the ghetto, there ain't nobody that don't have a bad reputation. And where am I gonna meet new people? Is the parole officer gonna take me into his home and introduce me to his friends? (Field notes, Folsom Prison, July 1966)

Condition VI states "you may not possess, use, or traffic in any narcotic drugs." Many parolees do not share conventional society's abhorrence and fear of narcotics, especially marijuana. Of those who were willing to answer questions on drug use, 38 per cent agreed that the laws against the use of all narcotics were unnecessary and unjust, and 80 per cent believed that the laws against marijuana in particular were unnecessary and unjust. Persons who have had considerable contact with deviant subcultures and deviant practices believe that marijuana is a harmless and innocent drug, much less dangerous both to the person using it and others than alcohol. Some parolees believe that other drugs, such as the opiates, although they may be more harmful to the individual himself, would not be a problem to society if they were not illegal and therefore expensive. So, many parolees do not have strong beliefs and values which prohibit drug use, especially in the case of marijuana. The only reason they can see for abstaining is the fear of arrest, and this is not a good deterrent for people who in the past have gotten away with many minor law infractions. A significant number of parolees (39 per cent of those who offered to answer the question) admitted that they had used some illegal drug while on parole.

Disparate Perspectives of Agent and Parolee

These particular points of disagreement are merely a few indicators of a broad disparity between the perspective underlying the official definition of the parole status and the perspective of most parolees. The parole conditions reflect the influence of an extremely conservative and puritanical segment of society. It has been suggested that the state legislature and governmental agencies are extremely vulnerable to the "crusades" of "moral entrepreneurs."[3] In a study of the temperance movement Joseph Gusfield has demonstrated how these persons or groups operate in our society. He submits that they usually represent and emerge from "the old middle class," and see their way of life and, therefore, their status challenged by "modernists." To regain their status they work vigorously to realize the "symbolic" publication of their mores; that is, the enactment of norms into law without, necessarily, the instrumental enforcement of the norms.[4]

Because of their zeal and dedication and because of a tendency of the public to be stirred or cowed on issues involving "sin" and public "decency," these "moral entrepreneurs" have had considerable influence upon laws and official policies of agencies in matters related to drugs, sex, crime, and abortion. The legal and official status of the parolee has, therefore, been unduly influenced by a conservative and puritanical perspective.

This status has for its underpinnings several premises which are often not shared by many deviants and ex-deviants. Two of these premises are self-evident axioms: (1) society, i.e., the existing political organization and government agencies, the laws and the government institutions, are both necessary and "good" per se; and (2) this society, especially the existing political organization and government agencies, has the right to imprison some of its members for acts which it has outlawed, to deny the ex-prisoner full citizen rights, and to impose special restrictions upon him. Furthermore, the conditions are underpinned by the belief that to be a worthy member of the society and, therefore, to be allowed to remain a free person, the ex-felon must live according to a puritanical code of conduct—he must work steadily ("steady employment is an essen-

3. See Howard Becker, *The Outsiders* (New York: the Free Press, 1963), Chapter 8; Joseph R. Gusfield, "Social Structure and Moral Reform: Study of the Women's Christian Temperance Union," *American Journal of Sociology* (November 1955); and Joseph R. Gusfield, *Symbolic Crusade* (Urbana: University of Illinois Press, 1963).

4. Gusfield, *Symbolic Crusade,* Chapters 6 and 7.

tial for anyone's satisfactory adjustment in life"), not drink to excess ("it is conceded that total abstinence from the use of alcohol would benefit most parolees"), not use narcotics or dangerous drugs, not associate with persons of "bad" reputation, and conduct himself as a "good citizen." [5] The derivation of these conditions is not self-evident. It may be argued that instead of deriving from a moralistic code of conduct, these prescriptions and proscriptions are derived from purely pragmatic considerations aimed at reducing recidivism. For instance, it may be argued that association must be prohibited because contact with former peers or with other deviants—by the principle of differential association—promotes continued deviance. However, treatment theories exist which are based on association.[6] Also, legalization and controlled distribution of drugs have been offered as solutions for the problem of narcotics addiction.[7] It has usually been the case that only notions of treatment that are compatible with conservative moral precepts have influenced legislation and official policy of government agencies.

The perspective of deviants or ex-deviants is quite different from that which underlies the official status of the parolee. For instance, parolees often do not share the belief in the "goodness" of society or the existing social organizations, agencies, and persons filling positions in these organizations. Some deviants believe that conventional society, conventional people, legitimate businessmen, and public organizations are corrupt. Often they believe that the laws and the workings of the public agencies are part of a power struggle where the big and powerful are protecting what they have from the small and weak:

> Because Beverly Hills is full of all the biggest gangsters living up there on those hills with their plush pool and the Adult Authority associates with them, ya know. (Taped interview, May 1967)

They, the deviants or ex-deviants, do not feel that the conventional society, the dominant society, the government agencies, are "right":

> I'm not changing because I now feel that they are right and I was wrong. I have never felt that I was wrong. I will always feel that they were wrong. But now I'm tired of losing, I've been losing a long time. You can't beat them, so I'm going to get trying to win their way. (Interview, Soledad Prison, June 1966)

5. Quotations are from the conditions and their interpretations in *How to Live Like Millions,* California Department of Corrections.

6. Donald Cressey, "Changing Criminals: The Application of the Theory of Differential Association," *American Journal of Sociology,* Vol. LXI (September 1955); Rita Volkman and Donald Cressey, "Differential Association and the Rehabilitation of Drug Addicts," *American Journal of Sociology,* Vol. LXIX (September 1963); Lewis Yablonsky, *The Tunnel Back* (New York: The Macmillan Company, 1967).

7. Alfred P. Lindensmith, "Addiction: Beginnings of Wisdom," *The Nation,* 1963.

They return the dominant society's accusations of immorality:

"You've got your nerve! Don't you realize that you owe a debt to society?" My answer to all such thoughts lurking in their split-level heads, crouching behind their squinting bombardier eyes is that the blood of Vietnamese peasants has paid off all my debts; that the Vietnamese people, afflicted with a rampant disease called Yankees, through their sufferings—as opposed to the "frustration" of fat-assed American geeks safe at home worrying over whether to have bacon, ham or sausage with their grade-A eggs in the morning, while Vietnamese worry each morning whether the Yankees will gas them, burn them up, or blow away their humble pads in a hail of bombs—have canceled all my IOUs.[8]

Parolees (that is, the criminal parolees) have other definitions of good and proper conduct. Even those who have resolved to live a conventional life—resolved to "straighten up their hand" and to "make it" in terms of a conventional life—are in disagreement with the conditions of parole and tend to believe that it is all right to break many of the rules. From their viewpoint, the only restrictions the agency should impose are on extreme criminal behavior:

I'm not doing anything wrong. I'm not running down the street robbin' and hittin' people in the head. That's what they ought to worry about, those guys beating people in the head and killin' people. (Field notes, San Francisco, May 1966)

The System's Flaw

In effect, the parole social system has brought into close contact, in an agent-client relationship, two people who represent different social worlds—one, the parole agency, which is unduly influenced at the formal level by conservative segments of society; and the other, a deviant subsociety. Officially, the agent is to demand that the parolee live according to a set of conditions which originate from the dominant and conservative segments of society, membership in which is barred to and/or rejected by the parolee. The parolee, especially if he is an ex-criminal, usually returns to segments of society which, even though they be noncriminal, such as the lower working class, do not share the conservative perspective underlying these conditions. This is an inherent disrupting factor which must be withstood if any equilibrium in the system is to be achieved. Though both role incumbents are involved in dealing with this potential disruption, the degree to which each makes adjustments and the styles of these adjustments are usually dominated by the performance of the agent as it is seen by the parolee. To understand this performance we must look closely at some relevant characteristics of the agent's position in the parole agency.

8. Eldridge Cleaver, *Soul on Ice* (New York: McGraw-Hill, Inc., 1968), p. 18.

THE PAROLE AGENT STATUS

The agent is a member of an organization which has the two-fold purpose of controlling and treating parolees. These two goals have been recognized by many as inherently conflicting.[9] Furthermore, there are no concrete criteria of success in achieving either one of these goals. Takagi in a recent study of the California Parole Agency suggests that in the absence of any direct measurements of surveillance and treatment these two abstract goals have been converted into the more tangible goals of: (1) avoiding general public and police criticism for lax handling of parolees[10] and (2) producing a low proportion of returns to prison for violation of parole.[11] However, these two goals themselves have proven extremely difficult. Parolee behavior remains unpredictable and successful treatment procedures are lacking. The agency, therefore, remains somewhat vulnerable to criticism from various groups and organizations which have different interests and investments in society. Takagi contends that the top administrators of the agency have protected themselves to some degree by passing on to the parole agent and his supervisor the responsibility and accountability for accomplishing the conflicting goals.[12] In doing this, however, they have necessarily, in a system of formal and informal demands and expectations, passed great discretion to the lower levels of the agency (i.e., the agent and his immediate supervisor). The dimensions of this discretion and their consequences for the parolee are the focus here.

The Formal Demands

The formal tasks of the parole agent appear to be two-fold. First, information related to public safety and the rehabilitation of the felon is to be gathered and passed on, according to defined procedures, to the higher levels of the agency so that decisions can be made involving the intensification or reduction of parole supervision, the granting or taking away of civil rights and privileges, and changes in parole "programs," such as nalline and out-patient clinics:

Parole supervision is an integral part of the correctional process. It is by this means that the true purpose of parole is satisfied. Every effort is made to protect society from further transgressions on the part of the offender; while at the same time attempts are made to assist the parolee in becoming a self-sustaining,

9. Donald Cressey, "Prison Organizations," in James G. March, ed., *Handbook of Organizations* (Chicago: Rand McNally, Inc., 1965), pp. 1023–70.

10. Paul Takagi, "Evaluation and Adaptations in a Formal Organization (unpublished manuscript, School of Criminology, University of California), p. 96.

11. Ibid., pp. 157–61.

12. Ibid., pp. 41–42.

law-abiding, and contributing member of society. Through the medium of supervision, Division staff is able to develop case information that is used in future evaluations and decisions as the parolee moves through the parole experience. The information gathered is frequently of great benefit to other agencies which may become involved from time to time in reaching decisions in reference to their particular interest.[13]

Second, the agent is to actively penetrate the parolee's life, make certain decisions for the parolee, afford assistance, grant permissions, and enforce restrictions.

The agent must also do something for and with the parolee. Environmental aspects of parole supervision cover areas in which the agent may be called upon to do something for the parolee, such as assisting in locating employment, residence, or providing him with financial assistance on a loan basis. Case relationships cover the areas where the agent will do something with the parolee, such as establishing an atmosphere where he can come and discuss his problems in a permissive setting and expect to receive reasonable understanding, support and possibly assistance in resolving the problems presented.

The concepts of parole place the agent in the position of setting and enforcing controls for the parolee in relation to the established parole conditions, or Special Conditions added on the basis of the individual case dynamics. The greatest amount of case decision making is brought into play in parole supervision.[14]

The definition in the first class of tasks—gathering information and passing it on to higher levels—in many instances is fairly specific. For instance, if a man has been arrested or if he has been convicted of a crime, the *Parole Agent Manual* specifically states who should be notified and in what form they should be notified. In other instances, however, it is more difficult to be specific and there is considerable leeway for parole agent discretion. For instance, the manual states that the parole board shall be notified and shall make the decision in cases where the following behavior is involved: all aggressive conduct, including deviant sexual behavior; possession of a deadly or dangerous weapon; possession of or use of narcotics (excluding marijuana); employment of any commercial or fraudulent scheme on a large scale; any violation of a Special Condition of Parole, including condition 5B (prohibition on drinking); and a Special Category Case where there is an arrest or serious violation of parole.[15] In many instances, there is considerable room for interpretation of actual behavior related to the above descriptions. Takagi cites the following example:

On a routine field visit on a warm summer evening, the door of the parolee's residence was ajar; and I saw my parolee brandishing a kitchen knife and speaking angrily to his wife. According to the rules this would be considered violent

13. California Department of Corrections, *Parole Agent Manual*, PA-III-00.
14. Ibid., PA-III-000.
15. Ibid., PA-IV-12.

behavior and would have to be reported to the parole board; but I didn't. I said "Hello" to the parolee and politely inquired: "Lovers' quarrel?" They both grinned. I talked to him for awhile, and it turned out the wife was riding him for not getting a job. I handled it by asking the parolee to come by the office tomorrow to work out a job.[16]

In the second task area—"working with the parolee" (the informal agency label for this phase of parole work)—the definitions are less clearly spelled out. In the case of some recurring problems such as parolee indebtedness, revealing parole status to employers, credit, legal advice to parolees, and operation of vehicles, there are some general guidelines.[17] For many problems that emerge in working with the parolee, however, such as those related to residence, travel, common-law relations, homosexual relationships, and employment, the guidelines are completely lacking or vaguely drawn. For instance, in the case of travel restrictions, the manual states:

Frequently parolees have legitimate reasons for traveling; however, some parolees should not be allowed to travel. If the agent agrees travel is necessary, permission to travel may be granted.[18]

Though the manual is vague in outlining the content of working with the parolee, it is fairly specific in outlining the minimum frequency of contacts for each supervisory class of parolees, the recording and written tasks, and the frequency of case consultations and summarizations. These aspects, which Takagi has called "the standards," receive considerable emphasis, especially by the agent's direct supervisor.[19] The agent and the district supervisor are protected to some extent from public and police criticism if these tangible facets of their tasks have been fulfilled.

The Informal Demands

A set of informal demands and expectations operate within (and at times outside) these fairly broad limits of the formal status. According to Takagi, these vary from district to district. He found that some districts consistently send high proportions of their cases back to prison for "technical violations"—violations involving only the conditions of parole. He suggests that certain offices, which he calls "cop-oriented" offices, are dominated by less tolerant, less flexible supervisors, and the agent's discretion and the degree of liberality in the interpretation of rules and definitions is less in these districts.[20]

Although this suggests that the degree of liberality in enforcement of the conditions of parole varies from district to district, in general, a less

16. Takagi, "Evaluation," p. 103.
17. *Parole Agent Manual,* Chapter III.
18. Ibid., II-3.
19. Takagi, "Evaluation," p. 86.
20. Ibid., pp. 97–101.

than strict interpretation of them is expected at all offices. In some offices, a very liberal handling of parolees is encouraged. The supervisors stress: (1) meeting the standards, (2) the employment and arrest record of the parolee, and (3) maintaining good relations with local police agencies.[21] Beyond this it is generally felt that it is impossible to strictly enforce the conditions of parole and produce successful outcomes—low violation rates:

If I applied the rules, I imagine half my caseload would be in jail. The parole rules are utilized only as general guidelines.[22]

There has been increasing informal pressure from "headquarters" to expand the limits set by the conditions of parole. It has been the case for some time that a high violation rate on the part of a particular agent could precipitate an investigation from above. Recently, the agency introduced a new parole experiment which has resulted in considerably more pressure to liberalize the conditions of parole. In 1965, the agency was appropriated $1.25 million by the State Legislature to hire new parole agents for the work unit program—a more intensive supervision experiment. The legislature had been convinced that both goals—treatment and surveillance—would be more successfully achieved by reducing the caseloads of the parole agents. In December 1965, the agency was faced with its first indication of the effectiveness of the program in regard to violation rates. There was no difference between work unit cases and conventional cases in violation rates for the first six months.[23] In a meeting following the release of these research findings the chief of the agency recommended that the supervisors of work unit programs "get more mileage" out of their cases. He added that all future promotions would be influenced by reduction in technical violation rates.[24] This in effect was direct informal coercion for supervisors to enforce a less stringent interpretation of the conditions of parole.

Other Agent Concerns

Other than the formal and informal pressure to enforce a liberal interpretation of the conditions of parole, there are two major concerns of the parole agent which influence his conception of his status and affect his performance in regard to the parolee. First, he is expected by his district supervisor and the regional administrator to be "on top" of a case. That is, in the event of a "blow up," he must be "prepared to answer queries on a matter of community interest." [25] The pressure is off the agent in a case which blows up if his records demonstrate that the mini-

21. Ibid., pp. 86, 90, 96.
22. Ibid., p. 103.
23. Agency document, "Work Unit Evaluation," December 27, 1965.
24. Takagi, "Evaluation," p. 159.
25. Ibid., p. 96.

mum standards have been fulfilled, that is, the agent has made the minimum contacts, has noted in his ongoing case file important incidents, has reported these to the proper levels, and has some written indication in his records of assisting the parolee.[26] This is sometimes done retroactively.[27] The important aspect of this concern in regard to the ongoing parolee and agent relationship is that, *due to the fact that he must be prepared for a closer inspection of his work relative to particular parolees, the agent maintains a readiness to move toward a more stringent interpretation of the parole rules. Often this means a retroactive enforcement of the conditions of parole.*

The second concern of the parole agent which influences his relationship with the parolee is that, in general, agents strongly desire to have their recommendations accepted by the parole board. Takagi found that 78 per cent of the agents questioned agreed that it matters a great deal whether the parole board follows their recommendations.[28] The reasons for this are not clear, since the parole board in California has no administrative control over the agency. The result, however, is a tendency for the agents to "bank" incidents of violations of the conditions of parole. The agents have discovered that the board, which also has demonstrated a concern for reducing the technical-violation rate, will not allow a man to go back to prison for a single or a few minor technical violations. Therefore, the agent tends to prepare for the possibility of building a strong case. He mentally notes or records in his daily log behavior which is in violation of the conditions of parole. For instance, an agent told me of incidents of association on the part of particular parolees. He stated that he wasn't going to do anything about this now, but if the parolee "gets into trouble" in conjunction with other parolees, he was going to include *association* in the violation report. The agents justify this procedure with the contention that the behavior which they have tolerated at the time, but have banked, will never precipitate the violation. It is always something more serious. They state that they are forced into doing this because (1) when they recommend that parole be suspended they have to build a strong case and (2) when they submit a violation report they must protect themselves by reporting other instances of violation which they had tolerated at the time, but now that the case is being reviewed more closely might not be tolerated by the board. This procedure, although some admitted that they didn't like it, is necessary in view of the system of demands made upon them.

In review, the main characteristics of the agent status which have an impact upon the parolee-agent relationship are (1) the agent is permitted in a formal system, and encouraged further in an informal system, to exercise great discretion and to enforce a liberal interpretation of the

26. Ibid., p. 94.
27. Ibid., pp. 92-93.
28. Ibid., p. 156.

conditions of parole; (2) he maintains a readiness to move to a strict interpretation of the conditions of parole in the case of certain emergencies; and (3) he deems it necessary by his conception of the parole board expectations to "bank" many potential rule violations and sometimes charge the parolee with these retroactively in violation reports. For the most part, therefore, parole agents, although there is quite a bit of variation among individual agents on this dimension, orient themselves somewhere between the official perspective and the perspective of the parolee. Unless some special event or events occur which result in the agent shifting towards the official perspective, he expects a performance which is less stringent and closer to the parolee's conception of how he is able to perform.

Limits on the Intensity of Supervision

One other more or less constant characteristic of the agent's position is important to the parolee's orientation: the agent cannot know what the parolee is doing most of the time. He cannot survey his client twenty-four hours a day. This is true in the maximum-security prison setting where there is up to one employee for every four convicts and is certainly true where each agent has a caseload of approximately thirty-five for work-unit agents and seventy for conventional-unit agents. Though the intensity will vary with the particular performance of each agent, the size of the caseload, and the emphasis in different supervisory programs (such as work-unit supervision *vs.* the conventional supervision), there is a limiting factor inherent in parole work—a strict enforcement of the conditions of parole and a full knowledge of the day-to-day activities of the individual parolee are impossible.

IMPORTANT VARIABLES IN THE PAROLEE-AGENT SYSTEM

The Agent Orientation from the Parolee's Standpoint

The parolee covers the remainder of the distance between the official perspective and his own perspective. The manner in which he does this varies with several dimensions. First it depends largely on his conception of his particular agent's orientation and/or performance. The agent's position is one in which a great deal of variation in approach has been formally and informally invited. Several writers have attempted to relate this variation to certain dimensions of the personal orientation of the agent. For instance, Ohlin, Piven, and Pappenfort distinguished three styles of agent performance and related these to three conceptions of parole work:

(1) The "punitive officer" is the guardian of middle-class community morality; he attempts to coerce the offender into conforming by means of threats and punishment and his emphasis is on control, protecting the community against the offender, and systematic suspicion of those under supervision.

(2) The "protective agent"—vacillates between protecting the offender and protecting the community. His tools are direct assistance, lecturing, and praise and blame. He is recognized by his ambivalent emotional involvement with the offender and others in the community as he shifts back and forth in taking sides with one against the other.

(3) The "welfare worker" . . . [with the] ultimate goal the improved welfare of the client, a condition achieved by helping him in his individual adjustment within limits imposed by the client's capacity. He feels that the only genuine guarantee of community protection lies in the client's personal adjustment since external conformity will be only temporary and in the long run may make a successful adjustment more difficult. Emotional neutrality permeates his relationships. The diagnostic categories and treatment skills which he employs stem from an objective and theoretically based assessment of the client's situation, needs, and capacities . . . [29]

Daniel Glaser has adopted this scheme, but has added a fourth type—the passive agents who see "their jobs as sinecures, requiring only a minimum effort." [30] He also changes the label and the description of the protective agent to the "paternal officer" which better fits, he suggests, persons in "corrections whose abilities derive mainly from experience, dedication, and a warm personality, rather than formal training." [31] His expanded and slightly revised scheme is derived logically by crossing two variables—emphasis on control and emphasis on assistance:

Emphasis on Assistance	Emphasis on Control: High	Emphasis on Control: Low
High	Protective Agent	Welfare Worker
Low	Punitive Agent	Passive Agent

29. Lloyd Ohlin, Herman Piven, and Donnell M. Pappenfort, "Major Dilemmas of the Social Worker in Probation and Parole," *National Probation and Parole Association Journal*, Vol. II, No. 3 (July 1956), as quoted in Daniel Glaser, *The Effectiveness of a Prison and Parole System* (Indianapolis: The Bobbs-Merrill Company, Inc., 1964).

30. Glaser, *The Effectiveness of a Prison and Parole System*, p. 431.

31. Ibid.

Takagi has recently devised a new scheme based upon modes of adapting to the particular pressures and conflicts which are inherent in the parole-agent status. He describes four types:

1. The "rebels" who dissipate most of their energies fighting the agency. These workers find themselves in conflict with the agency rules and their supervisors. Such agents believe that the organizational rules and procedures are silly and hamper their best efforts, and they criticize the supervisors for lack of knowledge and competence.
2. The "accommodator" also experiences severe frustrations and conflicts, but primarily in the area of providing services to the client. This is the agent who is committed to his profession and to the ideology of treatment which he believes can be implemented in an administrative structure . . . [and] attempts to work within the framework of organizational policies and administrative relationships.
3. The "noncommitted" whom parole agency administrators refer to as "bodies filling positions in the organization." His work style is guided by task objectives and ignores the goals of the organization. He is neither oriented toward the needs of the client nor the needs of the supervisor. He is thoroughly familiar with the routines of the job; and he can be depended upon to do the minimum; that is, eight hours of work for eight hours of pay.
4. Finally, the "conformist" who does not find himself in conflict with agency rules and procedures. He works within the framework of the administrative structure to achieve task objectives as well as the officially stated goals of the organization.[32]

None of these types are especially useful in explaining the different forms of parolee adaptation to the agent-parolee system. This is because these types are constructed from variables which (1) result in differences in parole-agent behavior which are not visible to the parolee and (2) are related to differences in agent behavior which though visible to the parolee are not important to him. For instance, in their actual performance in regard to the parolee it has been pointed out that persons with a "social-worker" orientation are in effect more "punitive" than "cop-oriented" parole agents.[33] An officer who is concerned primarily with the welfare of the parolee and has a treatment orientation to parole work can still be very intolerant of deviant behavior. Persons trained in social welfare usually have middle-class orientations and have often had much less contact with deviant subcultures than, say, an ex-policeman. Furthermore, other writers have suggested that authority can be a "treatment" tool.[34] Consequently, the treatment-punishment dichotomy does not

32. Takagi, "Evaluation," pp. 113–14.

33. Robert Carter, "San Francisco Project" (manuscript, School of Criminology, University of California, Berkeley).

34. Elliot Studt, "Worker-Client Authority Relationships," *Social Work*, Vol. IV, No. 1 (January 1959).

make a meaningful division in parole-agent behavior relative to the parolee.

Takagi's types are based upon the agent's orientation to the agency, not the parolee and, therefore, have very little to do with differences in agent-parolee relationships. When California parole agents were asked to choose "return to prison" or "continue on parole" in ten test cases, there was less than a 5 per cent difference between Takagi's four types.[35] In the same test, there was a 12.6 per cent difference between different positions in the agency—regional or headquarters, district supervisor, agent-grade II, agent-grade I—a 9.2 per cent difference between parole regions, and at least a 24 per cent difference between district offices.[36]

Furthermore, these particular schemes, which are based on variables related to ideologies of parole work and modes of adaptation to the frustrations of agent status, are not equipped to classify a wide variety of patterns of parole work which are related to many different variables (e.g., personality variables).

Variables Important to the Parolee

Three variables in parole-agent performance seem to this writer to be most important in effecting modes of parolee adaptation to the parole system. These are (1) the intensity of supervision, (2) the tolerance of the agent, and (3) the "rightness" of the agent. The *intensity* refers to the degree (from the parolee's standpoint) to which the agent penetrates the parolee's life. In part this comes from the frequency of contact initiated by the agent and the style of these contacts—e.g., were they arranged or surprise contacts and were they at home, at work, or some other social setting. It also is related to the pervasiveness of the supervision. Elliot Studt has suggested that the parole status is pervasive in the parolee's life:

> The parolee transitional status differs from many others in that it is a legally established social position that is pervasive in his life rather than intermittent, influencing and setting bounds upon all the roles available to him.[37]

Though this is theoretically true, in actual practice in the parolee-agent system the pervasiveness varies considerably. For instance, some agents never go to the parolee's work establishment because they do not want to embarrass the parolee. One agent told me of an incident in which he visited the parolee's home and found him in the company of several other adult men. Although he suspected that some of them might be

35. Takagi, "Evaluation," p. 118.
36. Ibid., pp. 147, 149, 150.
37. "The Reentry of the Offender into the Community," U.S. Department of Health, Education and Welfare, No. 9002 (1967).

parolees or ex-felons, he didn't ask them or the parolee. In fact, he took the parolee aside without publicly disclosing his own agent status, talked to the parolee briefly and left. He informed me that he did not feel that he had the right to penetrate the parolee's various social relationships. Another agent, upon encountering one of his parolees at nalline clinic, told him that he would like to give him a ride home. The parolee informed him that a girlfriend had brought him and was waiting for him outside. The agent, thereupon, insisted that the parolee wait for him because he wanted to meet the girlfriend. He went to the car after finishing his clinic duties, met the girl, made many personal inquiries, and then insisted that they all proceed to the parolee's room to see if he was living at the address the parolee had given him or if the girl had moved in with him. Clearly these agents pervade or obtrude into the parolee's life to a markedly different degree.

Tolerance is the parolee's conception of the agent's willingness to condone or ignore behavior which is deviant according to the parole conditions, conventional morality, and in some cases legal norms. Although agents tend to range on a scale from tolerance to intolerance, there are of course many different dimensions of tolerance. For instance, some agents tolerate common-law relationships, but may be very strict on some other behavior, such as association. The parolee will generally learn these particular variations in his agent's tolerance and will orient himself toward the agent by some conception of the agent's general tolerance.

Rightness is a complex concept related to the criminal's conception of high moral character, a "man." It includes the dimensions of being fair, keeping one's word, being dependable, and treating others (the parolee) with respect. An agent who squares with the parolee "in front"—that is, explicitly tells him what he is going to expect and what he will do in the case of various eventualities—who sticks by his guns, does not back down when superiors or other persons, such as policemen, put pressure on him, can be counted on for some assistance or at least when he promises assistance, fulfills his promise, is "all right." This concept is independent of punitiveness, tolerance, and intensity. The intense, intolerant agent can still be "all right" if he is "man." The main reason that this dimension is important to the parolee's own orientation is that it is related to the degree that the parolee feels he can predict the agent's behavior. With an agent who is "all right" the parolee "knows where he stands."

The following diagram indicates how some of the agent types described by others relate or fail to relate to these three variables—tolerance, intensity, and rightness:

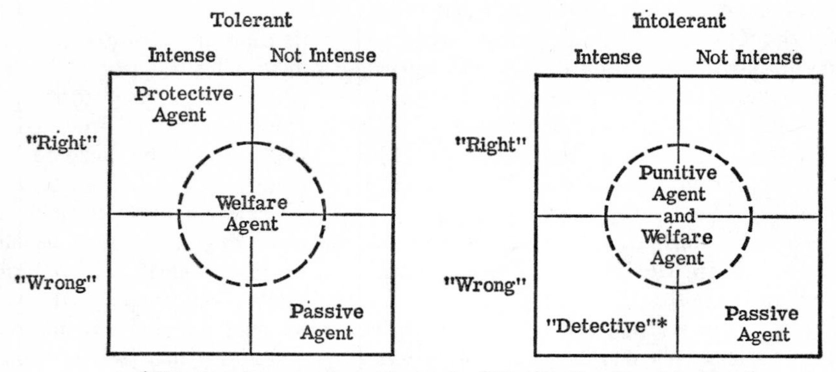

*This is a type suggested to me by Elliot Studt. The detective is concerned primarily with uncovering the deviations of his client.

Parolee Performance

According to these three dimensions, the parolee who does not jump parole, is not rearrested for a new felony and recommitted soon after release, and for a while at least achieves a working relationship with his agent, varies by three aspects in his own performance: (1) the amount and kinds of deviant behavior he will engage in (of course, these vary greatly if the parolee has decided to "make it" in terms of an essentially deviant or criminal style or an essentially "conventional" style); (2) the degree of deceit he will practice in his interaction with the agent; and (3) the amount of distance he will maintain from his agent.

The "successful" parolee (that is, the parolee who at least temporarily appears to be successful to the agent and agency), presents a performance which falls within the agent's tolerance limits. Those activities which are outside these limits are kept from the agent by deceiving him or by maintaining distance. For instance, if the parolee decides to live with a woman and believes that the agent will not tolerate this, he deceives the agent by renting a room which he does not actually use and placing some clothes and personal belongings there. Or he may just depend on distance, and he lives with a girl and does not tell the agent. If the agent visits the parolee while the woman is there, the parolee will offer no explanation unless the agent pursues the matter. The following ex-felon generally maintained distance from his agent:

He was just like a cop. I think he wanted to be a cop instead of a parole officer. He visited me regular. He used to meet me after work. Everyone knew he was a cop. Even when I had my car, he didn't know I had my car. He gave me a ride home one time and I had to take the bus back to get my car. I wasn't going to tell him anything. He didn't deserve to know. In fact I did all the things you aren't supposed to do, except I mean really get into trouble. I didn't get into any trouble. I wasn't supposed to drink at all. I was really supposed to abstain. I drank. I left the county. I phoned him one time for permission. They give you an argument, you know? Why? Is it really necessary and such things like that? There's no use telling them, you know. But just don't get in any trouble, you know. (Taped interview, April 1967)

For most parolees the most desirable agent is the nonintense, tolerant, and "all right" agent. The parolee can maintain distance and in regard to highly visible deviations he does not have to engage in so much deceit. He may, therefore, proceed in his everyday activities with maximum liberty. Furthermore, since the agent is "all right" the parolee feels that he can "level" with the agent when he has a problem and obtain a little assistance when he needs it.

The agent who is perceived to be intense, tolerant, and "all right" is not too difficult to adjust to. Some parolees, in fact, prefer and/or respond better to this relationship. It usually means that the parolee will have to reduce his deviations since, though the agent is tolerant, there is still a great deal of behavior—behavior that parolees "normally" engage in—outside the agent's tolerance limits. However, maintaining limits less than the parolee's own idea of what he should do or likes to do reduces the probability that he go off the "deep end"—be arrested or be caught up in some deviant dynamic, such as drug addiction, which leads to ever-increasing deviance. Furthermore, to many parolees this relationship can add meaning and importance to their lives. The agent can become a significant other whose approval is sought and when received is rewarding. He also can be one of the few or only connections with "educated people" or people who "have made good," who appears to have a better understanding of the world in general and who is more polished in social skills.

Perceived intolerance in the agent's orientation requires the maintenance of greater distance and more deceit. Intolerance coupled with intensity puts the parolee in the most difficult position. If any equilibrium is to be maintained, he must reduce his deviant activities greatly, which may greatly curtail and/or obstruct his pleasureful, satisfying, or meaningful experiences and relationships. This in turn may lead to his "blowing up."

Perceived wrongness in any of the combinations results in increased distance and deceit. The unpredictability and the agent's contempt toward him increase his fear, anxiety, and anger, and, perhaps, his tendency to "blow his parole"—to stop reporting and to go back to the deviant activities he engaged in formerly.

A successful adjustment to the system (that is, the maintenance of the proper amounts of deceit, distance, and deviance) will result, as time goes by, in the gradual reduction of the intensity of supervision and perhaps an increase in tolerance. It is also true, however, that the amount of assistance that can be expected is reduced. The "meaning," the support, the understanding, or other benefits that the parolee was receiving from the parolee-agent relationship diminish as well.

STUMBLING

There is a common relationship which does not fit this model of equilibrium. This is the "stumbling" relationship. Some parolees, often alcoholics and older, unskilled men who have extreme difficulty in finding and maintaining employment, cannot or do not try to hide their deviance and their failures. Instead they are very frank with the agent, carry all their troubles to him, and depend upon him for assistance in "solving their problems" and in meeting the bare exigencies of living, such as finding food and shelter. In presenting themselves to the agent as having no or too little self-control to contain their own deviance and insufficient resources to maintain themselves, they transfer to him the responsibility for controlling their behavior and locating funds, employment, and housing. In doing so they gain increased freedom to deviate. The agent, however, is left with the time-consuming and difficult task of solving the recurring crises of these men, placing them in jail to "dry out," and finding them new employment, housing, and funds. These men take up a disproportionate amount of his time and efforts and usually, after tolerating and "working with them" for some length of time, he will place them in jail and recommend that they be returned to prison or abandon them—which usually means ushering them to skid row to dereliction and ignoring them until they are rearrested for something serious, until they stop reporting and become "parole violators at large," or until they finish the parole period without something serious transpiring and are discharged.

THE FRAGILITY OF THE SYSTEM

Except in the few cases where the parolee has a strong commitment to conventional norms and has no "problem," such as alcoholism or sexual perversion which he cannot control, the equilibrium established in the parolee-agent relationship is precarious. This is because (1) the amount and types of deviant behavior in which the parolee engages remain beyond the limits of the official system and often beyond the legal limits of the community and (2) the actual performance of the parolee, although he has a tolerant agent and is successful in presenting a deceitful performance which is within the informal limits set by the agent, is usually outside the agent's tolerance limits. Because of this inherent flaw in the system, it remains fragile until the parolee is discharged. At any time a minor event may shatter it. This may mean a return to prison through cancellation of parole or a new prison sentence, a short disruptive stay in city jail—which results in loss of employment, perhaps loss of a particular employment career—or at least a major reorganization of his parole status—a change of residence, perhaps a move back into a halfway house, a change of jobs, assignment to special programs, such as the nalline clinic, the out-patient clinic, or group counseling. This reorganization almost always results in greatly increased intensification and decreased tolerance. This of course introduces new strains in the system.

Disruption of the System

Agent precipitation. The disruption of the system, which always involves a shift in the definitions operative in the system, can be precipitated and proceed in several different ways. First the agent, because of some discovery, some event or a spontaneous reevaluation, changes his conception of the parolee's performance. He believes that the parolee has stepped over the boundaries. Some event or behavior is brought to his attention or the parolee is arrested and the agent sees through the screens of deceit and distance erected by the parolee. When this occurs the agent usually conducts an investigation—he searches the parolee, searches his room, makes inquiries, questions employers, relatives and friends, and discovers a great deal of behavior that is beyond the official and his own limits of tolerance and rediscovers or reassesses behavior which he had been aware of and perhaps had tacitly or openly approved but which now, in light of his new evaluation, takes on new contours. Sometimes the investigation uncovers criminal acts, such as possession of drugs or drug paraphernalia, or possession of a weapon.

Depending on the agent's conception of the seriousness of the discoveries or the original information which precipitated the reassessment, different levels of the agency or different agencies, such as the police, are brought into the case. For certain behavior, such as those mentioned earlier (aggressive conduct, possession of a deadly or dangerous weapon, possession of or use of narcotics, etc.), or for crimes which result in a sentence of ninety days or more, the Adult Authority must make the final case decision. In cases where the parolee receives a sentence of from thirty to eighty-nine days, the regional administrator must make the final decision. Other than these, the case is in the hands of the agent, or the agent and the district supervisor. They, in turn, may decide to notify the Adult Authority and recommend continuance or discontinuance or reorganize the parolee's status themselves.

In any of these cases, however, the perspective which is operative is closer to the stricter official perspective of the agency. Because of the new discoveries and/or the reassessment, the parolee is called upon to answer to a set of conditions much more severe than those which were operative in the ongoing relationship with the agent. Importantly, not only is he now held responsible for behavior which he had kept hidden and which was discovered when the agent suddenly increased the intensity (i.e., investigated the parolee's life), but he is now held responsible for behavior which he believed, perhaps accurately, the agent had condoned.

Outside precipitation. A second manner in which the agent-parolee equilibrium can be disrupted and the definitions shifted is when the agent does not change his conception of the parolee's performance, but in view of the possible intrusion of demands and expectations from other sources, shifts his performance toward the parolee. Because the deviant acts of the parolee have become visible or are in danger of becoming visible to persons other than the agent and because of shifts in department formal or informal policies, the agent deems it necessary to protect himself by moving toward the official perspective. For instance, when the parolee, who has been given verbal approval to drive but was warned that the agent could not "back him up" is involved in an accident, the agent may write a violation report for driving without permission. When an incident such as this occurs and there is a possibility of closer scrutiny of the parolee's behavior by other members of the agency or the parole board, the agent often includes in his reports or consultations with superiors a great deal of behavior in violation of the conditions which he had implicitly or explicitly condoned and had banked for emergencies. The result is that the parolee, after thinking that he had achieved a working equilibrium and was meeting the minimum demands and expectations of the parole agent, finds that the structure of his status has shifted, sometimes retroactively.

Change of agents. A third way that the system can be threatened is from a change of parole agents. This can be quite serious to a parolee who has settled into a relationship with an agent who was tolerant and not intense and is then placed under the supervision of an intense and intolerant agent. To reestablish equilibrium he must make major revisions in his performance. This can be especially difficult as many parolees confuse the informal status—the expectations that emerge in their interaction with the particular agent—with the formal status. The tightening of restrictions and the intensification of surveillance which follows the change of the parole agent may seem extremely unfair and precipitate action which introduces additional strains in the new relationship. Furthermore, the new agent, in his more intense orientation, may discover intolerable deviant acts upon the part of the parolee which may or may not have been known by the former agent. The parolee is vulnerable to these discoveries because he has adjusted to the other agent's performance.

On the other hand, some parolees will suffer from shifts in the opposite direction. When they have adjusted to an intense relationship, whether it is tolerant or intolerant, it is possible that they may become dependent upon the agent's close supervision for various kinds of support. When this is withdrawn because of change of agents, the readjustment may be difficult.

THE SENSE OF INJUSTICE

When the system is disrupted and the parolee finds himself being judged and punished by a different set of standards than were operative in the ongoing relationship with the agent, when he finds himself being charged retroactively for acts which he feels were condoned by the agent, and when he discovers his agent acting differently toward him, apparently because of acts which the agent knew about all along, the parolee almost always emerges with a feeling that he received "a dirty deal." From his point of view, the system was rigged against him:

> They have that parole system set up to make you fail. I guess they have business going in this state and once they get you hooked into the system they don't want to let you go. They release you from the institution with a line on you and after a while they give it a jerk and you find yourself back. (Field notes, San Quentin, October 1966)

Even parolees who have committed new offenses often express bitterness and feelings of injustice towards "the system." Perhaps one of the most important unintended consequences of the operations of the parole agency is this sense of injustice. The agency, in attempting to pursue the two abstract and possibly conflicting goals of treatment and surveillance, and in attempting to impose, with great inconsistency, a conservative and moralistic behavior code on persons uncommitted to conventional values, has espoused a system to which the parolee must employ deceit and distance to adjust and in which the parolee remains in danger of being judged by a double standard and being charged *ex post facto* for acts which had been tolerated. This often produces or increases a sense of injustice and a further loss of commitment to conventional society. If it is believed that an increased commitment to conventional beliefs and values and an increased allegiance to society's institutions and agencies is a desirable and necessary goal in the rehabilitation of felons, then these sources of a mounting sense of injustice should be inspected more closely.

8

SUCCESS OR FAILURE

One of the chief objectives of the imprisonment of felons is their reformation. Ideally, changes are to be effected so that the felon will not continue to commit law infractions when he leaves prison. There is, of course, little agreement on exactly what changes will accomplish this reformation or how these changes are to be brought about, and sociologists have emphasized changes in criminal values:

> The central task of penal administration is to effect changes in the criminal value system of the imprisoned inmates.[1]

In measuring the success of any prison program, however, the chief and often the only indicator of reformation has been recidivism. The shallowness and possible invalidity of this measurement has been recognized. However, no workable alternative has appeared. Because of its clarity and because of administrative convenience, the statistically simple variable—rate of recidivism or rate of "lock up"—remains the chief measurement of reformation. For instance, in evaluating the effectiveness of a California special "treatment" program—PICO—Stuart Adams chose "return to custody" or "lock up" as the chief criterion of postprison performance because it

> appeared to be the best available indicator of quality of adjustment over the long term. It has the statistical virtues of a linear scale. It lends itself to the development of a weighted index based on qualitative institutions. Finally, it yields a realistic estimate of the economic gains or losses in a particular treatment process.[2]

Furthermore, in most studies related to reformation or postprison behavior, ex-felons have been divided, usually by the criterion of recidivism, into two groups—successes or failures. Again this is usually done for the sake of statistical crispness:

> To permit brief generalizations, it is convenient to classify released prisoners as either "successes" or "failures" with reference to their reformation. Such classifi-

1. Lloyd Ohlin, "Modification of the Criminal Value System," *Sociology and the Field of Corrections* (New York: Russell Sage Foundation, 1956), p. 29.

2. "The Pico Project," in Norman Johnston, et al., *The Sociology of Punishment and Correction* (New York: John Wiley & Sons, Inc., 1962), p. 215.

cation makes the statistical statements and tables in this book less complex than they otherwise would be.[3]

Glaser recognizes the shallowness of dichotomizing postprison performance in this way:

Nevertheless, the practice of merely dichotomizing post-release performance hides a tremendous amount of variation. Each case is unique in some respect, and the most intriguing details will be overlooked if one presses too hard for simple conclusions.[4]

He attempts to expand this classification and supply several types of successes and failures. However, his classification is somewhat lacking, mainly because of the inapplicability of several of his concepts—especially reformation and recidivism.

Reformation

When evaluating the postprison behavior of felons, criminologists often approach the area with a notion of reformation which is unrealistic, at least when applied to the criminal segment of the population of felons. What is expected or hoped for in reformation is a basic shift in values; i.e., the felon should return to conventional or law-abiding values. This is implied in Ohlin's definition of the central task of the prison administration:

This task involves the additional problem of devising methods for giving equal or greater legitimacy to the conventional value system represented by the administrative staff.[5]

Prison administrators have a similar but slightly more conservative model of reformation. "Penitence" is deeply imbedded in their notion in spite of the recent lip service paid to "treatment." The model ex-convict seems to be one who pursues a life of hard work for which he has been prepared by learning a trade in prison and who spends his remaining years penitent, puritanical, respectful of authority, and industrious, but not ambitious.

Neither of these ideals are realizable. The criminal very often changes his life, refrains from the type of criminal life he once followed; but he does not become a "square"; that is, he does not completely take on conventional values. The following comments were made by an ex-convict who had been out of prison and working for thirteen years with only one arrest for a minor misdemeanor:

3. Daniel Glaser, *The Effectiveness of a Prison and Parole System* (Indianapolis: The Bobbs-Merrill Company, Inc., 1965), p. 54.

4. Ibid.

5. Ohlin, "Modification of the Criminal Value System," p. 29.

I'm no less a thief than the day I went to prison. Let's say I don't have the nerve I once had. I still have a great desire to be a millionaire but not the nerve to take the chance.

You see, for me it was easy to steal. I don't mean that I am a kleptomaniac. You see, I don't think it's wrong to steal. I recognize the fact that if I am caught I will go to prison. I know that. I've also learned something I didn't know when I was young. I've learned the difference between pettiness . . . I've learned not to steal small things. Now something that is worth stealing isn't available to me. I guess that's the only reason that I'm not a thief now.

You must be yourself and you must see the whole thing, you must see it clearly. You must see—and you must understand yourself. You must know that you can't continue . . . if you continue to live your life the way you lived it before, then you stand a chance of going back to prison. If you want to stay out of prison you've got to find some other way to live your life. You can't be a flag waver, you never will be again. No convict will ever be a flag waver.

Fear makes us honest. Fear has made me an honest man. Fear and inopportunity have made me an honest man. That's what makes you honest. (Taped interview, May 1967)

Criminal ex-convicts do "straighten up their hands," but they do not approach the model of the reformed man held by behavioral scientists or prison administrators. In straightening up their hands, they refrain from the repeated commission of felonies of which society is especially intolerant. They discontinue being what *they* believe is a threat to society. However, they often continue to commit some felonies—felonies which they perceive as safe, such as receiving stolen property and marijuana use—and many misdemeanors, such as shoplifting. They maintain a latent criminal identity which prevents them from becoming a "flag waver" and from acting in certain instances as a conventional person, and which at times obtrudes into present situations and influences their behavior. For instance, on his job when a fellow worker deeply insulted him and then hit him with his fist, the ex-convict who made the statements above struck his coworker with a pipe and put him in the hospital. On another occasion, after being promoted to a foreman's position he was called into the supervisor's office and questioned about activities of some of his men. He refused to supply any information, telling the supervisor that he couldn't be a "stool pigeon."

Recidivism

An ex-convict who straightens up his hand is to some extent still highly vulnerable to reimprisonment, especially during his parole period. After completing his parole he still remains more vulnerable to arrest than the average square john because he tends to commit some felonies and misdemeanors.

It must be remembered that recidivism—return to prison—is ultimately an agency or court decision. It may or may not be related, in particular cases, to differential criminal activity. Ex-convicts who have straightened up their hands are returned to prison and others who have continued in their deviant modes are not. The strength of the relationship between recidivism and "crookedness" will not be estimated here, but it must be emphasized that it is far from a one to one relationship.

Success

Success as merely not returning to prison obscures a wide range of life successes and failures. An ex-convict who gravitates to skid row and lives out a short life characterized by alcoholism, ill-health, and short city-jail sentences is classified as a success by this measure. The dimensions of dignity, fulfillment, achievement of life goals, or level of gratification are not included in this measure of success.

Glaser attempts to rectify this by expanding the dichotomy into a typology with four major categories and fourteen categories in all:

"Success" Cases:
- Clear Reformation
  - (a) Late reformation after criminal career
  - (b) Early reformation after criminal career
  - (c) Crime-facilitated reformation
  - (d) Reformation after crime interval
  - (e) Reformation after only one felony
  - (f) Crime-interrupted noncriminal career
- Marginal Reformation
  - (a) Economic retreatism
  - (b) Juvenile retreatism
  - (c) Addictive retreatism
  - (d) Crime-contacting noncriminality
  - (e) Nonimprisoned criminality

"Failure" Cases:
- Marginal Failure
  - (a) Defective-communication cases
  - (b) Other nonfelony violations
- Clear Recidivism
  - (a) Deferred recidivism
  - (b) Immediate recidivism[6]

This typology, however, is still based on phenomenologically false conceptions of reformation, and other dimensions of success and failure only impinge upon it tangentially. The "Marginal Reformation" categories, those who are "only marginally pursuing a noncriminal life," include descriptions of life styles which seem to be failures by other criteria of success and failure. But this is only implicit in his typology. Furthermore, though his scheme does include *criminal* "successes" (that is, persons who

6. Glaser, *The Effectiveness of a Prison and Parole System*, p. 55.

have not been returned to prison though they are pursuing criminal careers), it does not take into consideration those "failures" (returned to prison) who had, in fact, straightened up their hands.

In this chapter a typology of postprison careers will be offered which approaches the subject with an entirely different viewpoint. The usual division—returned to prison or not—must be included in it, since, obviously, this is one of the most important facts in the lives of releasees. However, nonrecidivism will not be equated with reformation. In fact, reformation as it has normally been used will not be employed. Instead, the more accurate variable of "straightness" or "crookedness" will be used. Bear in mind that "straight" is not "reformed." Furthermore, "success" will be qualified by the degree of *goal achievement*, "failure" by the mode of return, agency precipitated or court precipitated.

Actual cases of the types formed by these variables are presented. It must be cautioned, however, that this typology of postprison careers is presented with a speculatory intent. It is impossible for me to estimate the exhaustiveness or the validity of these types or the distribution of the ex-felon population according to the typology.

At the close of the chapter, there will be a brief analysis of the termination of the criminal career. The focus of this section will be the final latency stage of the criminal perspective and important dimensions in this final stage, dimensions which seem to discriminate it from unsuccessful terminations of the career.

FAILURE

Straight or Crooked

It is possible for an ex-felon to be returned to prison even though he is pursuing what he considers a "straight" life. This is true because (1) he may be returned to prison while on parole by the agency without any crime proven against him; (2) he remains vulnerable to arrest and conviction because of his record; and (3) he continues to commit felonies and misdemeanors more frequently than those who are not ex-felons.

Actually discriminating between a straight and crooked life in particular cases becomes difficult. What is meant by crooked is the living of a systematic deviant life. Theoretically the distinction is whether or not at a particular time the person has returned to an active social relationship with other criminal actors who are involved in a criminal behavior system (e.g., drug addiction, stealing, hustling, etc.) and is consciously acting upon the meanings of the accompanying criminal perspective and his criminal identity within this perspective. In the vernacular, he has "gone back to the old bag." Finding a method to actually make this distinction is very difficult. The polar cases, as is the case with all polar cases, are clear. In the middle, however, are persons who are zigzagging and/or ambivalent toward "the old bag." To be accurate, the designation would have to be made by the person himself and those with whom he interacts. To find deviant peers, however, who would be willing to make this designation is next to impossible. The actor himself, when he is too close to the particular time period in question, because of fear of punishment or because of his ambivalence, would not be reliable. Probably the most reliable evidence would be the designation made by the actor himself several months or years away from the time period. Then he can afford to be honest and is removed enough to make reliable appraisals of his own activities.

Agency- or Court-Initiated Recidivist

While an ex-felon is on parole, the parole agency and the court both during or after parole can initiate a failure. It is sometimes hard to determine which actually initiated a particular man's return to prison. In the case of a new felony conviction, especially after the man has completed parole, it is clear. Also it seems clear in some cases of "technical violation"—violation of parole conditions—where there has been no contact with the courts. However, in many cases, the courts and the agency are in communication, and because of the court's insistence, the agency agrees to send the man back to prison for technical violations and then the court drops pending charges. For research purposes it is difficult to discover who actually precipitated the return because this is strictly an informal arrangement and the acts and decisions are not recorded or public.

Though both these variables, crookedness-straightness and court or agency initiation, are somewhat ambiguous, the distinction each makes is important in understanding failure.

Crossing these two variables which will be dichotomized here produces four types of failures:

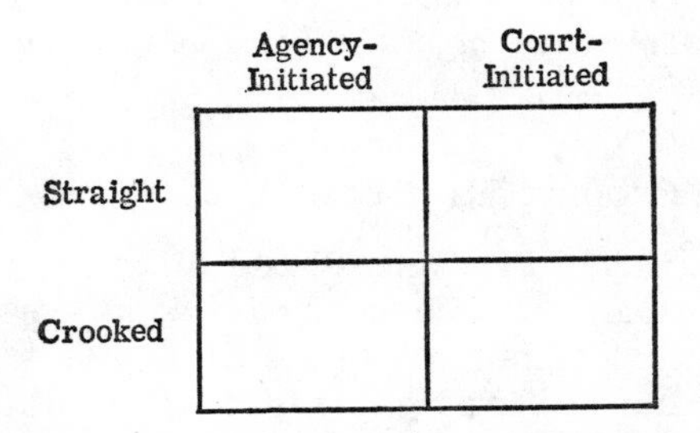

In this class of ex-convicts—those returned to prison—no consideration will be made if they were doing all right (that is, achieving gratification, fulfillment or respect), since being returned to prison completely disrupts their lives and usually cancels the gains they had made. Furthermore, in considering the recidivist, the crooked-straight variable is here dichotomized. When dealing with the nonrecidivist, however, a marginally deviant category will be added. Though this distinction could also be made in the case of recidivist, it doesn't seem necessary. In the case of the recidivist, the distinction between crookedness and straightness is made mainly to demonstrate that persons who have straightened up their hands may be returned to prison. To demonstrate that marginally deviant individuals are also returned would be redundant. However, in the case of the nonrecidivist, in examining the extended career on the outside, it is meaningful to explore more thoroughly the variations in criminal careers.

Court-Initiated, Crooked Recidivist

These are the least ambiguous failures. These men have returned to systematic deviance and have been arrested for some crime, usually a felony. If they are still on parole it may be a misdemeanor. The arrest and investigation reveals some or all of the details of their systematic deviant life and the court proceeds to have them sent back to prison. It may do this by convicting them of felonies and sentencing them to a new term, by convicting them of a misdemeanor and urging the parole agency to cancel the man's parole, or by dismissing charges against them *after* an agreement has been made with the agency to return the man to prison. Glaser offers an example of crooked, court-initiated failure:

> Ralph, Case V-926, is a professional burglar and proud of it. He was thirty-three years old when mandatorily released from prison on his fifth felony conviction, and he reports that he committed a burglary that night. He committed another three days later, but that same night he was investigated by the police when he drove into a gas station and appeared drunk. He was found to have over forty dollars in coins and over three hundred cartons of cigarettes in his car, in addition to burglar tools. While free on bond following arrest, he was caught in a gambling raid and found with identifiable stolen property. For this he served a two-year prison term before being returned to federal prison for mandatory release violation.[7]

Agency-Initiated, Crooked Recidivist

Often the agency discovers that a man has definitely returned to a deviant life and though he has not been arrested, or has been arrested but for something the court does not consider serious, the agency recommends that his parole be canceled for violations of the conditions of parole and that he be sent back to prison. Clearly this is the stated function of the parole agency as a surveillance agency. When the agency has in fact detected that a man has returned to deviance (that is, systematic devi-

7. Ibid., p. 8▴.

ance), and if attempts to direct him back to the "straight and narrow" fail, then it is appropriate according to the definitions of the agency's task to return him to prison. Though the man is called a "failure," it seems that the agency in fact has made a "successful" move; that is, it has performed its stated purpose. (The agency generally does not get rewarded for this kind of success.)

S., who had been a drug addict for many years, was released to a dishwashing job. For the first two months on parole he worked and reported regularly to the nalline clinic for his weekly inspection. However he was then picked up at a friend's apartment when it was "raided." He was not charged with a crime, but he was held for several days and he lost his job. He had been "chippying" with drugs before this arrest and when he was released he became "strung out." He did not report to nalline. He went to see his parole agent once and told him that he was going to "clean up" and report to nalline. However, he did not do so. He was picked up by the police several months later and the parole agency sent him to the Narcotics Treatment Center at San Quentin for 90 days to "dry him out." When he was again released on parole he never reported to the agent nor reported to the nalline clinic. He was listed as Parolee at Large and was picked up by the police several months later. He was again addicted to heroin and was living on the earnings of his "old lady," a prostitute and shoplifter. This time his parole was cancelled and he was returned to prison to continue serving his term. (Field notes, September and October 1966; interview with parole agent, September 1966; interview with S., December 1967)

Court-Initiated, Straight Recidivist

Some ex-felons are arrested for a felony or misdemeanor which in the court's opinion is serious but from the ex-felon's viewpoint is not serious. The ex-felon definitely believes that he has not returned to deviance, that he has consciously been avoiding the old bag and living a straight life. This occurs because, as was stressed earlier, criminal ex-felons even though they straighten up their hand, live in a manner unacceptable by conventional standards and, in fact, commit felonies more frequently than conventional people:

E. was released after serving 18 months at the California Institution for Men at Chino for possession of marijuana. He returned to his parents' home in a nearby community and went to work for his father as an apprentice plumber. During his first week on the outside a former friend stopped by to see him. After a short visit, the friend gave him three marijuana cigarettes, a simple gesture of friendship, since they had smoked marijuana together in former years. E. accepted the gift, he says, because he did not know how to gracefully refuse and not offend his friend. After the friend left he did not know what to do about the marijuana, since he had resolved before leaving prison not to smoke it again. But at this moment, he reflects, his reasons for not smoking it were not as clear to him as they had been. In his first week he was experiencing the usual disorganization of self. He decided to put off making a final decision and at least for the present not to return to the use of marijuana. After making this decision he still did not know what to do with the few marijuana cigarettes in his house. He "stashed" them in his room in his parents' home. Several days later, after he had actually forgotten about the marijuana, policemen came to his residence with a search warrant, searched his room and discovered the marijuana. It seems that his friend had been arrested for possession of marijuana and had revealed that he had given the cigarettes to E. E. was returned to prison with a new possession of marijuana charge. (Taped interview, August 1967)

Agency-Initiated, Straight Failure

The discrepancy between conventional society's definitions of reformation and the ex-criminal's definition of "straight," a discrepancy which is reflected in the discrepancy between the straight parolee's actual performance and the conditions of parole, often results in his being returned to prison for a technical violation. Generally this isn't simply a matter of violation of the conditions of parole, since most agents enforce these conditions with some constraint. Usually when a man is returned to prison for violation of the conditions of parole—a technical violation—the parole agent and the agency believe that he has returned to systematic deviance. This conclusion can be reached by the agent and the agency when in fact the parolee has not returned to systematic deviance for the following reasons: First, from the perspective of some agents, especially agents from the middle class, "innocent" activities according to a lower-class or criminal perspective can be seen to be indications of a generally deviant, unworthy, abandoned, and dissolute life. Second, when a full understanding of the parolee's behavior is not possible because of lack of information and a disparity of perspectives, some agents play it safe and believe the worst. The agent does this because it is a real threat to him when a case which he was not on top of blows up. Furthermore, "wiser," police-oriented agents are prone to ridicule others in cases where the agents were duped by a parolee who succeeded in hiding a generally deviant life from the other agents. The agents in these cases often feel that the parolee is laughing behind their backs when they succeed in deceiving them.

Finally, the agent tends to believe others' accounts of particular events rather than the parolee's. Where there are two or more versions which are contradictory, the parolee's version is the less likely to be believed. He is an ex-felon and is therefore considered less honest. Furthermore, the parolee has very often been caught in hiding *some* things from the agent, which is considered to be evidence that he is generally dishonest. Therefore, in matters in which there is another account, perhaps offered by a girlfriend or wife, the other's account is believed over the parolee's. In many cases, however, a belief in the other's credibility is no more warranted than that of the parolee, since the other, because of jealousy or vindictiveness, is often motivated to fabricate or distort stories about the parolee.

For various reasons the agent sometimes will construct a false impression of the parolee's life when presented with evidence of some deviations. He imagines much more deviance than is actually occurring, imputes immoral motives to the parolee, exaggerates the severity of some events, believes the false accounts of others, and, guarding against being duped or having his position threatened, constructs an image of an abandoned, reckless, irresponsible, and deviant life which the parolee has been living. He attempts to convey this image to the Adult Authority in violation reports when he recommends cancellation of the man's parole:

L. was released to San Francisco to report to a job which his sister had arranged for him, but which in fact did not exist. His intentions were to find work in a bakery after release. He had considerable experience in the prison in baking and cooking and was enthusiastically looking forward to learning more about baking. In the first few weeks he was not too successful in finding work and only worked a few days at two different bakeries, one of which did not give him a steady job because he was too slow. His financial situation was not too pressing because he had a grown daughter in the city who had turned her apartment over to him while she went on a long honeymoon with her new husband.

During the first month L. was not making a good impression on his parole agent. The agent was not pleased when L. reported to him that he did not keep the job he was released to. L. told him that the job was actually a janitor's job though he had been told in prison that it was a cook's job, so he had not taken it because he wanted to be free to look for work in a bakery. The agent stated that he should have kept the first job until he had another. The agent did not know that the first job was a "shuck" job. When L. failed to find steady work after a month and was actually laid off one job because he couldn't do the work, the agent stated that L. didn't seem to want to work. Once during the first month L. appeared at the nalline clinic for his weekly nalline shot with a small child in his arm. His agent, who happened to be one of the three agents present to supervise, became upset with him for bringing a child to this place and sent him home. "That was no place for a small child." During this period the agent visited L. at his daughter and son-in-law's apartment. On the door of this apartment he discovered a small poster which read: "We Hate Police." The son-in-law and daughter are active in civil rights organizations and this poster was a relatively common one among militant civil rights groups at this time. The agent was quite disturbed by this sign.

After being out about five weeks L. obtained a job as a cook. He was scheduled to report to work on Monday. On Friday he was in the company of a woman whom he had known for seven years and had lived with before he had been sent to prison on the last term. He had corresponded with her in prison and had seen her often since release. That Friday they and another female friend drove around the city. They bought some groceries and liquor. They proceeded to L.'s girlfriend's house, ate dinner and drank. Late in the evening, the third party left. Sometime between midnight and the next morning L. and his girlfriend, R., had a fight. He struck her several times. The next Monday L. was arrested for assault and rape. There are several different accounts of what transpired during that night and morning.

L. states that after drinking and sleeping he got up, was dressing to leave when he discovered that his forty dollars, his last money, was missing. He asked R. what happened to it and slapped her around. She implied that she had taken it by calling him a "cheap skate" for asking for it. She produced five dollars but that was all. L. admitted that he had slapped her in the face several times. He stated that he was very angry, because he had heard that she had been "pulling this kind of stuff" while he was in prison.

R. first told the police that late in the evening L. made advances on her which she repulsed and then he tried to rape her and beat her savagely. In court a week later she described the incident in this way: "I began to make a birthday cake for one of my sons and he (L.) began to jump on me and all of a sudden, all I know I was being punched, kicked and everything all of a sudden. I was threatened to be killed—threatened to be killed if I came to the court." The judge questioned her about the time discrepancy in the two stories.

The Court. Miss R., did this occur the following morning?

Miss R. Pardon me? Well, there was no sleep. This man tormented me for nine hours all night long.

D. A. I think that there is a relationship here, your honor.

The judge seemed to disbelieve her testimony and viewed the matter as a family battle. L. was given a 30-day suspended sentence for assault and battery.

The agent continued to investigate the case. He talked to L. who repeated his version to the agent. The agent received a 15-page letter from R. In it she elaborated extensively on her story. She accused L. of forcing her to commit acts of sexual perversion upon him (fellatio) and of committing cunnilingus upon her. She accused him of taking drugs she had in the house which had been prescribed for her, of keeping her prisoner until late the next morning, and of talking bitterly about the way he had been treated in prison.

The agent and the supervisor recommended that he be returned to prison. The agent stated in an interview that the parolee had not been trying to get established in the community. "He was running around with a Caucasian woman [R. was white, L. a Negro], he struck and drew blood on this woman, he couldn't keep a job."

In a subsequent investigation by the Department for the purposes of reviewing L.'s case before the Adult Authority, the following information was gathered. A written statement from the court revealed that "the judge felt this was a 'family' squabble, and the woman had precipitated the affair by rifling Mr. L.'s pockets and relieving him of his money. The judge gave him 30 days suspended and put him on one year's probation to *him,* to run concurrently with his parole." A letter from the parole agency stated that "we have no way of assessing the allegations made by Miss R. She has known this parolee for some time and probably has been intimate with him. On the other hand she has no police record while our parolee is a three time loser. Apparently the court believed him, not Miss R." (Field notes and interview, city jail, September 1966; interview with parole agent, September 1966; interview with L., San Quentin, October 1966; information from institutional files)

SUCCESS

Besides the variable crooked-straight with a middle category—marginal—added, successes will be inspected in terms of doing good or not doing good. In this way, there will be an attempt to discriminate between types of successes and nonsuccesses, in terms of the felons' own criteria of success. Crossing the two variables produces the following types:

	Doing Good	Doing Poor
Straight		
Marginal		
Crooked		

Crooked and Doing Good

This category, which contains those ex-felons who continue their deviant career in a successful manner and avoid arrest, probably constitutes a very small proportion of all ex-felons. Glaser classified only 2 persons out of 250 as nonimprisoned criminals after being out at least one year.[8] He did designate 13 more as crime-contacting noncriminals, some of whom, if all the facts were known, might be classified as criminals. However, it seems definite that a continued success at crime for an ex-felon is very difficult. His prior felony conviction(s) is (are) a serious detriment to him. The police have considerable knowledge which can relate him to particular crimes and help locate him. Once he has been convicted of a felony it is easier to convict him again, sinces judges and juries tend not to believe the innocence of one who has already been convicted of a felony.

Furthermore, the prison experience has reduced his criminal expertise. When he is first released he is not in the swing of things. He is generally disoriented, styles of criminal activities have changed, and many of his actual criminal contacts have disappeared. He is starting with no or ex-

8. Ibid., p. 84.

tremely limited resources. Considerable self-control is required to get started again.

The prison experience corrodes his criminal aptitudes in another more profound and intangible maner. It robs him of his "guts" or "soul":

You wanna know why these guys are coming back for petty shit, guys you thought could handle themselves outside? It's because a guy loses his soul in one of these places. When it really comes down to doing something he hasn't got it anymore. Oh ya, he can plan some heavy scores, but when it comes to executing them, he freezes. I remember two guys I knew inside before—dudes I thought were pretty heavy—they contacted me to pull this caper. They had this thing all set up and they wanted me to get a car and go with them. Well, we were going to take the place on Monday morning and Sunday night I grabbed a car and changed plates. The next morning we came wheeling up to the place and everything looked cool to me, but one of them said, "Man, there is something wrong. I don't know what it is, but something's wrong." So I said, "All right, man, if you wanna wait, I won't say anything." Ya know, a guy's risking his neck so I don't wanna push him into it. So, here we go again, next week, same story, I get the car, we come wheeling up to the place, this time this guy sees somebody heading for the door. I say, "It's all right, man, I'll take care of that dude." So I get out, they finally follow. Then this guy sees somebody coming down the street and now he really panics and gets back into the car. Man, I had to back away then and we drove off. I told these two motherfuckers not to come around me anymore. I finally figured out what was wrong with them. They had lost their nut sacks, their balls. Oh, they can still talk some heavy scores, but can't put them together anymore. That's what the joint does to a guy. Oh, these guys will walk by a candy store some day and on an impulse walk in and thump the guy on the head and half kill him. But when it comes to planning a caper, when there is time to back out, they'll back out every time. And then later pull some stupid shit and get busted anyway. (Field notes, San Quentin, March 1967)

A small minority continue crime in a successful manner on the outside. Those who do usually wait until they get back into the feel of the outside world. They wait until they have completed their parole or at least until they have established very good relations with the parole agent. For the most part the few who do all right at criminal pursuits are probably thieves or persons who in prison adopted the thief's identity and learned the techniques and patterns of this style.

Obviously, the successful criminal is still vulnerable to arrest and conviction, and at any time he may become a "failure." The skilled thief reduces his chances of returning to prison greatly, and if he is returned after a "long run" on the outside, he is still considered to have done all right, unless, that is, he has to serve a very long sentence on his return:

T. was released from prison on his second term when he was twenty-five. He had resolved to pursue some type of criminal activity. "I was gonna hustle something. I wasn't interested in getting married and raising a family and getting social security and becoming a communist."

He had learned baking in the prison and he found a job as a supervisor trainee at a large bakery. He lived in a boarding house, went to a local gym regularly, contacted the parole agent frequently—in fact, every day, since he was on an intensive parole program—and refrained from illegal activities until he had "set himself up." "I didn't know anything in Los Angeles, anyone in Los Angeles. I didn't know a lawyer, bondsman, I had nothing going for me in LA, and I wasn't going to do anything wrong. My idea of why most guys make a mistake is that they don't wait to set themselves up."

Though he was on an intensive parole program he felt that this didn't deter him from crime or help him get started in a conventional life. If anything, he feels that it deterred him from sticking to conventional life and pursuits. "If I had good intentions, it could've hurt them."

T. established good relations with the parole agent by appearing very cooperative. "I had discovered something, in my opinion, well, it's a fact. The parole—the Adult Authority doesn't care if I'm a good boy or a bad boy—just play their game. Keep out of their face and make it. Because Beverly Hills is full of all the biggest gangsters living up there on those hills with their plush pools and the Adult Authority associates with them, ya know. So I knew that. So I had to play according to the rules. I had to have some little job, I had to pretend to go for the program, the whole works."

By the time he finished his parole period, he had established contacts in a neighborhood near downtown Los Angeles. Upon completion of parole he quit his job and devoted all his time to various criminal pursuits. He had made contact with a very influencial lawyer, a bondsman and had acquired an "old lady"—a 17-year-old girl whom he "turned out." He centered his operations at a bar in this neighborhood which was a hangout for hustlers, thieves, bohemians and "swingers." He bought and sold this bar several times in the next eight years. His old lady became a very successful prostitute and built up a "book" which she and several other girls worked. T. bought and sold hot merchandise, made contacts for thieves, planned, organized and financed capers, and occasionally went on a caper himself. For ten years he avoided arrest except for misdemeanors for which he received fines.

He has driven new cars, owned a boat and an airplane. Though he has had short periods of "bad times," for the most part he has lived in relative luxury. According to the perspective of the "regular," he has done all right as a criminal. (Taped interview, May 1967)

Crooked and Doing Poor

This category, though it exists logically, in actuality seems not to exist. If an individual is not doing good at a criminal style outside, he abandons it or increases his efforts until he succeeds or is arrested. The price of mistakes, poor execution, pettiness, lack of expertise, and lack of finances in criminal pursuits is usually arrest and imprisonment. A criminal who does poor (that is, continues to fail at criminal pursuits), and who avoids reimprisonment in all practicality does not exist. This category, for all intents and purposes is subsumed in the court-precipitated or agency-precipitated crooked failures.

Marginal and Doing Good

There are a number of marginal occupations which are highly esteemed if the ex-felon does good at them. As mentioned earlier, success at these occupations fulfills many of the goals of the criminal. These occupations are seen to be profitable and they are sharp; that is, they involve ways of making money that are semi- or wholly illegal. Finally, they usually involve considerable contact with deviant worlds.

Some of these occupations are definitely illegal, but not necessarily felonious, for instance the production and distribution of pornographic material and religious and charity rackets. Others do involve felonies, but they are not highly detectable, convictable, or odious felonies. An example of this type of occupation is bookmaking, for which convicted persons usually receive short prison sentences (one year), jail sentences, or fines.

Not so clearly illegal, but still on the margin between legality and illegality are various automobile, encyclopedia, home improvement, and furnace sales. These are defined by many ex-criminals and others as "hustles" and are seen, therefore, as sharp, marginal occupations. In pursuing these marginally deviant ventures the ex-criminal continues to interact a great deal with other deviants and continues to act upon deviant categories. Therefore, as far as the extended felonious career is concerned, his deviant identity remains active. He continues to be susceptible to return to a more deviant and illegal style and to rearrest for a new felony.

During his parole period if he is following an occupationally marginal style, he is also susceptible to return to prison for technical violation. Consequently, continued success at a marginally deviant style is extremely difficult, and only accomplished by the more gifted ex-felons. More frequently, the ex-criminal pursues a marginally deviant style for a time, but after continued contacts with other deviants, and possibly some financial setbacks, he returns to the old bag. He is then more vulnerable to rearrest and return to prison.

When a shift to a sustained, successful, marginally deviant style is accomplished it seems probable that it is done by thieves, hustlers, and (less often) heads. Often this shift is related to gleaning in prison. The committed deviant who plans to prepare himself for alternate avenues often chooses one of the ventures described above which offers him a compromise between his former purely deviant commitment and a nondeviant life. Sometimes his orginal aim is something less marginal, such as a more respectable sales career, ownership of a small business, or a position in the business world in general. It turns out, however, that the realities of the outside opportunity structure force him to scale down his ambitions, and he turns to something for which he is better prepared morally and vocationally, and which is more available to him.

Aside from the marginal occupational styles, some criminal felons shift to one of the unconventional, nonconformist styles described in chapter 4. These are the styles of the intellectual, bohemian, artist, writer, political activist, and celebrity. These must be included in the marginal category because so many of the patterns of these are illegal, such as use of marijuana and LSD. These styles are most attractive to heads and dope fiends because of an affinity they have for intellectual, artistic, and/or glamorous activities.

These outsider marginal styles are viewed unfavorably by the parole agency. The bohemian style often includes periods of unemployment, patterns of grooming and dress, and an antiestablishment, anticonventional society posture which offend the parole agent. Likewise the political activists often antagonize the agent and the agency because of their political attitudes and their political activism, such as civil disobedience. The "celebrity"—musician, athlete and actor—often keeps late and irregular hours, travels a great deal, and is in contact with undesirable people, all of which causes the parole agent considerable consternation and actual difficulty in his supervisory tasks. All in all, the outsider careers are generally disapproved of by the parole agency and the person following these styles is in danger of having his parole cancelled.

The ex-convict improves his chances of remaining outside if he delays his outsider activities or at least camouflages them until he is discharged from parole. Once he is off parole his chances of not returning to full deviance, and therefore prison, are better because the outsider perspective devalues the more serious crime patterns of the hard-criminal styles. If he is returned to prison it is likely that it will be for drugs—usually marijuana.

J. was sent to prison for possession of heroin and burglary when he was 19. He gleaned in prison and planned to complete college when he was released. While in prison he inherited $4,000 and he made plans to invest this and support himself while going to school. Upon release he did enroll in a state college and invested some of his money in the stock market. Soon, however, he was diverted from these plans by several obstacles. He met a young lady who moved into his small apartment. The parole agent discovered this and, after a warning which was unheeded, placed him in city jail. When released, J. did not return to school and he continued to live with the young lady who had become pregnant. He established two residences to hide the situation from the parole agent. He did not earn money on his investments, and soon his savings were depleted. He had minor legal difficulties at this time. He received numerous traffic tickets until he finally lost his license, but he continued to drive.

He went to work selling encyclopedias and proved to have some aptitude at this work. After a year's experience he was able, when he applied himself, to earn a good salary. For the next five years he worked at various high pressure sales jobs. In one job, furnace sales, the methods approached fraud. The "pitch" in these sales was to pose as a furnace inspector and warn the occupants that their home was in danger of exploding unless they had their furnace cleaned. The cleaning crew would then discover parts that needed replacing, which they replaced at high prices. J. was successful at this work, in fact, at times too successful. He was fired from one company for being too forceful and receiving too many complaints.

J. married the young lady previously mentioned, but after three tumultuous years of home life he placed her on a bus and sent her back to her former home in Washington. For the next few years he lived a relatively libertine life. His friends were mostly other salesmen, ex-convicts and bohemian heads. At the end of this period he began to gravitate more and more to the city's bohemian circles. He moved into a large dwelling which housed a small community of young bohemians. Soon he was the manager of the building and he assigned rooms and collected rents for the owner, for which he received his rent free. He shared his room off and on with numerous young bohemian girls who moved into the building. He also participated in the active drug life of the house. He finally quit his sales job completely and swung over to a full bohemian existence. He allowed his hair to grow and participated fully in the emerging "hippy" community. He was arrested for possession of marijuana when the house was raided and he moved from it to a moving van in which he built a small living quarters. Two years later the possession charge is still pending and J. has gone back into high pressure sales. He works for a circus and travels to small towns promoting.

Except for the one setback, which still may send him back to prison, J. feels he has done what he wanted to do. He does regret not following his plans for college. However, he does seem relatively content with his life so far, and his life has had many of the valued dimensions of the convict perspective. (Taped interview, April 1967)

Marginal and Doing Poor

Most individuals who return to a deviant or marginally deviant routine and do not do good accelerate their efforts—even to the extent of taking desperate chances—or abandon their deviant pursuits for conventional ones. Some, however, accept the dishonorable alternative—a very petty, marginally deviant life. This is a routine which tends to keep them out of prison and at the same time allow them to continue some deviant patterns.

The drug addict probably takes this alternative more often than other ex-convicts. This means that he will have to refrain from the use of heroin, morphine, and other opiates which are available only in the illegal market and which are expensive and highly addictive. He usually turns to drugs which are legally available without prescription, such as "turps" (turpinhydrate, a cough syrup which contains codeine). In this way, he has a relatively inexpensive and legal source of drugs.

This acceptance of what is clearly an unprestigious, in fact, a somewhat contemptible, style of life seems inconsistent with the argument presented earlier, that not doing good would usually result in a return to the old bag—a fully deviant life—and/or prison. However, some do accept this devalued alternative which is thinkable though not dignified. It is thinkable because for some there is one worse alternative—return to prison:

Ya, did you hear about ______, man, is he doing bad. The raggedy motherfucker is on his ass hustling quarters and taking turps. He won't make a move. Several guys tried to help him, tried to shove a little action his way. He turned them down. Says he can't do no more time. You know, I can't blame him, the poor motherfucker did a lot of time. Had nothing but bad luck. At least he's out. (Field notes, San Quentin, November 1966)

Glaser has described a case which fits this category:

"Arthur," Case S-918, first said he was not well enough for an interview, but when our interviewer mentioned that he could pay a small amount for his trouble, Arthur eagerly cooperated on condition that the interviewer first buy him a large bottle of a particular cough syrup. Arthur visibly recuperated from his apparent illness as he gulped most of the bottle during several hours of conversation in the interviewer's car. When he revealed that he had been consuming a pint of codeine cough syrup a day, it seemed probable that his illness had consisted of mild withdrawal symptoms.

Arthur's criminal and narcotics record spanned over twenty-five years. He was handicapped by loss of his left forearm and supported himself mainly by peddling pencils. He was nominally employed at a restaurant of a relative, but only called there for free food. He was provided with a free room in a slum building by another relative, who was the absentee owner. He claimed to have sometimes made as much as fifteen dollars a day by selling pencils, mostly by going into taverns at night where drunks gave him as much as a dollar for a single pencil. Nevertheless, it was difficult to sell these long in one neighborhood, and unless he traveled widely he often did not even earn the three dollars per day needed for his cough syrup. However, he periodically supplemented this income by procuring nylon hose from a shoplifter and selling them to prostitutes.

Arthur also had difficulty buying enough cough syrup in his home community, for he sought only one type, and most druggists knew him and would not sell it to him. Therefore, he made regular trips to other cities, sold pencils there and purchased a supply of cough syrup. On these trips he traveled by hitchhiking or freight-riding. He would sleep in skid-row missions at his destination.[9]

After he was interviewed Arthur was sent back to prison on a technical violation. This would shift him into a failure category, but until this time he fits among successes who are doing poor. If he hadn't been on parole he would probably have continued this life for years and will possibly return to it upon release.

Straight and Doing Good

Most criminals who manage to overcome the obstacles of reentry, the parole experience, and who get started on the path to a "good life," do

9. Ibid., pp. 68–69.

so by straightening up their hands. They avoid the old bag and venture into a relatively conventional career.

Continued success at the other modes—crooked or marginal—requires considerable skill, knowledge, and finesse. The probability of rearrest and imprisonment is high, and a sizable proportion of those following these modes are removed from the success category by social control agencies.

Furthermore, the "outsider" styles are only acceptable and available to a small percentage of ex-convicts. Art, writing, entertainment, and sports require special skills that few possess. The bohemian and political-activist styles are unacceptable to most ex-convicts because of their strong, politically conservative, racially prejudiced, materialistic, and competitive attitudes.

Therefore, the only feasible, practical and acceptable modes of doing good are straight ones. The great majority of criminal ex-convicts who remain out of prison and reach some level of fulfillment, gratification, and dignity do so by finding their way into some relatively conventional career.

The business career. Different identities may be related to different patterns of conventional careers. For instance, the thief places high value on financial prosperity and autonomy. He very often seeks a career in the business world, most often ownership of a small business. If he gleaned, which is rare among thieves, this is not changed; it merely means that his aspirations in the business world will be higher:

P., after serving one term for safe burglary and another eighteen months for parole violation, was discharged from prison. He was then thirty years old. He had been a relatively successful safe burglar since he was twenty years old. He was highly respected in one urban neighborhood as a thief, but he did not return to an active career in crime. He worked as a house painter for several years, began contracting and finally obtained a contractor's license.

He maintained contact during these first few years after release with his younger brother and other younger thieves in the neighborhood. Occasionally he participated directly or indirectly in actual capers. However, after several years he participated in crime less and less. His group of criminal associates dissolved. His brother and some associates were sent to prison. Others moved away from crime.

During this period he was remarried—his two former marriages were terminated when he was sent to prison—and began building a family. His wife had inherited a medium sized home from her father. They lived in this house for several years and then sold it, buying a home on a large lot. He moved this house to one side of the lot, bought another house which was in the path of a freeway construction, moved it to this lot, and rented the second house.

The building trades slumped so P. went to work for a catering company. Soon he bought a catering truck of his own. He bought other trucks and after a few years built a very lucrative business.

Now after being out of prison for seventeen years he owns two houses, a small business which earns approximately $15,000 to $20,000 a year. He has three children in their teens, one of whom is a member of the DeMolays. From the exterior he appears to be a respectable, conventional and, in fact, conservative member of the community. It is doubtful that he will ever commit another major crime, such as the crimes he was still committing in the first few years after release. However, when he meets a former criminal associate, he gives indications that the criminal identity is operative. He examines his present status from the old criminal perspective, and discusses with relish his former criminal activities. (Taped interview, June 1967)

Working-class success. Disorganized criminals and state-raised youths, even if they gleaned in prison, probably do not have the preparation, determination, and/or high aspirations of criminals. They tend to have minimal contact with the middle-class world and therefore are generally ignorant of middle-class patterns. Even after gleaning and coming into contact to some extent with middle-class persons—square johns—in prison they still tend to find the subtleties of the middle-class and especially the middle-class occupational world foreign to them.

If they do good they usually obtain a good job with good pay and possibly a wife and family. If they overcome the other obstacles and obtain these they have usually fulfilled their goals. Glaser describes a state-raised youth who achieved this level of doing good:

"Ichabod," Case S-514, was a rather transient individual but did not incur any serious difficulty with the law until he was nineteen years old. At that time he received a state prison sentence for an auto theft which he and some other youths committed while hitchhiking across the country. He was paroled in fifteen months but was not closely supervised, and he continued his transient pattern by joining a traveling magazine-sales crew. Again he and some friends stole a car, and this time he received a Federal Youth Correction Act sentence, on which he was confined twenty months. Ichabod had spent much of his earlier life in orphanages, and he told a prison psychologist that he followed delinquent activities and got into trouble in order to be placed in an institution, as he was happier in institutions than anywhere else. In the Federal prison he worked well as a hospital orderly, but he never persisted in the educational programs in which he enrolled.

Ichabod was twenty-three years old when paroled. In keeping with his prison record and because he had no family to offer him a home and job assistance, employment was procured for him by the prison Employment Placement Officer as an orderly in a hospital. He worked there about fifteen months, and during the latter part of this period he courted a young woman from a town sixty miles away whom he had met when she was a paraplegic polio patient where he worked. He then procured employment at a hospital closer to her home and in a few months married this woman, despite being counseled by the probation officer to defer such a marriage until he was in a better position to handle the responsibilities it involved. Shortly after his marriage he started to seek factory work because of its higher pay rates, and after unsteady employment at first, he progressed markedly in pay and job security. He seems to have procured a new lease on life from the marriage, as well as from good relationships with relatives by marriage and with blood relatives whom he discovered only when his marriage was publicized in local newspapers. He is now a much more self-sufficient person, in sharp contrast to the dependent individual who earlier sought refuge from responsibilities in institutions.[10]

New careers. Some criminal ex-felons have found their way into the new field of social work—new careers. In the overall picture their numbers are extremely small. In my sample of 116, none were working in a new career. In the future, however, this may become a very significant doing good, straight termination of the felonious career. For this reason it bears looking at here.

New careers are seen as doing good by almost all criminals. The work, even though it is social work, does not smack of do-gooderism or police work. It is work aimed at helping the lot of the oppressed lower class and this is highly valued. Furthermore, the pay is good enough and the work is not routine, not "slave"-like and, therefore, the career has a bit of "sharpness" to it.

This termination of the felonious career seems especially suited to the particular characteristics of the dope fiend and will probably show a relationship, if it doesn't already, with this identity. The dope fiend has the special problem of avoiding monotony and frustration. He has a low tolerance for both. His solution for these has often been a "fix," and this is all that is required to precipitate a rapid descent into the old bag. The dope fiend seeks conventional jobs which have some excitement, glamor, or intrinsic interest. Examples of these would be commercial art, advertising, and public relations. These are not generally available to him, however, because of his record and his lack of training and experience. New careers have these valued qualities and are becoming available to him. It must be noted that Synanon, one of the earliest forms of new careers, originally was exclusively an organization of dope fiends.

Although it seems that there will be a strong relationship between the dope-fiend identity and new careers, these jobs and their attendant life styles are acceptable to criminals with other identities. Disorganized criminals and heads tend to find them very acceptable. Furthermore, there will be a strong relationship between gleaning in prison and this future life style. One project—New Careers Development Project—has already trained eighteen inmates in California prisons for this work upon release.[11] There are also a growing awareness and interest in these careers among gleaning convicts or those with an interest in gleaning:

F. was born in a Mexican-American colony in Los Angeles. He didn't learn English until he started attending school at five years old. By the ninth grade he was having trouble with his school work partly because of his poor language skills, and he quit school. He started using drugs soon after this and after many

10. Ibid., pp. 61–62.

11. J. Douglas Grant and Joan Grant, *New Career Development Project, Final Report,* National Institutes of Mental Health Project OM-01616, August 1967.

years of addiction, county jail sentences for heroin and various forms of theft, he was sent to state prison.

In prison he gleaned. He completed high school, read extensively and prepared himself for college. He enrolled in city college immediately upon release. After two years with very good grades, he transferred to the state university. He was married at this time to a "middle-class" girl he met at a public swimming pool who was also beginning school at the state university. By working summers, with the help of a small scholarship and some help from his mother-in-law, F. finished his work on a B.A. in social welfare.

Upon graduation he discovered that most social work agencies would not hire him because of his extensive arrest record. After a few months he did obtain a position with the Catholic Youth Organization, but he was released because, he related, he departed considerably from their approaches to social work. He worked much closer with the delinquents and was more tolerant of some of their deviant behavior. Furthermore, before being dismissed he was arrested for shoplifting and was acquitted in a jury trial. This additional arrest, though he was acquitted, seemed to end all possibilities of entering social work.

The next five years were very difficult for him. Seeking a new vocation he turned to the California Vocational Rehabilitation Program and sought support for learning a new trade. He qualified for their support, since it was decided that he was "psychologically" handicapped. This decision required considerable manipulation of the agency's guidelines. He went to barber college and after six months went to work as a barber. For the next four years he worked in various barber shops in neighborhoods close to the colony in which he lived as a youth. He was in constant contact with his former deviant peers, most of whom were still caught in the cycle of release, addiction and return to prison. He didn't return to the use of heroin, even though he states he was often depressed in these years. In spite of having a family and relative financial security, he was very disappointed because he had struggled to obtain a college education which he couldn't use. His deviant peers often indicated that they were disappointed in him. They didn't understand why he had all that education and was still "slaving."

His discontent and his growing bitterness of the "middle class" had its toll on his marriage. His wife had become increasingly neurotic and finally developed paranoiac delusions in which she imagined that F. was plotting against her. She was hospitalized for a short period and then remained in out-patient treatment.

At this time F.'s life changed. New programs financed by the O.E.O. emerged. A counselor at California Vocational Rehabilitation who had handled F.'s case and who had been very favorably impressed with F. contacted him to offer him a position as a Community Aid worker. F. accepted and for the last two years he has been working in an agency close to his community. He earns a good salary, enjoys his work and seems to have the respect of the agency. He believes that he serves as a bridge between the agency and the lower class Mexican community. He also has the respect of his former peers, many of whom he has succeeded in placing in the program. Now they feel that he is doing good. He has an office, dresses well and doesn't seem to them to be "breaking his back." Now they come to him often to seek advice. Also his family situation has improved considerably. His wife has improved and is now making plans to return to school to complete work on a B.A. (Taped interview, June 1967)

Straight and Doing Poor

Not all ex-felons who stay out of prison and straighten up their hands are a success by the criteria of the social perspective of the prison reference world. Many who succeed in "making it" do not get started, do not do good. They fail to achieve their goals or succeed in one of the acceptable life styles. In the early years of their failure there is a strong tendency for them to return to the old bag. However, because of fear of returning to prison, exhaustion from years of a desperate criminal life and a deprived prison life, or because of the simple inertia of a mundane life routine, many do not return to systematic deviance and they finish out their lives in a style which is disappointing to both the prison reference world and themselves.

Retirement. A common doing-poor termination of a criminal career is that of retirement. The criminal has reached an age when it is somewhat acceptable to retire. Because of his advanced age and his long prison sentences, expectations of sexual and financial successes have been reduced. He is free to some extent from the success obligations which push younger criminals. He may retire with some impunity. Many criminals, especially thieves, who have served one or two sentences do retire after the age of forty. This is reflected in the drop of recidivism after that age.

The thief whose life John Barlow Martin recorded was in retirement when he told his story to Martin:

"Since I got out of Joliet this last time I've been a little careful. My luck hasn't been any too good, and I can't afford to take the chances I took when I was younger."

For five years he had been unable to find a good job. At the age of forty when last released from prison he had no work experience.

"After I lost my boiler job, I got a job in a garage. I just happened to be walking by and I got talking to the night manager. He seemed to think it was worth while to give me a try at it—floorman, hiker. One of the highest-class garages in the city of Chicago. I was there about three and a half years. I was finally night manager.

"I lost out in a reorganization. The garage was being operated by a bank for the bond-holders and they finally sold it and it was reorganized and they changed the whole setup. Then I was night manager of another garage for about a year and a half but I run into the same thing—reorganization."

His health was becoming poorer and this reduced his chances of obtaining a good employment. He lived alone in a small boarding house and had few friends. He has never married and felt that there was no chance of ever getting married.

He does not seriously consider going back to crime. He stated that he did not have the motivation he once had and though he seemed to be regretful that things turned out as they did, he did consider himself lucky to be alive and not serving life.

"The best out for a person like me would be on a job that's not too important where I can do well and not attract any attention to myself and just go along.

"And I've got to a point where things that were important to me twelve, fifteen years ago aren't important now. I used to have a lot of ambitions, like everybody has—different business ventures, stuff like that. But today, why, with what I have to buck up against, why, I could be just as happy and just as satisfied with a job that I'm getting by on, where I knew I wasn't going to run into trouble or anything. I'd get just as much pleasure out of that as I would out of something ten times as good. I don't have any obligations, I've just myself to take care of. It could be a good chauffeur's job, out in the country, away from Chicago. Or it could be a caretaker's job, a stationary job, anything, you know what I mean. I don't have any doubts I could handle a job like that real well and be pretty satisfied with it. Because you get a little older, like I say, I don't drink like I did a few years ago, a lot of things that were important to you then aren't so important. I can get more enjoyment out of walking down to the lake and sitting around, fishing, something like that than I could out of spending a thousand dollars in a night club.

"Why am I lucky? Well, I'm thinking of guys I know that've been hung, been electrocuted. I'm thinking about guys down there doing life under habitual that are never going to get out. I'm thinking of guys that have been broke, sick, and had twenty times more bad luck than I had. So I still think I'm darn lucky." [12]

Dereliction. Another common doing-poor termination of the felonious career is dereliction. The derelict lives out his life as a skid-row or neighborhood bum or alcoholic.[13] The skid-rower lives in a cheap room and sleeps outside or in parked cars. He works sporadically or not at all, drinks or takes drugs he purchases in drugstores, such as codeine cough syrups. He is arrested frequently, serves city and county jail sentences up to six months, is committed or commits himself for short stays at various rehabilitation centers or hospitals, and then returns to skid row and drinking. The neighborhood derelict often stays with a friend or a relative who tolerates him and who supplies him with a room and some food. He then spends his time at a town bar, a pool hall, a corner where he meets other nonworking local alcoholic derelicts. He panhandles, "borrows," or "scrounges"—engages in petty hustles—for money for drink. He too is arrested frequently and spends months in city and county jails and other institutions.

The toll on his health is heavy and the derelict generally dies at a fairly young age—forty to fifty. Furthermore, as time passes, a return to another life style becomes less and less probable due to his irreparably degenerating health:

B., after many years of drug addiction, served one prison sentence for posses-

12. *My Life in Crime* (New York: Signet Books, 1951), pp. 180, 180–81, 187–88.

13. Jacqueline Wiseman, in her study of skid row, related to me that many skid-row persons were ex-convicts. For a full description of this life, see *Stations of the Lost: The Treatment of Skid-Row Alcoholics* (Englewood Cliffs, N. J.: Prentice-Hall, Inc., 1970).

sion of heroin and when released he returned to San Francisco. He was in his early forties at this time. For the next four years he worked as a waiter. He did not return to drugs but started drinking excessively. He finished his parole with no difficulty, but by the end of his parole period he was drinking so heavily that he couldn't hold a steady waiter's job. He lived in a small hotel room near the waiter's union and reported there daily for banquet jobs. These one meal jobs paid from seven to fifteen dollars and a few of these each week would support his drinking and pay his rent. After several years of this, however, he was barred from many of the hotels who hired banquet waiters. He then moved to Venice, California, a site of another waiter's union and a skid row. Here he continued to work banquets and drink. His friends were other waiters who were following the same routine and alcoholic inhabitants of the Venice skid row.

He has been arrested several times for being drunk and one time received a six-month sentence at the County Honor Farm. He returned to Venice after this and continued his former pattern.

At last contact with B., he was still living in Venice and still drinking excessively. He was very thin, looked much older than his years and had the alcoholic parched red skin. He had suffered one stroke which left one arm and one side of his face slightly paralyzed. He was at this time a derelict. (Interview, July 1966)

The slave rut. A routine which is hated and feared by most criminals actually succeeds in capturing many of them. This is the working-class family rut. This life involves an "old lady" who, although she may have once been desirable, has become a "bitch" or a "dog"; children; a job which is hated and which pays poorly; a crowded and dirty house or apartment; unpaid bills; and disharmony in the family interaction. Two conditions set the general tone of this routine: (1) the relatively low wages which place material restrictions upon the life and (2) the narrowness of scope and interest of one or both marriage partners.

This style, though most convicts are cognizant of its ugliness and vehemently derogate it, succeeds in capturing some of them—especially state-raised youths and disorganized criminals—because it takes shape around them slowly and subtly. Whatever their plans were when they left prison, they are forced to accept relatively undesirable work because of stigma and lack of vocational skills. They are lonely and desirous of sexual activity. They marry women who are available to them and who at any other time would not meet their expectations of beauty, intellect, and interest. They very often start having children and as they become increasingly discontented with the situation, a net of obligations is trapping them. They incur debts and have children to whom they have become attached or toward whom they feel obligated. Furthermore, they fall into a routine—a rut—which becomes a habit easier to follow than to break:

E. finished his second term for possession of marijuana during which he devoted himself to learning to paint. When he left prison he was committed to pursuing a career in art. Before he could get started, however, he had to find some means of support. He obtained his first job, after several weeks, as a busboy in a large hotel. He worked a split shift—three hours at lunch and four or five hours in the evening. The work was hard and the waiters for whom he worked were usually very irritable. He earned only $75 a week and he could not paint because he was too fatigued after work. Furthermore, it soon became apparent that he could not rise to a better job in this field because he was not temperamentally suited for food service.

He lived in an inexpensive boarding house which was filled with recent migrants to the city. He became acquainted with a small group of these people and soon was going with a plain, withdrawn, mid-western girl. They started having sexual relations and she became pregnant. He received permission from his parole agent to marry and they moved into a small apartment.

After one year he quit his job and started to look for another. He drew unemployment and didn't find work for one year. During this time he began to paint again. He displayed his paintings at a co-operative art gallery. A well-known water colorist who held classes in the city was impressed with E.'s paintings and gave him free lessons for several months. E.'s paintings began to sell.

But after a year of unemployment, his financial situation was desperate, and he had to find employment. He had experience with his father as a plumber, so after considerable persistence at the plumbers' union, he succeeded in obtaining a job in the shipyards as an apprentice plumber. This work was hard and again he found that he couldn't paint. After six months, however, he was laid off. He returned to painting and at this time he won first prize in an important art show. From then on his paintings sold very well and he received about $200 or $300 for a water color. However, he was not a prolific painter; one painting sometimes took him several weeks.

He was becoming more and more discontented with his home situation. He started to smoke marijuana regularly and his painting productivity dropped off. At this time he met a friend from prison who was interested in photography. They became close friends, and E. and his friend stayed away from E.'s house a great deal of the time.

He quit painting entirely and he and his friend tried to enter commercial photography. This did not succeed and E. returned to the shipyards. His friend died of an overdose of heroin.

His wife was becoming more and more withdrawn and finally required a short hospitalization when she developed paranoid delusions. After a short stay in the hospital she returned home and remained in out-patient care.

E. states that he is presently trying to cope with his home situation and be more attentive to his wife whom he had "taken for granted." However, he has an outside girlfriend whom he still sees. At work he has risen to a foreman position and works very hard. After work he has to stop at a nearby pool hall and drink several beers and play pool for an hour or two to "unwind." He is not painting; he says that he is now just waiting for retirement. (Taped interview, June 1967)

Suicide. Some ex-felons, perhaps after several years of doing poor, dereliction, or a slave rut, commit suicide:

B. had planned to work when he left prison, save his money, fix up an apartment and buy things, like a hi-fi, movie projector, TV so that he would be content at home and would not have to hang around the neighborhood. Upon release he soon obtained a job as a teamster and was driving a truck on local deliveries. He roomed in a small hotel in the meat packing section of the city—"Butcher Town." He had grown up close to this hotel. The downstairs of the hotel was a neighborhood bar where male "working stiffs" hung out. B. fell into a pattern of working days and sitting in this bar drinking every night. He stayed in this hotel about seven years. The pattern of his life, once established, didn't change. He worked, drank at the same bar each night, and slept. He had virtually no other activities. He occasionally ran into old friends but they did not draw him away from this rut. After being out of prison for ten years and while still in his thirties, he jumped from the San Francisco–Oakland Bay Bridge. (Field notes, April 1967)

SQUARE JOHNS AND LOWER-CLASS MEN

The cycles described above generally do not apply to the noncriminal identities. Square johns and lower-class men, since they were not committed to a criminal social world, do not follow the criminal course of failure to make it and/or to get started and then the return to the old bag. In the true sense of the concept they do not have an old bag. Before prison they followed conventional styles or working-class styles from which they deviated one time or only occasionally.

The nonalcoholic, sexually "normal" square john returns to respectability, resumes his former position in life, and is usually never seriously tempted to return to crime. His prison record and his advanced age may cause him some difficulty in regaining admittance to his former occupation. In some instances, however, he received additional training and education in prison and is vocationally better equipped, which can compensate for his stigma. He very often finishes out his life refraining from crime and looking back upon his prison experience and his association with other criminals as a thoroughly distasteful experience. Case examples in Glaser's category of "Crime-Interrupted Noncriminal Career" display this pattern:

"Ivan," Case S-573, came from a relatively poor family, but by dint of his own strong ambition and family encouragement he worked his way through law school. Within a year of his admission to the bar he changed from a law-clerk position to his own law practice, operating in office space rented from a large law firm. He married a woman who seemed to equal or exceed him in social-climbing aspirations. They lived lavishly, and thus acquired large debts. Ivan, as a lawyer, became trustee of several thousand dollars paid for claims against the federal government. When he "borrowed" from these funds beyond his capacity to repay, he was sent to federal prison for embezzlement.

Ivan was a model prisoner and contributed the benefits of his education to fellow inmates by serving as an instructor in the prison school. On release he was employed at analysis and correspondence work by a large corporation and quickly advanced to a position to considerable importance there. He has been assured that if, upon completion of his parole, he procures readmission to the bar, he will be welcomed into the legal staff of this corporation.

Ivan was divorced by his wife while he was in prison, but he remarried her after release. He then left her when he could not discourage her excessive spending, but they have once again reunited. Since she is reported to have become more moderate in her expectations, and he now seems able to resolve their crises without jeopardizing his future, it does not seem likely that he will have further difficulty with the law.

Another example of this pattern, in a prisoner with a less distinguished profession, is provided by "Irwin," Case S-508. Irwin left school at seventeen to work in the printing trade. He progressed well in learning this trade, and three years later he and another youth opened their own printing business. The business did not prosper. When Irwin could not earn enough money to meet expenses of his wife's pregnancy, he and his partner printed their own money. The government, to discourage competition in this printing specialty, soon placed Irwin and partner in federal prisons.

Irwin was paroled in less than two years, and rejoined his wife and the son born during his incarceration. After a few months of diverse employment, he received a job as a printer again. When interviewed by us two years later he had been advanced to a foreman position, had paid his pre-prison debts and was saving money toward purchase of a home.[14]

The alcoholic or sexually deviant square john, although still committed to conventional values, remains vulnerable to new "trouble." The alcoholic, often after a short period of control of his problem, returns to alcoholic bouts, has employment difficulties, and difficulties with his agent; and after a few arrests or perhaps a crime or crimes committed while drinking—check-writing or assaultive behavior—is returned to prison on a new felony charge or technical violations. The sexually deviant ex-felon often continues to progress on parole until detected in new sexual offenses and is then returned to prison.

The lower-class man typically returns to working-class life, often with more stability than he possessed before prison. Though he does not have an old bag to avoid, he does have the "trouble" syndrome which is often related to unemployment and drinking. Prison, however, has often equipped him to avoid this trouble. He very often enhances his vocational and educational skills, gains "insight" into his drinking and other problems, and acquires a strong distaste for prison. The stigma of the ex-felon is of little consequence for him. In the occupations he pursues, usually semiskilled labor, it is seldom important. In his informal social world it is no stigma.

Clearly, the lower-class man has the lowest recidivist rate of all the identities. For instance, while 36 per cent of the 116 had been returned to prison and another 8 per cent had absconded after a year, *all* of the 7 lower-class men were still successfully continuing their parole.

14. Glaser, *The Effectiveness of a Prison and Parole System*, pp. 63–64.

TERMINATION OF THE CRIMINAL CAREER

If he makes it, copes with parole, and does good in a straight style, as years go by the criminal identity does not disappear but submerges to a latency state. As it submerges, deviant activities which are common among criminal ex-convicts, even those who have straightened up their hand, subside. They slowly refrain from shoplifting, commission of traffic violations, contacting and aiding criminal ex-convict friends, and planning criminal activities.

This final latency stage of the criminal career is still quite different from "reformed" as conceived by penologists, sociologists, and the public at large. For instance, there is no denial of, or regret for, the past. In fact, the past criminal life is looked back upon with pleasure and excitement. There is an awareness of the latent criminal identity, a tendency to view oneself in some instances as a thief, dope fiend, hustler, head, etc. An ex-convict interviewed after being out of prison for more than ten years, during which he married a "square girl," worked steadily in the office of two construction companies and raised a small family in a middle-class community stated:

I've been stealing all my life nearly, hold-ups since I was a teenager. So, I don't know anyway . . . so I consider myself a thief, good or otherwise, a good thief or not is immaterial. The point is I was. Kleptomaniac, perhaps not, but a thief, yes. And I still see this tendency. Ah, I laugh at myself about it. I open a supply closet at work and I'll take three pencils instead of one. Like I say, I fight it but, I feel . . . I knows it's there. Hell, I may give this all up and go pull some caper. You never know. (Taped interview, June 1967)

Furthermore, there is an enduring affinity for ex-convicts, others with the same experiences and an inability to become completely immersed in another social world. Another statement by the ex-convict quoted above reveals this final dislocation of the criminal ex-convict:

Whether I have meant to or not I have gone very strongly into the average man category. I mean just really into it. Tremendously so. Maybe it is a little different. Like I dwell in an apartment instead of a home. That is just finances. But type job, the 8 to 5, the regular holidays, ah, the social drinking, the occasional visit to the topless bar, the go out and eat once a month, the little league, the cub scouts, the PTA. I know a lot of people, a lot like me and I like them, but I'm just not one of them. It's like I said, I'm the gregarious loner. When I came to Los Angeles, the first thing I did was look up ________ (former prison buddy) and drove fifty miles out to ________ to see him. That's how much I wanted that association. I can't get this identity feeling with some of the guys I was with there. I never had it there. Look, I never had reform school, see, never had it, never had the county jail bit until the four months when I was going to the joint. So I never had that background with them. Still, I have much more background with them from the one deal that now

I can't really fit with these people. I can't fit with these and I can't fit with them. (Taped interview, June 1967)

Important Dimensions in the Final Termination of a Criminal Career

In the cases interviewed where the criminal career appeared to be terminated and the criminal identity has passed into a latency stage, the persons' lives seemed to have the following two aspects which differentiated them from the others who continue to do poor and remain susceptible to a return to prison.

The first is an adequate and satisfying relationship with a woman, usually in a family context:

I am now settled in the warmth and congenial atmosphere of my own home with my wife and child. For once in my life I have something worthwhile to work for. I want my child to have all the advantages that were denied me. Already I have taken out a life insurance policy for him, which will mature when he is old enough for college. My hopes and plans for the future are all tied up in him. I want him to have a college education and be a refined professional man. Nothing in the world could take the place of my wife and child in my life, as they mean everything to me. . . .[15]

If he does not have home and family, his life is not a sexually barren one. Until he is past a certain age—forty or fifty—the expectations of sexual fulfillment are too strong to permit this. He is at least successful in dating females or maintaining temporary relationships with a woman or women.

Secondly, he is involved in extravocational, extradomestic activities. Examples of these activities are sports (bowling, golf, swimming, skin-diving, camping) or hobbies (photography, woodworking, painting, etc.). It may also be an activity involving his entire family or his children. An ex-felon interviewed after twelve years with no arrest spoke of his leisure activities:

So, I seek other things—physical—to keep me going. Well, I have my little boy now, who is ten, a little girl eight, another little girl four and a half. Ah, . . . get wrapped up to a certain extent in their stuff, little league, cub scouts . . . work with the kids, enjoy working with them, especially the little boys, talking, teaching, kind of buddies with them. (Taped interview, June 1967)

CONCLUDING REMARKS

In closing this final chapter, and thereby the book, allow me to devote the last few lines to the two major themes of the study. In review

15. Clifford Shaw, *The Jack-Roller* (Chicago: The University of Chicago Press, 1930), p. 182.

these are the continuity of the felon's life from phase to phase because of perspectives acquired earlier and the series of misunderstood and officially constructed obstacles. It was seen in this chapter that from the standpoint of the felon a successful postprison life is more than merely staying out of prison. From the criminal ex-convict perspective it must contain other attributes, mainly it must be dignified. This is not generally understood by correctional people whose ideas on success are dominated by narrow and unrealistic conceptions of nonrecidivism and reformation. Importantly, because of their failure to recognize the felon's viewpoint, his aspirations, his conceptions of respect and dignity, or his foibles, they leave him to travel the difficult route away from the prison without guidance or assistance; in fact, with considerable hindrance, and with few avenues out of a criminal life acceptable both to him and his former keepers.

APPENDIX

INSTRUMENTS FOR CLASSIFICATION OF FELONS ACCORDING TO CRIMINAL BEHAVIOR SYSTEMS, AND PRISON-ADAPTIVE MODES

The instruments below, which were directed towards information from an inmate's central file, were designed to classify men according to their major and most recent participation in one of the criminal behavior systems or prison adaptive modes. Each category combined several indicators—criteria and correlates—which gave evidence of participation in the criminal systems or adaptive modes. The weighting was designed to maximize the mutal exclusiveness of the categories. A total score of five for the criminal behavior system and four for prison-adaptive modes were required to classify an inmate in that category.

Felonious Identities

Thief	*Weighting*	*Total*
A. Sophisticated crime for money on present conviction	— 1	
B. Labeled professional by probation officers or arresting officers	— 3	
C. Record of several (2 or more) professional crimes: burglary, forgery, hijacking and robbery where at least $400 was involved	— 3	—
D. If A, B or C then over 30 years of age	— 1	
E. If A, B or C then White	— 1	

Dope Fiend	*Weighting*	*Total*
A. Evidence of opiate use in the three years prior to present incarceration	— 2	
B. Admission of extensive opiate use in the three years prior to present incarceration	— 3	
C. Two or more arrests for opiates in the three years prior to present incarceration	— 3	—
D. If A, B or C then arrests for shoplifting or petty theft	— 2	

Hustler		*Weighting*	*Total*
A. Several (3) arrests for gambling, pandering, picking pockets, forgery, fraud or bunco	—	2	
B. Labeled by arresting officers, probation officers or judge as "con man"	—	1	
C. If A or B then evidence of very little or no evidence of opiate use.	—	2	—
D. If A or B then Negro	—	1	

Head			
A. Presently convicted of sales or possession of marijuana, methedrine or dangerous drugs	—	2	
B. Two or more arrests for sales or possession of marijuana or drugs other than opiates and cocaine	—	2	
C. If A or B then no evidence of opiate use or evidence of no opiate use	—	2	—
D. If A or B, and C then less than three adult convictions of burglary, robbery, grand theft, petty theft and forgery	—	1	

State-Raised			
A. At least one commitment to juvenile prison	—	3	
B. If A then no stay as an adult of more than 1½ years on the outside	—	2	—
C. If A or B then under 25 when arrested for present charge	—	2	

Lower-Class Man			
A. All employment at less than skilled level	—	1	
B. Less than 7th grade placement level	—	1	
C. Present conviction for murder, assault, felonious drunk driving or manslaughter	—	1	—
D. Negro or Mexican	—	1	
E. If A, B *and* C then less than three convictions for theft and/or narcotics	—	3	

Square John			
A. Not more than two arrests for theft	—	1	
B. Present conviction for sex crime, murder, manslaughter, forgery, bribery, escape or other felony which doesn't seem to be related to a "criminal"	—	1	
C. High school education	—	1	
D. White	—	1	
E. Employed as skilled worker or above	—	1	
F. No arrests other than misdemeanors before present conviction	—	1	—
G. If C or E then evidence of sexual deviation, alcoholism or other "problem" (compulsive gambling, dire financial problems, etc.)	—	1	

Disorganized Criminal	*Weighting*	*Total*
A. No arrest for crimes for money which indicate sophistication, several arrests for theft, and no indication of extensive narcotics use in the three years prior to present incarceration	— 4	
B. If A then 25 or older at time of arrest for charge of present commitment	— 1	—
C. If A no juvenile prison commitment	— 1	

Prison-Adaptive Mode

Jailing		
A. Prison power job assignment (captain's clerk) or prison wheeling and dealing job assignment (store room clerk)	— 2	
B. Disciplinary actions (2 or more) for "wheeling and dealing," gambling, contraband, possession of knife, rioting, instigating riots, gang fighting, fighting with a knife in last two years	— 2	
C. Juvenile prison record	— 1	
D. Over 5 years served on present sentence or total of 8 years in adult prisons	— 1	
E. If A, B or C then no extensive trade training (less than two out of last three years or less than 2/3 of sentence if shorter than 3 years) or no extensive educational efforts (high school diploma or high school attendance for last 2 years in prison)	— 1	—

Doing Time		
A. Good prison job—a job which offers privileges, leisure time, interest or which is related to work before coming to prison—but not power or wheeling and dealing job	— 1	
B. One or less "beefs" per year	— 2	
C. No extensive trade training (less than two out of last three years or less than 2/3 of sentence if shorter than 3 years) or no extensive educ. efforts (no high school diploma or less than 2 years attendance)	— 2	—
D. Square john, lower class man or thief	— 1	

Gleaning		
A. Completed high school, attended until paroled or received 2 years trade training in a vocational shop	— 2	
B. Consistent AA attendance	— 1	
C. Extensive therapy (2 years group counseling, individual therapy or, until paroled, participation in ICE programs or other voluntary therapy programs)	— 1	—
D. If A or C then one year before release with no "beefs"	— 1	
E. Consistent attendance in religious programs	— 1	
F. Board reports indicate significant "self-improvement"	— 1	

CONDITIONS OF PAROLE AND THEIR INTERPRETATION

These are the standard Conditions of Parole which you agree to follow when you get out. The Adult Authority may impose special conditions as appropriate. After each of the following conditions an explanation is added.

I. *Release:* Upon release from the institution you are to go directly to the program approved by the Parole and Community Services Division and shall report to the Parole Agent or other person designated by the Parole and Community Services Division.

Brief Interpretation: This ordinarily will require the parolee to report to his Parole Agent on the day of release or the day following. This depends on the distance between the institution and the District Parole Office. In case of emergency (illness) which prevents the individual from reporting to the designated person on time, he immediately should contact the parole office by either phone or telegram.

II. *Residence:* Only with the approval of your Parole Agent may you change residence or leave the county of your residence.

Brief Interpretation: It is essential that the parolee keep his Parole Agent informed of his whereabouts at all times. Any emergency situations can be handled by telephone. Talk to him before you make the change. Failure to do this possibly would not justify the return of the parolee to prison; however, a violation of the condition, considered with a series of other violations may be ample reason for return as a violator.

III. *Work:* It is necessary for you to maintain gainful employment. Any change of employment must be reported to, and approved by, your Parole Agent.

Brief Interpretation: This does not prevent the parolee from changing his job, if the change is beneficial and approved by the Parole Agent. The Parole Division is anxious to assist any parolee to better his working situation. Changes may be made for reasons of better pay, better working conditions, work for which the parolee is better trained, or work more convenient from a transportation standpoint.

In exceptional cases an immediate change of jobs may not be allowed, for example, approval to leave a job may be withheld if the employer had agreed to hire a parolee for a specific period or until a replacement can be trained.

Under certain circumstances a parolee may be allowed to accept employment outside the continental limits of the country. Work in the Merchant Marine may be arranged. The Parole Agent may grant continuing permission for a parolee to leave his county of residence if the job requires it.

Steady employment is an essential for anyone's satisfactory adjustment in life. A parolee is no exception. Unemployment due to illness or inability to find work is not the cause for violation, but refusal to work may be reason to recommend a return. There are no limits on maximum earnings.

From *How to Live Like Millions,* California Department of Corrections publication no. 272 (38135).

IV. *Reports:* You are to submit a written monthly report of your activities on forms supplied by the Parole and Community Services Division unless directed otherwise by your Parole Agent. This report is due at the Parole Office not later than the fifth day of the following month and shall be true, correct and complete in all respects.

Brief Interpretation: Failure to receive this report usually indicates to the Division the parolee has absconded or some other serious problem exists. This report is required for all newly released parolees. The decision when, and if, the form is no longer required will be made by the Division. Failure to submit a monthly report is not sufficient reason for violation, but coupled with other problems, such failure may be adequate cause to recommend return to confinement.

V. *Alcoholic Beverages:* The unwise use of alcoholic beverages and liquors causes more failures on parole than all other reasons combined. *A. You shall not use alcoholic beverages or liquors to an excess. B. You shall not use ANY alcoholic beverages or liquors. (*Strike out either A or B, leaving whatever clause is applicable.)

Brief Interpretation: It is conceded that total abstinence from the use of alcohol would benefit most parolees.

This parole condition is intended to meet the individual problems realistically.

A parolee not strictly prohibited from drinking or taking an occasional drink will not be returned as a parole violator for drinking occasionally. The excessive use of alcholic beverages, however, can and frequently will be adequate ground for revocation of parole. Further, any abuse of this privilege will probably result in the "A" clause being altered to the "B" clause. The attempt to make this condition realistic is not intended to be construed as a license to drink.

Penal Code Section 3053.5 defines restrictions concerning the use of intoxicants by individuals convicted of certain offenses. In other cases it is optional with the Adult Authority. In such instances, the "B" clause will be specified on the person's parole papers.

VI. *Narcotics and Dangerous Hypnotic Drugs:* You may not possess, use or traffic in any narcotic drugs, as defined by Division 10 of the Health and Safety Code, or dangerous or hypnotic drugs, as defined by Section 4211 of the Business and Professions Code, in violation of the law. If you have ever been convicted of possession, sale, or use of narcotic drugs, or have ever used narcotic drugs, or become suspect of possession, selling or using narcotic drugs, and are paroled to a section of California where an Anti-Narcotic Program is, or becomes available, you hereby agree to participate in such program and agree to conform to the instructions of your Parole Agent regarding your participation therein.

Brief Interpretation: The use of drugs prescribed by a member of the medical profession is not a violation of parole. However, if you have a history of illegal use or possession of drugs, assignment to the Anti-Narcotic Program may be required. This is because early detection of use and the immediate removal of an addicted person from society are essential. If the Parole Agent determines that Anti-Narcotic testing is necessary and tells the parolee so, refusal to report for testing constitutes a violation of the parole conditions as specified by the Adult Authority.

VII. *Weapons:* You shall not own, possess, use, sell, nor have under your control any deadly weapons or firearms.

Brief Interpretation: Permission cannot be granted to any parolee to carry a weapon capable of being concealed on his person. This is defined by law.

This rule also covers such firearms as rifles and shotguns. It includes deactivated souvenirs. A parolee occasionally may be granted permission to use a rifle for the control of rodents and other predatory animals. Such permission will be allowed only when the parolee resides in an area where there is a definite need to control such animals.

VIII. *Associates:* You must avoid association with former inmates of penal institutions unless specifically approved by your Parole Agent, and you must avoid association with individuals of bad reputation.

Brief Interpretation: Parolees visit the District Office, frequently work on the same job, often live in the same quarters, meet in group meetings and constantly see former inmates on the street. The contacts which are not acceptable are those contacts which are voluntarily arranged or continued, usually during the parolee's leisure time. A passing and brief greeting is not objectionable, but the greeting should not become a conversation. A parolee is not allowed to visit or correspond with inmates of a penal or correctional institution without the permission of his Parole Agent and the institution Superintendent.

IX. *Motor Vehicles:* Before operating any motor vehicle, you must have written permission from your Parole Agent, and you must possess a valid operator's license.

Brief Interpretation: Even though an inmate has a valid operator's license when released on parole, it is necessary for him to secure approval from his Parole Agent before driving.

X. *Cooperation and Attitude:* At all times your cooperation with your Parole Agent and your good behavior and attitude must justify the opportunity granted you by this parole.

Brief Interpretation: A close working relationship between the Parole Agent and parolee is essential to a successful parole. A parolee should learn to confide in his Parole Agent and trust in the Parole Agent's guidance and recommendations.

XI. *Law and Conduct:* You are to obey all municipal, county, state and federal laws, ordinances and orders; and you are to conduct yourself as a good citizen.

Brief Interpretation: No exceptions can be allowed any parolee regarding the compliance with all the laws and ordinances of any community in which he resides or visits.

XII. *Civil Rights:* Your Civil Rights have been suspended by law. You may not marry, engage in business, nor sign certain contracts unless your Parole Agent recommends, and the Adult Authority approves, restoring such Civil Rights to you. There are some Civil Rights affecting your everyday life which the Adult Authority has restored to you, but you may not exercise these without first getting written approval from your Parole Agent. You should talk to your Parole Agent about your Civil Rights to be sure you do not violate this condition of your parole. The following Civil Rights only are hereby restored to you at this time.

A. You may make such purchases of clothing, food, transportation, household furnishings, tools and rent such habitation as necessary to maintain yourself and keep your employment. You shall not make any such purchases relative to the above on credit except with the written permission of your Parole Agent.

B. You are hereby restored all rights under any law relating to employees, such as rights under Workmen's Compensation Laws, Unemployment Insurance Laws, Social Security Laws, etc. (Reference here is made to Adult Authority Resolution No. 199)

Brief Interpretation: A man released on parole ordinarily is short of money. This may mean that the parolee will have to establish credit for some special purchases. The Adult Authority must restore the parolee's rights before he can make any contract.

Adult Authority Resolution No. 199 restores most Civil Rights to parolees subject to the determination of the Parole Agent. The Parole Agent understands that a goal of a parole is to help that adjustment and if society will not be adversely affected by such restoration, the Parole Agent will obtain the necessary clearance for the parolee.

XIII. *Cash Assistance:* In the time of actual need, as determined by your Parole Agent, you may be loaned cash for living expenses or employment, or you may be loaned such assistance in the form of meal and hotel tickets. You hereby agree to repay this assistance; and this agreement and obligation remains even though you should be returned to prison as a violator. Your refusal to repay when you are able may be considered an indication of unsatisfactory adjustment.

Brief Interpretation: Inmates preparing for release on parole and many parolees have misunderstood the purpose of funds loaned from the Revolving Fund. Such loans for special emergencies, tools, meal and bed tickets, etc., are not gifts or gratuities, but loans in the strictest sense. Reimbursement is necessary.

Parolees and dischargees will be expected to repay loans. In addition, the Director and the Adult Authority have approved procedures whereby violators returned to confinement will make payments from funds available to them.

XIV. *Special Conditions:*

Brief Interpretation: If special conditions are specified, they become a vital part of an individual's parole. Special conditions can be removed only by the Adult Authority.

XV. *Certification of Rehabilitation:* The Penal Code makes provision for an inmate to file for a Certificate of Rehabilitation at the time of his release on parole or discharge. The Certificate automatically becomes an application to the Governor for a pardon, which, when granted results in restoration of your Civil Rights. Parolees are urged to initiate filing procedures as soon as possible after release. You will be assisted by the Parole Division. Other agencies are also available to provide counsel and assistance to you. There is no cost to you for the services provided. The procedures and requirements involved will be discussed in more detail in your pre-parole classes.